COLORADO
14ER DISASTERS

COLORADO
14ER DISASTERS

Mark Scott-Nash

The Colorado Mountain Club Press
Golden, Colorado

Colorado 14er Disasters, Second Edition
© 2016 by Mark Scott-Nash

PUBLISHED BY

The Colorado Mountain Club Press
710 Tenth Street, Suite 200, Golden, Colorado 80401
303-996-2743 e-mail: cmcpress@cmc.org

Founded in 1912, The Colorado Mountain Club is the largest outdoor recreation, education, and conservation organization in the Rocky Mountains. Look for our books at your local bookstore or outdoor retailer, or online at www.cmc.org/store.

Takeshi Takahashi: design, composition, and production
Jodi Jennings: copy editor
Clyde Soles: publisher

CONTACTING THE PUBLISHER

We would appreciate readers alerting us of any errors or outdated information by contacting us at the above address.

DISTRIBUTED TO THE BOOK TRADE BY
Mountaineers Books, 1001 SW Klickitat Way, Suite 201, Seattle, WA 98134, 800-553-4453, www.mountaineersbooks.org

Topographic maps were created with CalTopo software (caltopo.com)

COVER PHOTO: Longs Peak from the northwest by Dave Christensen.

We gratefully acknowledge the financial support of the people of Colorado through the Scientific and Cultural Facilities District of greater metropolitan Denver for our publishing activities.

Second Edition

ISBN: 978-1-937052-36-2
Ebook ISBN: 978-1-937052-37-9

Printed in USA

TABLE OF CONTENTS

PREFACE

I wrote the original *Colorado 14er Disasters* seven years ago. Since then it has become somewhat of a Colorado hiker's classic and remains unique in that it is an unflinching examination of a topic that has both fascinated and frightened people for as long as humans have climbed mountains. Over the years the book has received overwhelmingly positive feedback. I felt that this new edition was necessary to help focus and reinforce what the first edition of *Colorado 14er Disasters* began: an honest revelation of what really happened in mountaineering accidents. This book is not a "part 2," or an "even more disasters" book. The original stories are archetypes of preventable mountaineering accidents on Colorado 14ers. Readers seeking a comprehensive annual publication of mountaineering accidents should consult *Accidents in North American Climbing*, which is published by the American Alpine Club (AAC). The AAC also publishes accident reports on its website, www.americanalpineclub.org.

This book aims to objectively evaluate official accident reports, which may be colored by legal constraints in reporting or agency politics. For instance, a rescue manager in a national park who approves an expensive helicopter evacuation during a rescue operation must justify the use of the helicopter, when some might have the opinion that it was not necessary. A ranger or rescue manager fills out the report; many times it is someone who may not have the time or resources to do more than a cursory investigation and is under pressure to justify decisions made during the rescue. I have extensive experience with this sort of reporting as a climbing and rescue team member, as both a reporter and a subject of a report, and have directly witnessed the challenges of objective reporting many times.

Accident reports have an element of subjective bias. This is also present in personal accounts of accidents from witnesses and victims that appear regularly on web forums, whether expressed from embarrassment, lack of a big picture view, or simply because the poster did not fully analyze the situation. Of course this is not always the case, but it is hard for the average reader to determine if a personal account is correct.

An accurate evaluation of evidence is important to understanding an accident. It is difficult to come by this evidence by "crowdsourcing" accident analysis, which happens on many social media sites. One reason for this is a natural human tendency to elevate mountaineers based solely on their social popularity or reputation as successful climbers. There are examples in this book of highly respected hikers who became victims of surprisingly simple mistakes. Good mountaineering practices do not come from reputation or success, but rather by sticking to techniques that have been proven to work by many people over the years.

By examining evidence from different sources, this book goes beyond conventional analysis to show how accidents may be prevented.

Colorado 14er Disasters, Second Edition contains all the original material, plus updates, and additional archetypal accidents such as lightning hazards that have happened since the first edition was published. This book is not intended to deter anyone from the great joy, fascination, and glory of mountain climbing, but rather serves as a another guide to understanding the mountaineering environment and some aspects of the psychology of mountaineering.

Mark Scott-Nash
June 2016
Boulder, Colorado

FOREWORD

By Lou Dawson

The first death I heard about on the Maroon Bells was when, about forty years ago, a couple of guys started climbing too late in the day and tried to descend in the dark. Without headlamps or flashlights, they pushed down unfamiliar and ever steeper terrain until footing ran out and gravity took over.

Why did they not simply stop and wait for morning? And why were they in that situation in the first place?

In *Colorado 14er Disasters*, Mark Scott-Nash details what can only be described as a series of funereal tragedies—many of which are similar to those poor boys on the Bells so many years ago. He asks "why," and attempts to answer the question.

Most accidents that happen on the 14ers can be divided into two categories. The less common form is when a well-trained and equipped climber makes good decisions, and still gets in trouble. The second and more common type is when, as happened with the young men who fell down the Bells, some combination of over confidence, poor training, or bad thinking is the cause. It is mostly the second type of trouble Mark details within these pages.

In the case of the expert who does everything right, it is excruciatingly sad when the results are tragic, but at the same time somehow okay. After all, one thing that makes us human is taking calculated risks. Well-executed mountain climbing honors and sustains that part of our humanity, and we see that in our fallen heroes.

But the second type of accident is just plain grim. You parse the decision-making, the gear choices, the level of competence, and you come up with an ugly picture that's uncomfortable to behold. The victim's epitaph might read, "He died doing what he loved." But it would be much nicer if it read, "He died in the mountains with poise and grace, after a long and successful career of alpinism, practiced with methodical excellence."

I'd like to think the second type of accident (that of incompetence) is easier to prevent than the first. After all, is it not easier for us to avoid doing stupid things than it is to avoid the unavoidable? Sadly, this doesn't appear to be the case.

At this point, it's only fair that I mention my own biggest mistake in the mountains. I wasn't on a 14er, but in a similar fashion to much of the incompetence Mark details here, I blithely skied into an avalanche slope that was obviously primed and ready for a slide. Orthopedic surgery and a year of recovery got me back on my feet, but I came within inches of dying. Definitely my fault—stupid—not a chance thing at all.

Thinking back on 14er accidents (and most mountaineering misfortune), I have trouble coming up with even one event that is simply a "chance" act of God. I'm sure we could find such an accident if we looked hard enough, but in truth, it wouldn't be that instructive.

So, if most accidents on the 14ers tend to be the result of human error, what is the key to prevention? Shouldn't it be easy? Consider some of the accidents Mark writes about.

What could have kept David Worthington from pushing to the storm-blasted summit of a 14,064-foot mountain, ineptly camping at the apex, then mortally injuring himself on the descent the next day because he carried no ice axe and foolishly decided to attempt a controlled slide down steep wind-packed snow—with cliffs below?

What could have kept climber Valerin Anton from leading his party higher and higher on Pyramid Peak when it was obvious the avalanche danger was extreme, and his group had no avalanche rescue gear or experience? He's dead, so we can't ask him.

What could have kept Eric Sawyer from inviting a novice woman hiker along for what she assumed would be a fun hike in the 14er sun, but which, through their own actions, was transformed into a difficult epic—during which Eric's companion disappeared and was never seen again?

And consider my own brush with death. What could have kept me from skiing into that avalanche slope as casually as sitting down to dinner?

By all accounts, the people at cause in these "accidents" were not stupid. Yet as pop psychology informs us, intelligence comes in different forms. Perhaps in mountaineering, intelligence equates with respect. And if that's the case, many (if not most) Colorado 14er climbers appear to be sorely lacking.

Just navigate a peak on a summer day. Observe the numbers of obviously under-equipped hikers for whom even a severe rainstorm would be a survival epic. They appear to regard mountain climbing as some sort of jumbo Stairmaster with a view—required equipment being only a t-shirt and water bottle. Their hubris is so insulting that you can almost see the noble mountain wilt beneath their feet.

Indeed, respect. In my view the causality for most of the accidents Mark writes about can be traced to a lack thereof. Take the mountains seriously and you tend to dial back your goals, perhaps realizing you're not quite ready for a safe and sane ascent of a more difficult peak such as the Bells. And if you're ready, educated, and trained in mountaineering, respect leads to small but essential details, such as starting early, snowclimbing (or descending) with caution instead of clueless exuberance, carrying things such as a headlamp, and simply bringing enough clothing to survive a rainstorm.

In most mountaineering cultures with which I'm familiar with, respect is the norm. Traveling prepared is common, going under-equipped or exceeding your skill level is considered poor form. Somehow, on the Colorado 14ers we've lost much of that ethic. It's time to get it back, and studying this book will help.

Speaking of respect, another related subject is how does one report human tragedy in a respectful way? In this book, I believe Mark Scott-Nash takes a leadership role in not only improving mountain safety, but in how mountaineering accidents are reported with genuine respect. This, rather than the fake qualifiers that news reporters use, wherein most victims are "experienced" or "experts," and little mention is made of just how badly they messed up even though in most cases, they did mess up royally.

Thankfully, Mark avoids misleading labels and purposefully details the often deficient experience and preparation of those he writes about. But in doing so, he indeed ends up being somewhat critical of people who have died tragic deaths. Such criticism may not be appreciated by the victim's family and friends, and is often derided as "Monday morning quarter-backing." But is it wrong and insulting, as detractors claim?

I submit that analysis and criticism of mountaineering accidents is not wrong. Far from it. Instead, picking apart the causality of an accident is one of the best ways to honor and respect the victims. Why? Simply because doing so could save lives and more heartache. In writing this book, Mark does exactly that and I applaud him. Read, learn—and respect.

—Lou Dawson
Carbondale, Colorado
www.Wildsnow.com

ACKNOWLEDGMENTS

For relating accounts of what were very difficult times in their lives, I want to thank Dylan Hettinger, Bowmann Judd, Caroline Moore, and David Sweedler.

For their assistance in gathering and confirming information, I'd like to thank Lt. Kim Andre and the Eagle County Sheriff's Office, Dale Atkins, Shawn Keil, Scott Kelley, James Kramer, Josh Friesema, L. David Lewis, Jamie Nellis, Julia Taylor, Sarah Thompson, and Kevin Wright.

Thanks to the Alpine Rescue Team, Lou Dawson, Cindy Gagnon, Howard Paul, and Paul "Woody" Woodward, for their valuable contributions.

Thanks to Dave Christenson, for photo contributions.

And special thanks to Gillian Collins, Anna Fowles-Winkler, James Gallo, John Joseph, Scott Papich, Shelly Scott-Nash, and Jack Zuzack for their comments and suggestions resulting from many hours of reviewing these stories.

INTRODUCTION

When a non-climber asks me what the summit of a 14er is like, I sometimes answer that it is like being nowhere. On a summit you will find no shelter, no food, no water, no trees, and no one living there. There is no warm bed to rest in, no fortune to be found, and no adoring crowd cheering your accomplishment. You will find cold, wind, harsh sunlight, hard ground, rain or freezing snow, and lightning.

To get to "nowhere" and back you must experience pain and soreness; be tired, cold, dehydrated, hungry or perhaps nauseated. You potentially

Mountain accident victim being loaded on an air ambulance by rescuers.

face a long trek that you just want to finish, to be back at the trailhead where you can find relief from both your physical and mental suffering. If everything goes as planned, that is the best outcome possible.

All this is true, of course, but not really dwelt on by 14er hikers—they accept this as simply the price they pay to climb a mountain. And there is an undeniable motivation to climb, the reasons for which alone could fill volumes. In Colorado, we witness an additional strong motivation to climb all the 14ers in the state: *The List.*

Fourteener mania, the phenomenon characterized by a seemingly obsessive drive to summit *The List* of all 54 of Colorado's 14,000-foot peaks, is an older tradition than many may realize. It was invented when Carl Blaurock and William Ervin completed *The List* in 1923. Their ascents were done before the existence of guidebooks, signed trailheads, internet trip reports, convenient transportation, or easy communication. Interestingly, though Blaurock and Ervin were credited as being the first two to climb the 14ers in aggregate, neither made a first ascent of any of them—they had all been climbed previously. However, until 1923 no one had collected ascents of all of the 14ers—no one had completed *The List.*

It was not until 1968 when the number of people completing *The List* surpassed 100. The next 20 years saw the number climb to 500. Today, in 2016, that number is approaching 2,000.

The Colorado Fourteener Initiative (CFI), a non-profit dedicated to preserving the 14ers, declares a staggering statistic: the 14ers receive a half-million visitors per year. And they claim that number is a conservative estimate, based on survey numbers from 1984, 1994, and the late '90s, which show a 10 percent growth per year. The estimate number could be as high as 750,000 visitors per year. Hiking the 14ers is transitioning from a lonely, self-reliant wilderness adventure into something like a crowded marathon run.

Other aspects of the climbing experience have changed over the years as well. *A Climbing Guide To Colorado's Fourteeners* by Borneman and Lampert, published in 1978, was the first guidebook written solely for 14ers. It was unique for a guidebook in that it not only described routes but also related historical stories and legends surrounding these mountains.

Fourteen years later came *Colorado's Fourteeners, From Hikes to Climbs* by Gerry Roach. This guidebook focused on the thing serious hikers want in a guidebook: factual route information—directions to trailheads, physical descriptions of the routes, photos, maps, distances, and inventive ways of measuring difficulty. It contained information for the standard routes as well as those more obscure. Roach interspersed his descriptions with his eclectic lessons on mountaineering that became known as "Roachisms." It became a bible for 14er baggers.

Right on the heels of Roach's guide came *Dawson's Guide to Colorado's Fourteeners*, written by Lou Dawson in 1994, a two-volume series that provided information about winter ascents and skiing descents, and year-round condition information. The 14ers were not just for summer weekends anymore.

Now the internet is providing yet another information portal for climbers. The web site *14ers.com* disseminates information in the form of trip reports, up-to-date condition and access information, discussion forums, and interactive climbing guides. The site provides a convenient way for hikers to gain information and interact.

Equipment and clothing have also improved greatly. Forty years ago, state-of-the-art clothing consisted of cotton windshells, nylon rainshells and wool insulation. A decade later, climbers benefited from material advances that brought us waterproof/breathable shells and lightweight synthetic fleece. Pliable kernmantle ropes replaced stiff braided ropes. However, these improvements were a trifle compared to the current onslaught of new material, gadgets, food, equipment, and information.

Thirty years ago, a typical trip to a 14er might have gone something like this: Pick out a climb maybe a week before from Borneman and Lampert, the only 14er guide available. Check to see if any of your friends have climbed the mountain (they probably had not and thought you were either a kook or a superman for attempting it). Buy several U.S. Geological Survey topographic (USGS topo) maps covering the intended route. Check the news the night before for general weather conditions in the mountains. Drive to where you think the trailhead is, based on your interpretation of the guide, and search around a bit.

Shoulder your 25-pound pack of essentials. Begin the climb and, if it's a mountain far from the Front Range or not in the summer season, be prepared to navigate with a map and compass. Continually attempt to interpret the guidebook or make your best guess as to the route. Summit. Hike back to the trailhead in a storm, find a phone booth, and call your friend to say you're off the mountain. Drive back home.

Today it might go something like this: Decide to climb a 14er the night before. Get on the internet and pick a route based on perhaps dozens of trip reports available. Click on the website guide and print out the step-by-step route description including multiple color photos with arrows and lines showing the *exact* route and difficulties. Go to another website and print out a one-page USGS topo of the area. Go to yet another website and get an up-to-the-minute pinpoint weather forecast for the mountain. Enter waypoints found on the 14er website into your GPS receiver. Wake up early. Drive to trailhead. Try to find parking.

Shoulder your 15-pound pack of essentials (same as three decades ago but lighter material). Follow a bunch of people on a well-marked trail to the summit. Call your friend from the summit with your cell phone; send a photo of yourself doing a handstand. Hike back to the trailhead in a storm (some things never change). Drive to Interstate-70 and get stuck in traffic for four hours, unlike 30 years ago.

All of these changes are truly revolutionary, especially compared to Blaurock's era. But while technology has improved, crowds have increased, and information has exploded, two things have not changed: the growing popularity to complete *The List*—the holy grail of Colorado climbing—and the fact that the 14ers remain difficult to access in remote wilderness. These two factors conspire to draw ever-increasing numbers into what can be an extremely dangerous environment from which there may be little chance of escape.

The 14ers have been fonts of joy, icons of beauty, monuments of accomplishment, taskmasters of suffering, and doorways to visions and epiphanies. It is no mystery why hundreds of thousands have been drawn to their summits. But along with these intensely positive experiences is the possibility of the opposite extreme—to become stranded, severely injured, or even killed, in disturbingly easy ways. Many climbers are unaware of the harsh reality of the dark side, and very rarely experience it firsthand. *Colorado Fourteener Disasters* explores this dark side of climbing. When an accident happens on a 14er, the victim is far from help and in an environment where rescue is difficult at best.

One myth about mountaineering accidents should be immediately dispelled: Except for the most minor incidents, self-rescue is far too difficult to manage for the vast majority of 14er climbers. If immobilized by serious injury, a victim will require medical care beyond the skills of novices. Safe evacuation of a victim, even down an easy hiking trail, requires a coordinated team with specialized gear to care for the victim.

It is one thing to help out a friend who has twisted an ankle a quarter-mile from the car. It is quite another to carry a victim with a broken ankle several miles while preventing further injury to the ankle and avoiding making the matter worse by injuring a rescuer. This kind of effort is unlikely to go well, even with a group of the best-intentioned Good Samaritans. Evacuation essentially relies on the efforts of a mountain rescue team.

Although there are more mountain rescue "home teams" around the state than there used to be, which can provide a faster, organized response to mountain emergencies, there are still sparsely populated areas that have no teams and essentially remain in the same situation they were in 25 or even 50 years ago. Places that have rapidly increased their team numbers and capabilities, such as Summit County, still have to contend with the inescapable physics of rescue—victims generally must be hand-carried out of the mountains.

Helicopters, the only quick means of evacuation from roadless areas, cannot fly in bad weather or at night. Altitude also presents a major problem for flight control, and many helicopters cannot safely fly even at altitudes as low as the trailheads of some 14ers. Also, very few helicopters can help a victim on steep or cliffy terrain, as winches and specialized—and highly expensive—crew training are not available.

Front Range mountain rescue teams covering 14ers, such as El Paso

Blanca Peak from the summit of Little Bear and the connecting ridge. Rescuers are few and far between in this remote part of Colorado.

County SAR that handles the famous Pikes Peak 14er, and Alpine Rescue Team that covers the popular Grays, Torreys, Evans, and Bierstadt 14ers, have become some of the premier mountain rescue teams in the state because of higher funding levels and large population bases to choose from.

More remote counties such as Custer County, which borders the difficult Crestone Peak and Needle, Kit Carson, and Humboldt 14ers, have teams that are ill-equipped, understaffed, or insufficiently trained to handle large operations such as searches or long, technical evacuations. The poorest and most sparsely populated counties such as Huerfano or Conejos, which border the remote Blanca Peak, Little Bear, Ellingwood Point, and Mount Lindsey 14ers, have no teams at all.

Thus not all 14er rescue situations are equal. When Alpine Rescue Team calls for help for a large, complex rescue operation that may involve 50 rescue team members on Torrey's Peak, they are assured of having a critical mass of their own team members scattered throughout the field to efficiently control the operation.

This isn't true for counties that rely heavily on external help for large operations, a fact pointedly illustrated in Part I of this book. Evacuating someone with a broken leg on Mount Lindsey will in all likelihood take many hours, if not days, longer than if it happened on Grays Peak.

However, when faced with helicopter-grounding bad weather, even Alpine Rescue Team, with all the help it can muster throughout the Front Range, will require many hours or perhaps an entire day to respond to, find, and evacuate an immobilized hiker on any 14er in their territory. Imagine that your car crashes in a snowstorm and you are thrown onto the side of the highway. You have a broken leg but must wait, lying in the snow, six hours for an ambulance. When the ambulance at long last arrives, they lift you into the pram, cover you up, and instead of driving you, they push you for 18 hours along a bumpy road while the snow continues to fall.

All climbers of 14ers should be well aware of the rescue situation when they leave the trailhead. *Colorado Fourteener Disasters* is not about mountain rescue per se, but because it is important for the 14er climber to understand how rescue attempts can affect the outcome of a disaster, I have integrated the events of a failed rescue into the first section.

The roots of 14er disasters take hold long before a rescue. They grow in an environment that has many dangers in forms both obvious and subtle.

Mountaineers face hazards of two sorts: the objective dangers of the mountain environment, and the subjective factors that are dependent on the climber.

—Mountaineering: Freedom of the Hills

This passage, from the widely recognized authoritative book on mountaineering, expresses the classical philosophy of the dangers of mountaineering. Basically, the theory states there are two kinds of dangers: objective and subjective. Objective dangers are defined as uncontrollable hazards, such as rockfalls, lightning, and avalanches. Subjective dangers are defined as humanly controllable, those that can be avoided with the proper knowledge and experience.

There is an inherent problem in this way of thinking: It implies there are two separate and distinct classes of danger; one almost random, beyond our control and unavoidable, and the other within our control so much as to be completely preventable. Analysis of mountaineering accidents reveals a better way of understanding the dangers of mountaineering. Simply stated, the environment contains *hazards* that are mitigated or exacerbated by the decisions made by the climber.

Mountain hazards vary widely based on factors such as location, difficulty of a route, and weather conditions. Mountaineers manage these hazards by the decisions they make, such as which route to ascend, at what time of day, during which season, with which equipment; and a myriad of others. The mountaineer must decide, when faced with a hazardous condition such as an approaching storm, whether to continue to the summit or turn around and try on another day. But we are not machines making decisions based on the logic of a flowchart (if we were, we would not be climbing in the first place). Decisions are made in a mental flux stirred by an array of psychological factors including group dynamics, past experiences, drives and desires, and a potentially altered state of consciousness due to

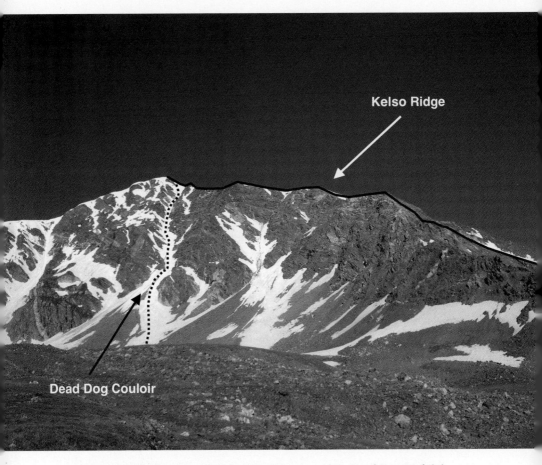

Torreys Peak showing Kelso Ridge and Dead Dog Couloir. Dead Dog Couloir is notorious for late spring avalanche danger.

factors including altitude, fatigue, insufficient calorie intake, dehydration, and hypothermia. Everyone can recall a time when they made a "stupid" decision, did something they would never do again, or can't figure out why they did it in the first place.

It can be argued that all mountain danger is subjective, implying all accidents are the result of decisions and actions taken by the climber. The example of being in the wrong place at the wrong time, such as when a rare rockfall kills a climber, is trivial in both decisions made as well as lessons learned. The climber made the decision to be in harm's way, so to speak, and therefore was responsible for his accident. And of course there isn't much to say about it. The stories in this book assume that climbers are aware that they expose themselves to this type of omnipresent hazard.

Other accidents are due to a climber failing to follow "common sense" rules that don't require any special mountain education at all to understand. Every 14er climber who has been at the game for more than a season will recognize this scenario: During an afternoon descent from a summit you see a massive black cloud bearing down on the mountain. You are well above treeline and the vision is ominous. It is a plainly visible danger lurking in your near future. You are glad to have summited before the storm but notice several other groups still ascending. They are 30 minutes below the top and are well aware of the impending maelstrom. Thunderstorms do not approach instantaneously; there is time to think about the situation and retreat. You notice that some hikers hesitate, while others turn and descend. And yet there is inevitably the third group that continues up, sometimes convincing others to follow by their apparent confidence in their decision.

The sight of a massive black cloud bearing down on an open mountain slope, releasing fingers of lightning and sheets of rain, is usually enough to send any flatlander fleeing for shelter. Why is it that an extraordinary number of hikers refuse to follow instincts that would lead them to safety, something they would likely do in any other situation? Are they too vested in the climb, willing to place odds on their demise versus getting to the summit? Are they so tired or so focused that they aren't thinking straight and venture into one of the most plainly obvious mountain hazards? Why are some willing to let other hikers they've never met, and who are expressing a severe lack of sense, make critical decisions about their lives?

This behavior is present to some degree in climbers of all ability levels. For example, in an interview with John Marshall of "The Daily Beast" published in October 2009, Viesturs states, "Up until that point, I'd always been conservative, believing that no mountain was worth dying for. When it started snowing hard on K2, I kept asking myself, 'Is it really that bad?' Scott Fischer and Charley Mace were going up the mountain, but I was real hesitant to make that call—to tell them, 'You guys go on, I'm turning back.' Not making that decision and carrying on was my worst decision ever. Coming down the mountain the danger of avalanches was so great from that snow that I was convinced that we were all going to die, although that also produced a sense of calm since there was nothing left to lose. My instinct had always been so important that I told myself then: Don't ever question that again! It was a big fuckup!" The storm that materialized created conditions that nearly killed them on their descent.

This lack of good decision-making, whether momentary or long term, is probably why there is no discrimination in mountaineering accidents. If you examine the background of a random group of victims, no one stands out as being the most vulnerable. There are roughly as many novice victims as those considered very experienced. This makes it difficult to lay the blame for accidents on either the victim's experience level or risk-taking behavior.

Except for the random event of being in the wrong place at the wrong time, victims follow a decision process that leads to their accident. The stories in this book illustrate how these hikes and climbs progress, from their beginnings to the tragedies that follow. The routes are not extraordinary. The climbers and victims are not extreme; they are like most hikers of 14ers. The decisions they made during their climbs are also not uncommon. These are accidents that could happen to any average 14er climber, and indeed, most of the victims would have correctly counted themselves as part of the average group, not a beginner and not an expert.

My objective in *Colorado Fourteener Disasters* is not to simply show who made a poor decision and when it was made. It is to tell a story to reveal the psychology affecting the decision-making processes of climbers, and to raise the questions to you, the reader: Could you fall into the same flawed decision-making process that would lead to an accident? Do you understand how you would make decisions in the same situation?

Throughout the book, the abbreviation "14er" is used to denote a mountain whose summit rises more than 14,000 feet above sea level.

I have used the terms "hike" and "climb" interchangeably throughout the text. This may seem confusing at first, but the practitioners use the terms interchangeably. "Scrambling" is a term used to indicate climbing where both hands and feet are necessary, but not so difficult or dangerous that ropes are needed. Use of ropes and other specialized climbing gear is referred to as "technical" climbing.

PART I: **FLIRTING WITH DISASTER**

"Do you think he slipped?"
"No, on a climb the week before, Shawn said he did the same and ended up flipping down the slope, but he was OK then."

—From interview *with Caroline Moore*

The Beginning

On Sunday evening, May 6, 2007, a man living in the mountains west of Denver saw a short news story on television. The story prompted him to turn on his computer and log on to the 14ers.com forum using the screen name *colopilot2002*. He started a new thread titled, "Climber injured and stranded on Humboldt Peak." The body of his terse missive repeated:

> Climber is stranded above 12k on Humboldt Peak.

Nineteen minutes later, a user with the screen name *SDKeil* posted a second message to the thread:

> Hmmmm I hope this isn't what I think it is about.
> USAKeller and TalusMonkey went to climb Humboldt
> this weekend. Neither is answering their cell phones.
> Let us all hope for the best.

SDKeil was Shawn Keil, a 14ers.com forum member and friend of *USAKeller*, screen name for Caroline Moore, and *TalusMonkey*, the moniker used by David Worthington. Shawn was aware of his friends' plans to climb Humboldt that weekend. Not many people would choose to climb the 14,064-foot mountain, located in remote south-central Colorado, in early May. The weather would be unstable, changing from sunny and windless to gray and overcast with blizzards in a matter of hours. Deep snow remained from winter and would make the access road impassable by car. The waist-deep snow on the mountain would require any climbers attempting the peak to use skis or snowshoes. These conditions rendered the climb more difficult than it would be in summer, one short month away.

Shawn worried that the accident involved his friends. And he was right.

But what neither Shawn nor anyone else expected were the unprecedented events that would transpire over the next few days. The internet was about to lay bare to the world the real-time drama of a remote 14er accident and rescue, eliciting a rollercoaster of emotions ranging from sad empathy to maddening ignorance, from thrilling hope to heart-wrenching letdown. It would reveal the difficulty of a remote mountain rescue where

Late spring storm on a 14er.

rescuers were delayed and endangered by lack of training, resources, and leadership, none of which had ever been witnessed in an unfiltered, spontaneous manner before.

Introducing *TalusMonkey*

The mountains now exist in cyberspace. There are numerous websites centered on everything from news about specific mountains such as Everest to the activity of climbing itself. These sites contain news, photos, trip reports, maps, videos, and everything else that can be pushed through a digital pipe. They often include an interactive forum, where registered users, signing up under screen names that many times represent their alter egos, can post their thoughts and ideas.

David Worthington entered the 14ers.com environment an inexperienced yet enthusiastic hiker, and in less than two years ascended to the position of guru. He was strong, motivated, and hell-bent on climbing the 14ers. He was an extrovert and was energized by the younger climbers he met through the website, and mentored many of them.

David was a fanatic. He did not tend to moderate his climbing style or his sense of humor. He climbed mountains nearly every weekend. He pushed his fast, lightweight style to the limits, testing and trying new techniques often. He named himself *TalusMonkey* to display his speedy deftness on talus, the loose rocky slopes so common in the mountains.

He had no patience for non-committal wishy-washy partners who planned trips and then bailed at the last minute. If you said you wanted to go on a trip with him, you went "or else." Anyone who he felt was frivolously canceling out on a trip would be verbally raked over the coals for wasting his time. He was strong, focused, and motivated to climb mountains, especially 14ers. The hundreds of postings he wrote on 14ers.com witness his enthusiasm.

At age 39, his personality overwhelmed and infatuated many of his younger 14ers.com friends. He was seven to 15 years older than most of his partners. They looked up to him as an expert and a coach—and an irreverent clown. He was an entertainer, whether you were a male friend with whom he shared his most "inappropriate" raucous humor, or a female friend with whom he flirted endlessly. He was someone you just wanted to hang out with.

"I'd never met anyone like him," a friend and climbing partner related to me. "He was motivated and would not deviate from his plans. His experience spoke for itself; he'd climbed all the 14ers in less than one year. He was astonishingly fast on a climb."

Another partner, Scott Kelley, remembered meeting him for the first time on a climbing trip to Culebra Peak, which they had set up over a 14ers.com email exchange. "About 10 minutes into the drive of our first trip together he says something completely inappropriate," Scott laughs. "He always had a thing for girls in high heels. I knew then we were going to get along just fine. Then he told me about all his climbing plans. He was old enough to be my father [Scott was 23] but people would think we were brothers when they saw us together. Aside from climbing, he didn't take life too seriously."

He was famous for two attention-grabbing costumes. The "pimp" outfit, a knee-length purple jacket and matching wide-brimmed hat, accented with a hand-sized gold "$" pendant hanging around his neck. He turned more than a few heads as he sauntered up 14er trails, and meticulously posed for summit photos, taking as many as necessary to propagate his carefully crafted image as an intense, fun, and sometimes shocking character, to the world.

The second costume was his "14er Jihad" t-shirt, flaunted during the peak years of the Iraq war. "He wore it for shock value," a friend said. It was intended to draw attention, but mostly it represented his fanatical drive to conquer the peaks. Local television news stations, broadcasting images of David in the aftermath of his accident, airbrushed the writing out of the photos. They thought the shock value of the word "jihad" would detract from David's personality and predicament, when in fact it was a powerful part of him.

"He was always the gung-ho instigator of trips and had no patience with people who would not commit to climbs. He would come down on you with a fury if you canceled," a friend said, and added, "he was also extremely obsessed with ultra-lighting." This is a style of travel that focuses on carrying as little weight as possible. It is achieved by selecting lightweight food and equipment and only taking what is absolutely necessary. By shaving off ounces, the practitioner also shaves off time and energy expended on a climb. A few ounces may not gain much in energy expenditure, but if every piece of equipment is scrutinized, pounds may be saved and that does make a difference. Reinhold Messner, considered by many to be the greatest Himalayan mountaineer ever, was an ultra-light practitioner. Messner would go to the extreme of even cutting manufacturing labels from his clothing to save weight.

But this style can be rather tricky when it comes to going with a lighter version of gear or leaving it behind altogether. It should temper a hiker's decisions over the course of a climb. For example, when considering a three-hour climb up Mount Sherman on a cloudless summer morning, a hiker may reasonably leave behind his headlamp and choose a rain shell instead of his heavier parka. But if the hiker is then tempted to continue on a seven-mile, 4,000-foot vertical gain high-altitude ridge traverse to Horseshoe Mountain and back, the hiker should consider the possibility of becoming stuck out overnight in a rainstorm, a time when his parka and headlamp would be critical.

David was experimenting with his ultra-lighting technique. He was able to climb faster, but he also began displaying an unnervingly casual attitude toward the increased risks he was taking.

New Friends

Not long after *USAKeller* (Caroline Moore) joined the 14ers.com forum in 2005, she noticed the postings of *TalusMonkey* and sought his advice.

"My dad wanted to climb Snowmass but dreaded the 22-mile hike from Snowmass creek," Caroline recalled as to how she first met *TalusMonkey*. "David had posted a trip report on that climb. I sent him a message asking about it. He said 'let me know if you ever want to hike.' There was something that was very intriguing about him so I had to meet him."

Soon they were hiking together. And predictably, David quickly became infatuated with Caroline, who was 16 years younger. "He would have said we were dating," Caroline said, avoiding a direct answer about their relationship. She was 23 and had just graduated from the University of Colorado. She said, "I would say we were dating too. There was a big age difference so there were issues, but we were dating."

Shawn Keil, who had been Caroline's friend for many years, said, "David had been chasing her for months and she did not reciprocate until March. He wanted to spend the night with her on that 14er. He loved her a lot more than she thought she loved him."

On April 13, three weeks before David and Caroline's climb of Humboldt, *ray06* started a new 14ers.com forum thread titled "3 Mile High Club":

I was wondering if anyone has (or will admit to)

making love at the top of one of these bad boys
[14ers]. :P

As the thread progressed, *USAKeller*, playing along with the bawdy humor, proclaimed it was on her "top 3 list of things to do on a 14er" and followed with:

I also really want to:
1) Do a night ascent to watch the sunrise from a
summit*, and
2) Camp overnight on a summit*
*Both may not be as exciting as the subject of this
thread though!
But, I think that combining all 3 into one trip would be
the ultimate experience!

TalusMonkey responded on April 17:

USAKeller! I'm looking forward to that overnight camp
on the summit of Humboldt next month that we've
been planning all spring. We can watch the sunrise
the next morning. And mark all three goals off of your
list and mine. ;)

We'll be in the 2.65 mi high club, or, as I like to say,
the "4,267 meter club!"

Your Monkey

Flirting along in the public forum, *USAKeller* replied:

You would say something like that! Is that a pick-up
line? You've never told me your goals on 14ers! I'd
bet you'd posthole* for that goal, wouldn't you?! ;-)
What am I going to do with you boy?! ;-)

(* "Postholing" is what happens when a hiker walks through snow
several feet deep, punching through the layers to create deep "post holes."

It is highly energy consuming and an undesirable form of travel. Flotation in the form of snowshoes or skis is used to mitigate this while traveling over snow.)

Incident on Lackawanna

Though David hotly anticipated his tryst with Caroline on the summit of Humboldt, there were still weekends to fill with mountaineering in the meantime. David planned a trip with friend Shawn Keil to climb "Lackawanna Peak," the unofficial name for a moderate 13,823-foot peak near Independence Pass, for April 21st.

David chose the peak because it fit two of his objectives. It was a "centennial," one of Colorado's highest 100 peaks, yet another list to pursue after the 14ers were completed and a list that David was working on. And it was a snow climb that he thought would help him train for his planned trip to Mount Rainier, a glacier-covered 14er in Washington state, later that summer, a climb done almost totally on snow. Shawn, who was also a long-time friend of Caroline and a 14ers.com member, considered David far more experienced and so followed David's lead on the climb.

"David hated to climb on the snow," Shawn recalled. "He hated wearing snowshoes and we didn't need any for this trip. The snow was extremely hard that day. No mountaineering boots, crampons, or ice axe was technically required to climb the peak." David consulted with friend and 14ers.com member Sarah Thompson, who had climbed Lackawanna one week before. She told David about the hard snow conditions and that he probably did not need snowshoes. That sold David on the climb. It would be a snow climb, training him for Rainier conditions, but with hard snow conditions that would not require his despised snowshoes, so they did not take them.

That decision is questionable given that, with rare exceptions, the snowpack on the high peaks of Colorado requires flotation from autumn through late spring. Although the snow is beginning to melt, April is one of the deepest snowpack months. And it is also a month when snow conditions change rapidly. Sarah's week-old snow report could easily have been obsolete, though in this case it happened to be accurate.

David also chose not to take his ice axe. This decision was even more questionable than the snowshoe decision. An ice axe is a fundamental tool of both climbing and descending the steep snow slopes ubiquitous in Colorado, where the snow conditions can vary from hard-packed and icy to fluffy and deep on the same route. Some snow slopes run out into gently flattening terrain while others abruptly end in a boulder field, a stand of trees, or a cliff. But no matter what the topography of the slope or how benign it may look, falling uncontrolled down hundreds or even thousands of feet is likely to cause injuries or even death.

An ice axe helps overcome the danger of falling down a snow slope. It helps mountaineers ascend by attaching themselves to the slope as they climbs. It can also be used as a "self-belay," holding a climber fast to the slope during rests. If the mountaineer does fall down a snow slope, an ice axe can be used to stop the slide by a technique called "self-arrest." A self-arrest is accomplished by digging the pick of the ice axe into the snow to slow and eventually stop an accelerating slide. Self-arrest is one of the most valuable safety techniques a mountaineer can learn, and is required to safely travel on any steep snow in Colorado.

An ice axe can also be used to control a "glissade," an intentional slide down a slope, usually in a sitting position. Glissading is both a fun and efficient way to descend a mountain. The slide can be fast or slow depending on the skill and daring of the glissader, and in minutes the mountaineer can get down a slope that may have taken hours to ascend. The ice axe is used as a speed-control device as well as an emergency brake device.

There are several other uses for an ice axe ranging from chopping steps in steep snow to digging emergency snow shelters. It is so useful that experienced mountaineers will often carry one even if they don't anticipate seeing snow on a climb. One never knows when a route change is necessary, or what the exact conditions are on varying mountain snow.

But David still chose not to bring his axe on Lackawanna. "Carrying an ice axe was extra weight he didn't feel he needed to have," Shawn explained, despite the fact that David owned a lightweight axe. "He had a very lightweight aluminum ice axe he could have taken." It was a CAMP XLA, 45cm length, weighing 7.4 ounces. This is just over half the weight of a can of soda.

"David was a 'go light-er' to the extreme," Shawn emphasized.

Even without snowshoes and David's ice axe (Shawn brought his ice axe), they ascended one of the snow slopes cascading down from the summit of Lackawanna without incident. After a short rest, David walked over to the top edge of the steep slope and looked down. A long glissade back down was tempting him. "We made the climb, and there was a long snowfield we could descend nearly half our elevation," Shawn told me. The thrill of the slide down would be one of their rewards for achieving the summit.

"I had my ice axe but David would use his trekking pole to slow himself," Shawn explained. David had climbed the mountain using a single trekking pole, essentially a ski pole, to assist him. This is a common technique that actually saves energy by helping climbers balance themselves over uneven ground. David intended to use the end of his trekking pole to control his slide by digging it into the snow, similar to the ice axe technique. The

SNOW CLIMBING IN SUMMER

Though there are no big glaciers in Colorado, there are permanent snow-fields that can be climbed any time of year. The condition of the snow changes depending on temperature, recent accumulation and location of the snowfield. Generally, some of the best snow conditions occur in late spring to mid-summer. The avalanche danger decreases and the snow consolidates to form malleable yet solid footing, not yet becoming near-solid alpine ice of late summer and fall.

During this time, many climbers take advantage of the snow conditions to ascend long, steep and direct lines toward the summit. Many of these climbs are very steep; some popular routes approach 60 degrees. Carrying and understanding how to use an ice axe is very highly recommended. Crampons and ropes are used on many of the steeper climbs to add further protection. Understanding of late spring/early summer avalanche conditions is also highly recommended.

trekking pole, however, was missing an important feature: it had no pick for self arrest if the glissade got out of hand. "David felt comfortable with the trekking pole self-arrest method," Shawn said, despite the fact that it is nearly impossible to self-arrest with a trekking pole.

David didn't give it a second thought; he sat down and was off down the thousand-foot slide. "David was always first on a glissade. He got going pretty quickly and I lost sight of him," Shawn said. It surprised Shawn how quickly David slid out of sight, and he was somewhat shocked at David's apparent recklessness, but chalked it up to David's greater experience. "I just thought he knew what he was doing. I wouldn't have glissaded without an ice axe."

"It was FAST," David wrote of the glissade later in a trip report on 14ers. com. It was so fast, in fact, that he had problems controlling his speed, something he did *not* mention in his trip report. Shawn began his glissade and used his ice axe to maintain a slow speed until the slope relented, and met David at the bottom. It was fun; they had both gotten the thrill of the ride. Standing at the bottom, they breathlessly exchanged reports of their experience.

Laughing, David told Shawn, "I got going too fast and tried to stop but flipped." Trying to slow himself by dragging a ski pole into the slope, David discovered how awkward the maneuver could be. Instead of a controlled slide in a sitting position, he caused himself to tumble. "I didn't think too much of it at the time," Shawn recalled. They continued trekking through the forest to their car parked on the road, packed up, and drove back to Denver.

David's trekking pole self-arrest failure was forgotten. It was a minor incident on a slope with a long, flat runout. Even if David had used no braking method at all, there was no danger of him hitting anything before his slide stopped. It was no big deal. David added one more summit and one more glissade to his résumé. His next climb would be with Caroline on Humboldt, another climb where David would think ice axes wouldn't be needed.

"Looking back maybe I should have said something," Shawn told me.

Decision to Climb

In his meticulous, take-charge manner, David planned the overnight climbing trip to Humboldt Peak for Caroline and himself during the first weekend of May. "He knew I wanted to finish my 14ers, and he chose a peak I had not done before and one I could do in winter conditions," Caroline said. Humboldt is located in the Sangre de Cristo range in south-central Colorado. The Sangres, as they are called, are a steep, narrow, north-south oriented spine that rises out of the high plains that surround them. They are so steep, narrow, and tall that on a map they appear to form a wall dividing the San Luis Valley on the west and the Wet Mountain Valley on the east. Nine of Colorado's 54 14ers are located in this remote, rugged range, and these are some of the most difficult 14ers in the state.

Humboldt is located in a cluster of 14ers in the center of the Sangres called the Crestones. The Great Sand Dunes accumulate at the western base of the Crestones, while the town of Westcliffe is huddled on the eastern slopes. Of the four 14ers in this cluster, Kit Carson Peak, Crestone Peak, and Crestone Needle are considered very difficult, while Humboldt is relatively easy. Its slopes can be steep but don't contain the giant cliff faces characteristic of the other three peaks.

Winter weather tends to linger on the 14ers far longer than in the lowlands, and early May 2007 in the Sangres was no exception. Humboldt was still covered in its mantle of snow, and spring storms were sweeping the area every few days.

"I had been checking the weather all week, it didn't look good, lots of precipitation and wind," Caroline recalled. She was concerned about the weather and told David about it. "He said, 'don't back out!' I heard from his coworkers that he really wanted to spend the weekend with me in the mountains. When I sort of hinted I would be fine without going, he again said, 'don't back out!'" David was expressing to Caroline his well-earned reputation for wanting commitment from his climbing partners. As usual, he wanted to stick to his trip plans. But he had yet another motivator with Caroline: he wanted to be the one to fulfill Caroline's wish list and to consummate his relationship with her.

Willow Creek Route

Kit Carson Peak from the west. The summit is the square topped mountain on the left. Humboldt is viewed further left, out of the photo.

Aside from her "wish list," Caroline had her own motivations to climb and didn't need a lot of encouragement from David. She wanted to climb all the 14ers, and this was one she needed. David was helping her climb, and their new relationship seemed to be working to a degree. So she did not back out and met him at his house in Lakewood on Saturday morning, May 5, as planned. From there they began the four-hour drive to the small town of Westcliffe and then up the South Colony Lake Road, a rugged four-wheel-drive track toward Humboldt. They knew it would be snowed-in at some point but were pleasantly surprised at the conditions on the lower road. "We were happy because we were able to drive a long way up South Colony Road," said Caroline. "We started at noon; I was on skis and David on snowshoes."

Their climb started out at a sluggish pace. "My energy was low. I look back now and say, wow, we should have just turned around. I don't know why I felt so drained." But she did not bring up the possibility to David. They were, after all, already on the mountain and going for it.

Caroline had a difficult time ascending the steep slopes while on her skis. It was "too steep, and I kept sliding backwards into the trees," she wrote of her climb later. This difficult struggle further sapped her energy. She was fighting just to stay upright on steep ground in a forest.

Soon Caroline experienced another setback. While crossing a partially frozen stream below treeline, her foot slipped into the water. She wasn't used to hiking in her ski boots and awkwardly slipped off a rock, soaking one of her feet. "I changed my sock, but the liner was wet," she said. They still had a long climb ahead and her foot would remain cold and wet for the entire climb.

Eventually they reached treeline where the snow conditions changed from soft and unconsolidated to wind-packed and hard, interspersed with exposed ground. They could hike all the way to the summit without flotation from here, so Caroline cached her skis and David his snowshoes, to be recovered on their descent.

The wind picked up considerably as they ascended out of the trees to the exposed, bare slopes. Caroline was now having a hard time keeping warm. "At one point I lost a mitt while trying to put a handwarmer in my glove." Now cold and weak, she slowed considerably.

David, who was always well ahead of Caroline, kept moving and kept her moving. He would wait for her at times but then plod on ahead as she caught up. They pushed on as the wind picked up and snow blew horizontally. At no time did David suggest they turn around; he drove them forward despite Caroline's alarming slowness, the rapidly deteriorating weather, and fading light. They finally summited in the dark at 9:15 p.m.

They climbed a total of four miles with a 4,000-foot elevation gain, a distance that could be covered by a fast hiker in four hours, a slower hiker in six hours. Caroline took an excruciating nine hours in her weakened state. She was near to collapse at the summit.

"I fell to my knees and started crying, happy to be up there and done," Caroline recalled. But they were not done. They would not survive without shelter. "It was blowing snow, freezing. He said 'You did it! You're going to be fine. We're going to get the tent set up. I want you to get in the tent and get warm.'"

They could have high-tailed it off the summit at this point, having achieved a hard-won 14er. Even when exhausted, descending is much easier than climbing up, and Caroline's strength would likely have recovered as she moved to lower elevations. They could have descended 2,500 feet in a single hour, but instead spent that critical time struggling to erect a tent in the dark, with strong wind. David's determination to camp on the summit prevailed over reason.

Camping on the summit of a 14er is never a good plan. Storm winds rage unobstructed across the highest points on land. Rarely felt at lower elevations, wind speeds at 14,000 feet can exceed 100 miles per hour, which is equivalent to a category-3 hurricane. In summer, thunderstorms can sneak up at 3:00 a.m. and blast the summit with bolts of lightning. There is a popular saying that 14ers are "big enough to create their own weather." Whether that statement is accurate or not, it is a fact that their high, exposed summits experience the worst conditions of the storms surrounding them.

David and Caroline fought to control the tent fabric as it whipped in the wind. David fumbled with a tent pole and it slithered away over a cliff like a thin black snake escaping in the night. It was gone. There was no way to find it in the nooks and cracks below them.

Caroline was shivering violently in the wind, so David directed her to unroll her sleeping bag in the tent shell and crawl in. She removed her boots and snuggled into her shelter, still cold but finally out of the wind. "My foot was freezing," she said. It had not recovered warmth since she punched into the creek earlier in the climb. David continued to wander around the summit as Caroline began to thaw.

A few minutes later, David told Caroline he had found better shelter from the wind behind a rock wall a few feet away. Concerned that their makeshift bivouac would not withstand the wind through the night, he told Caroline they should move to the better location. Caroline had just started to warm and did not want to emerge from her sleeping bag but finally had no choice. She dragged herself out of her bag and immediately began shivering again. She pulled her boots on with numb fingers and emerged into the frigid storm. They hauled the tent behind the wall and crawled in again. David joined her in the confining wrap of the flapping, collapsed tent.

After their difficult day they were finally able to physically rest, generate some warmth and be somewhat more comfortable, but energy recovery would be more difficult. There was no possibility of lighting their stove in such conditions. Caroline recollected, "Snow kept blowing into the tent and it was loud. I was freezing. We didn't eat any food; it was the last thing on our minds.

"I don't remember sleeping at all that night."

First Morning

The summit of Humboldt Peak was spectacular the next morning. The hellacious wind of the previous night had relented to stillness before sunrise. Both were uncomfortable and cold, but the imminent sunrise raised their spirits like the proverbial light at the end of the tunnel. The mountain would grant them a stunning view that morning.

"I really wanted to watch the sunrise and we were able to, it was really cool. Perfectly calm, blue skies, and sunny. Except for the cold, we could not have asked for a better morning." David set his camera to automatic and snapped a photo of them kneeling on the summit, blue sky and snow-covered Crestones in the background. It appeared to be the start of a perfect day, something they would remember for the rest of their lives.

Despite the inspiring sunrise, however, they were not feeling their best; the previous 20 hours had taken their toll. They wanted to descend, to get going, to eat a good meal and recover in the comfort of a restaurant in Westcliffe. "We didn't eat breakfast. We didn't bother with our stove. Our water was frozen."

This was another mistake. Though many times on long climbs eating and drinking needs to be delayed for hours and sometimes days, this should only be done when there is little choice. David and Caroline had the means and ability to fuel up and hydrate that morning.

But their hunger and thirst had been muted, a phenomenon that happens after hours of suffering. Feelings of thirst and hunger come in waves, and they happened to be in a trough. But these are merely feelings; they were actually far deeper into calorie deficit and more dehydrated than the day before. This condition can easily affect clear thinking and decision making.

Within minutes they were packed and ready to descend. To speed things up, David decided they should descend down a couloir to the south. This was a change of plans—they had originally intended to descend the route they hiked up. From the summit, they could see the road heading up to South Colony Lakes and thought they could walk out from there. David thought it would go much faster that way. "I want to take the south couloir down. From the bottom, we'll go down to that road," David said. Caroline agreed.

They began their descent down the rocks below the summit, crossing short patches of snow as they went. Caroline became concerned about the possibility of glissading down the couloir; the snow did not feel right, and she did not have an ice axe. After 20 minutes, Caroline raised her concern with David. His answer was intended to placate her.

"We both agreed the snow was not safe enough to glissade. The snow was hard packed; I wouldn't have felt safe even with an ice axe," Caroline emphasized later, almost in an attempt to reinforce to herself that she would never do such a thing. Glissading hard-packed snow requires great skill and care. It is faster, like sliding down ice, and more difficult to control speed. An ice axe will easily stick, ripping it away from the glissader if she doesn't have the strength to hold on. But this point was moot since neither had an ice axe—David explicitly chose to leave them behind the day before.

"It wasn't even five minutes later that he sat down and glissaded," Caroline said.

The Price of Momentary Negligence

There have been joys too great to be described in words, and there have been griefs upon which I have not dared to dwell, and with these in mind I say, climb if you will, but remember that courage and strength are naught without prudence, and that a momentary negligence may destroy the happiness of a lifetime. Do nothing in haste, look well to each step, and from the beginning think what may be the end.

—Edward Whymper, "Scrambles Amongst the Alps"

9:04 p.m. *OBX Fisherman* (Gary Rohrer)

> I spoke with USAKeller this evening and in fact TalusMonkey did suffer some severe injuries while descending the peak today. I've only had a brief conversation from USAKeller and she left him with 2 sleeping bags, not sure if they got the tent erected. SAR has his GPS coordinates so finding him should not be a problem. I'm hoping for the best...

"He was 30 yards ahead of me to my right. I was watching my own descent but I could see him out of the corner of my eye. There was about a 30-foot stretch of snow below him. *He did not slip*, it was an intentional glissade."

One hundred feet below her, David crouched on the edge of the snow-field evaluating the contours of the smooth white surface below him. Bracing his ski pole against the firm snow as he had done two weeks earlier on Lackawanna, he squatted down on one foot as if beginning a Russian folk dance. He didn't say a word, he just launched downward. He accelerated to a frightening speed as he increased the pressure on the end of his ski pole. He suddenly lost control and tumbled head over heels. He slid and rolled faster and faster down the snow toward a rock band. With a bone-snapping impact, his body was launched into bounding cartwheels.

"I saw him tumble over small rock cliffs, turn completely over and project into the air two or three times. His body tumbled and tumbled down the couloir."

She heard loud howls of "Caroline! Help! Help! Caroline!" from a voice wavering with adrenaline and fear. He was roaring down the slope away from her. He hit another set of rocks and slid to a stop some 200 feet below where he started. The entire event spanned a few seconds. David lay in the snow, his body skewed at impossible angles. Caroline recalled, "I don't know how he stopped. I thought, 'oh my god.'"

She heel-plunged down the edge of the snow slope. She could see his hat, gloves, and trekking pole strewn randomly down his fall line. She wondered how they would get out of this; she was sure his body was broken and there was no way she could carry him out. Within several minutes she had descended far enough to be even with him. She had to traverse out on the snow to reach him. She kicked steps laterally across the slope and finally arrived where he lay. She pulled back his parka hood and checked for blood. His right arm was in too much pain for her to manipulate. He could not initiate any movement from his right hip. He felt something was sticking out of his lower left leg.

"I'm so sorry, Caroline," he apologized in a voice probably trembling with the remorse and pain of someone who would have given anything to get back those last few minutes.

Perhaps David thought he had mastered the ski pole glissade, or thought that another failure such as the one he experienced on Lackawanna would again result in a no-worse-for-the-wear tumble down a smooth, soft slope. This was a terrible misstep the mountain would not forgive.

The first action Caroline took in their initial shock and confusion was to try to get David off the snow. He was still on a 40-degree slope. Caroline could not drag him across the slope alone, but he could use his one good arm to help her move. It took an hour to move him 15 feet. If he had let go, they would have both fallen down the couloir.

They were now alone above 13,000 feet in the Colorado wilderness, one with life-threatening injuries, the other a novice in unknown, dangerous conditions. Because their party consisted of only two, no one could wait with David to comfort him, keep him warm, fed, and hydrated. Because they climbed a remote peak in off-season, no other climbers were on the mountain who might have come to their aid. Though Caroline had carried a cell phone, its frozen battery was dead, so she could not call for help and wait with David.

They had one choice. All the options open to David before that moment had been funneled down to one. "Caroline, you are the only life that I have right now," David pleaded to her. The weight of those words opened up the curtains on the enormity of Caroline's next responsibility.

"I zipped two sleeping bags together. Getting him into the bag was a really hard thing to do. His legs were still hanging out, dangling down the slope. He said he didn't want any food or water, the water was frozen anyway. I took his GPS, he marked his coordinates. He told me, 'Go straight down and hit the road.'"

David would now have to wait alone, to fight for his survival alone. He most certainly throbbed in pain from his injuries and could not adjust himself to get much relief. He also probably suffered from a certain mental anguish knowing he did it to himself. He knew he had cut away every lifeline except one, the thin line held by Caroline. He more than likely prayed his last line would not be too fragile, would not break, would hold him in the world of the living.

"Up to that point I was terrified of soloing anything," Caroline said.

She left David and began a descent into the unknown. She no longer had David to follow and for the first time on this trip had to make all of her own decisions. She faced an unknown route to their car. Fortunately, skies were clear and she could see the South Colony Lake Road below her. All she had to do, she thought, was hike to the road and follow it out.

At the bottom of the couloir she came upon a huge cliff band. She tried to climb around it on one side but was trapped by a stream cascading down the mountain. She scrambled back up and traversed over the rock and snow to the other side of the cliffs where she found a hikeable route leading down to the road.

"I saw fresh bear tracks at the top of the road," she said. It startled her but did not take her focus away from getting out. "I kept yelling out, 'help!'"

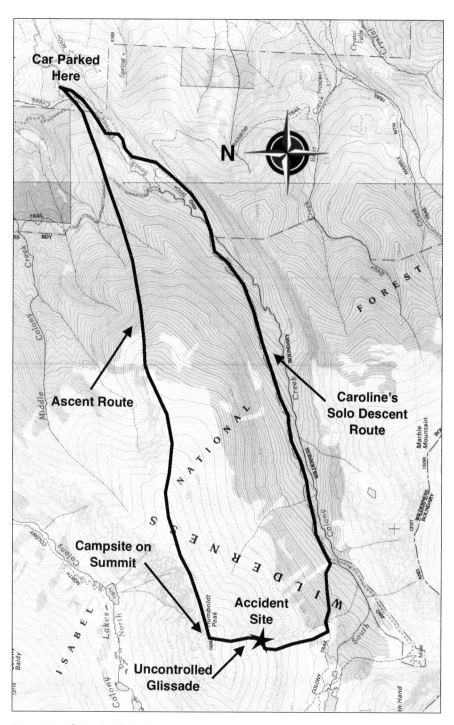

Topo map of Humboldt Peak.

But there was no one in the entire basin to answer her. She continued down the road, postholing in deep snow. She tried to locate her skis that they had stashed the day before, but she soon gave up the hopeless task. She had descended a different route, was confused by the terrain and trees on the mountain, and had no idea where her skis were. She continued postholing in the deep snow until finally reaching their car five hours after leaving David. She opened the door and immediately dug up some Gatorade and an energy bar, quenching her thirst and hunger for the first time in 24 hours.

She found David's phone in the car and dialed 911 as she drove toward Westcliffe. She arrived in the small town just as she connected with help. They told her to stop at the "Rescue Barn," the headquarters for the Custer County mountain rescue team, and it turned out she had just driven right by it.

She described what had happened over the phone. It was not long before a few rescuers arrived at the Barn and debriefed her. She described the accident and gave the rescuers the GPS coordinates of David's location. The team was not immediately prepared to go out that day, but the rescue coordinators began calling other members and packing the rescue gear they would need to take up to the slopes of Humboldt Peak. It was a desperately slow process.

"It took them two-and-a-half hours to get their stuff together and get going," Caroline said.

A Difficult Position

David and Caroline knew they were remote, but they did not understand the magnitude of their isolation and the extremely difficult problem of rescue. Nearly two decades before *TalusMonkey*'s accident, I observed the difficulties of a mountain rescue for the first time. Not much has changed since.

MOUNT SNEFFELS, AUGUST 1988

I found myself lost on an old mining road in a high, rocky valley above the town of Ouray in southwestern Colorado. Well above treeline, the gurgling snowmelt-fed streams were lined with green grass sprinkled with wild-

Crumbling rock visible looking toward the summit of Mount Sneffels.

flowers of intense yellow, violet, and burgundy. Above me rose gray rocky slopes like the walls of a mighty fortress. The walls rose into the clouds, and I could only imagine what the vast, jagged skyline above me looked like. But I continued hiking up on that crisp, wet morning, my body generating enough heat to keep me comfortable in a t-shirt.

I was attempting to climb the 14,150-foot-high Mount Sneffels, a relatively easy peak in the grand scheme of Colorado 14ers. I felt the climb was so straightforward that I didn't even bring a guidebook (or map). Surely I could follow other climbers up the popular route to the summit.

Ahead of me lay one of the walls that seemed to lead to the highest summit in the valley. It must be Sneffels, I thought. I approached the wall and the trail evaporated into ridiculously steep scree. I decided the gulley above me couldn't possibly be the summit route—it looked too dangerous and was full of loose rocks that could easily tumble down on me. I continued to explore the wall of broken rock for the next half hour, but nothing seemed to be correct. The sky cleared as the morning flowed on.

When I had exhausted all the options that seemed reasonable for a summit route, I heard the simultaneous sounds of rockfall and yelling from across the valley. My reaction to the sound was of disgust, because it sounded like a bunch of hooligans trundling boulders down the mountainside, yelling and carrying on. Don't they know they could kill someone? This must be what the local punks do for fun in Ouray, I thought. Nice.

I then looked around and saw several people strewn down the slope of a mountain across the valley. Bingo. They were on Sneffels, I was somewhere else. I learned later that I was at the base of Gilpin Peak, the 13er just south of Sneffels. I had not yet learned the value of carrying navigation tools such as a map and compass.

After about 15 minutes I saw a man bounding down the scree on the far side of the valley. He was moving fast and it sounded like he was laughing and talking to others climbing up the mountain. He was probably the guy rolling rocks down the face. He kept running down as others ascended. I thought nothing more of it.

Because I had burned so much time searching for a route on the wrong mountain, I decided to forget the Sneffels climb and just explore the basin. I continued on the trail and hiked over a ridge to a lake. While sitting on the shore, the whop-whop-whop of a low-flying helicopter broke the silence. The chopper shot over the ridge and circled the summit of Sneffels. Strange, maybe it was a tourist flight.

Hiking back to the ridgeline, I again had a view of the basin in which I had started. Sneffels was on my left and a string of people was hiking the trail up the basin toward the summit. I could see a helicopter on the ground near the end of the road where cars were parked. Hiking closer toward Sneffels, I came upon a man hiking up with a heavy metal litter strapped to his back. "I'm with Ouray Mountain Rescue," he said. "Is it possible for you to help us with a rescue?"

It all came together at that point. The rockfall I heard was not some errant teenager trundling boulders, it was someone falling near the summit. The victim was yelling in pain as an unstable boulder rolled over his leg, breaking it. His partner was the one I saw running down to get help. The helicopter tried to land on the summit but was unable to, and now the mountain rescue team was on their way to evacuate the victim.

The Ouray rescuer was the first one of his team up the trail, and was probably carrying the heaviest load, a 70-pound litter. He was successful in recruiting me, mainly because I still desired the summit of Sneffels and this would give me a good excuse to keep climbing. I took a turn schlepping the heavy load up the steep, loose scree gully rising above us.

Along the way we discussed mountain climbing and mountain rescue. I asked him if he had climbed Sneffels before. He said yes, many times including a winter ascent. But the most fascinating stories he had were about mountain rescue. When I told the Ouray rescuer about how I mistook Gilpin Peak for Sneffels, he said I wasn't the first. As a matter of fact, he had recently helped recover the body of someone who fell from Gilpin.

I soon reached my anaerobic exercise limit and bent over heaving breaths. He took the 70-pound load while I followed. He continued his story of the Gilpin accident. He said that someone had, just like me, mistaken Gilpin for Sneffels but instead of turning around when the scree got steep, he continued on, hell-bent for the summit. The slope became much steeper as he neared the summit—almost vertical. The victim, alone on Gilpin, had climbed into a dangerous position such that climbing down would be just as risky as continuing to ascend.

No one knew what his exact actions were, the Ouray rescuer said, but the result was that he fell. It was obvious that the victim had frantically tried to stop his fall, to grab onto something, he told me, by the evidence that most of his fingers were sheared off at the first knuckle. The adrenaline that surged into his muscles as he fell stiffened his grip to the point that his fingers broke off like dry sticks under the force of his body falling down the cliff. He handed me the load.

We continued up and arrived at the summit. Ouray Mountain Rescue team members arrived sporadically over the next half hour. They prepared for a long evacuation. At the summit I saw the victim lying in the rocks, bundled up in coats and being made as comfortable as possible. I then thought of the time: He had fallen before 8:00 a.m. that morning, and it was now after 4:00 p.m. He'd been lying on cold rocks, waiting in pain for over eight hours for rescuers to arrive. There were still hours ahead, hours of being lowered down potentially dangerous scree slopes.

The Ouray team finally got him to the trailhead around midnight, 16 hours after his accident. The weather was mild that day, no thunderstorms, 65 degrees near the summit, and very little wind. Though unlucky in his accident, the victim was fortunate in having good weather and the fact that Ouray Mountain Rescue was located very close to the base of the mountain—they were able to respond as quickly as any team near a 14er. And yet it still took 16 hours, far longer than if he had been in a car accident in an urban area, or twisted his ankle in a neighborhood park. The victim was lucky he did not suffer a life-threatening wound such as an arterial bleed, or severe head injury. He would have likely died before help arrived. As it turned out, he only had to wait and worry in pain for a day.

I experienced this reality check almost as a matter of luck. I wasn't hurt and really not even inconvenienced. But I witnessed the victim's painful situation, participated in the difficult rescue, and realized the dark side of mountaineering. It was a lesson David had not learned until he himself was caught in the trap.

Gathering the Cavalry

9:26 p.m. *OBX Fisherman* (Gary Rohrer)

> From what USAKeller said the SAR was called off tonight because of too much danger of avalanche. I know David will do the best he can in this situation. I hope he can stay warm tonight.

Josh Friesema got a call at 6:00 p.m. Sunday evening at his home in the small town of Divide, Colorado, asking for help. Josh was a member of

Teller County Search and Rescue, and his team was asking some of their highly skilled volunteers if they could help with a rescue in Custer County, their neighbor to the south.

He had just settled down to relax and have dinner with his wife and young children when the call came in. Josh, an unpaid mountain rescue volunteer, knew the rescue would mean leaving the comfort of his warm home and entering the cold darkness of the mountains. He would give up the cozy, relaxed sleep that Sunday night for backbreaking physical labor and potential life-threatening danger. He would have to cancel his plans for the next day or two, pack enough gear to survive in the wilderness for 48 hours, drive through the night, and prepare for a planned early morning start. Josh did not hesitate.

"They were looking for people to start at six the next morning. Two of us decided to drive down that night and spend the night there," he said of that evening. They decided it was better to get the drive out of the way and be as fresh as they could for the early start. They started driving at 7:00 p.m. and immediately ran into their first trouble, a blizzard.

"It normally takes about 45 minutes to drive to Westcliffe," Josh said. "But it took us four-and-a-half hours that night. We were driving 20 miles per hour down the highway because the blizzard was dumping so much snow." The roads were slick and visibility was very low through the dense, blowing snowflakes. But without Josh and others like him putting in the extra effort to respond in difficult conditions, David would have had no chance at all.

Each county in Colorado is responsible for setting up its own search and rescue (SAR) team. Counties in the northern Front Range, such as Boulder or Clear Creek west of Denver, are extremely well covered. Their teams, one being Alpine Rescue Team, are the best in the state due to members' experience level and a large population base to recruit from. "Best in the state" is not a commentary on individual skill level, but on the overall quality of a rescue. This includes how long it takes to respond and evacuate a victim, as well as medical care along the way. Mountain SAR usually requires dozens of people for each incident and because every team in Colorado is voluntary, the more populated areas have the advantage.

And therein lies a major problem: The vast majority of 14ers in the state are in remote, exiguously populated counties. The 2000 census shows the entire population of Custer County, where Humboldt Peak is located, as 3,503 people, whereas in comparison, Boulder County had a population near 300,000.

Due to the remoteness and ruggedness of the Sangre de Cristos peaks, Custer County is notorious for large, difficult rescues, any of which can require upward of 75 skilled people. This number of people would be a strain on even the most populated counties in Colorado and is impossible for Custer County to provide alone. When facing this kind of emergency, they call the Colorado Search and Rescue Board (CSRB).

The CSRB coordinates mountain rescuers from throughout the state and summons help for major rescues. Custer County is not alone in its need for help, as every county in the state occasionally calls the CSRB. The smaller counties, however, must ask for higher numbers of "out of county" rescuers and on a more frequent basis. Members showing up from a diversity of teams can overwhelm a smaller "home" county team. Big rescues involve a patchwork group made up of individuals from many different teams. For David's rescue, Custer County had extra help from El Paso, Teller, Douglas, and Gunnison counties, as well as from Alpine Rescue Team located in Clear Creek County, approximately 200 miles away.

All 14ers climbers should consider this situation. Even a relatively simple but immobilizing injury such as a twisted ankle can grow into a life-threatening situation for a hiker unprepared to wait out a mountain storm for a day or two.

Josh had other worries. Heavy snowfall triggers one thought in the mountain rescuer's mind: avalanche. Their concern grew as the snow accumulated. "We wanted to help the guy out there in it but we were pretty nervous about the rescue; the terrain was avalanche prone."

Josh and his partner arrived in Westcliffe after hours of contemplating their future while driving in mesmerizing white darkness. There was an eerie feel to the town. "There were no lights on in town," he remembered.

Heavy wet snow caused power lines to collapse and overload circuits. They saw flashes of light in the opaque distance. "Transformers were blowing everywhere." It was like arriving at a war zone.

They crept through the surreal town, finally arriving at the Rescue Barn. Relieved to get out of their car seats, they stretched their legs for the first time in four hours. It was chaotic at the Barn with people arriving from different points around the state. "Some El Paso County rescuers showed up who wanted to go out that night and get in good position for the morning," and Josh felt the same way. Though it was late, they were awake and fully charged to get going on the rescue immediately.

Also arriving at the Rescue Barn were members of the Custer County rescue team who had already attempted a rescue that night. The Custer County team had gotten all the way to the base of Humboldt but it was dark and snowing heavily. "Their plan was to reach the victim, stabilize, and shelter him," Josh said. "They thought they heard an avalanche, decided the risk was too great to continue, and turned back. They carried in rope and litter and left them cached at the base of the mountain."

NUMBER OF TECHNICAL RESCUERS

Why does it take a large number of rescuers when they extract a single individual from the wilderness over technical terrain? To perform a rescue such as David's requires route finders, technical anchor experts, belayers, rope handlers to keep the ropes running free, safety officers to watch for hazards both natural and rescuer-made, a medical officer or two, equipment and mission coordinators. Also required are members to carry all the equipment into the field, carry the victim out, and carry all the equipment out.

Though many members of the mountain rescue team may perform multiple duties, the number of people adds up quickly when you consider how strung out the team may be along the route and the manpower needed for patient and equipment hauling. See the chapter "The Challenges of Mountain Rescue" for further details.

The El Paso/Teller County group heard the story and wanted to start hiking right then. Josh was also ready to go, and the improvised group took the initiative. "Instead of waiting until morning, we would hike up to the gear and wait for daybreak. They told us where to find the cache," Josh recalled. The group packed their gear and began driving into the night toward the trailhead.

"We left at midnight."

The Wait

10:18 p.m. by *AzScott* (Scott Kelley)

> If anyone can come through this, it's our man David. And I haven't met a better-equipped climbing companion either. Hang in there man.

10:26 p.m. from *OBX Fisherman* (Gary Rohrer)

> Caroline said David was glissading down a section of mountain and picked up too much speed and could not stop due to no ice ax and went over an edge and landed on some rocks. She said he could not move one arm and one leg. I know he will make it.

Monday, 6:51 a.m. by *FlyGirl*

> Oh no! TalusMonkey! Where was your Reddi-Whip? You could have engaged the emergency switch on the side of the can which releases the motherload of cream and landed in a big puffy pile of the whipped stuff.
>
> No seriously! I am concerned. I know you'll pull through A-OK! I want a full trip report on your safe return!

9:11 a.m. from *Jeffro*

> TalusMonkey: I am **certain** you'll come out of this just fine.

Unaware of these words of encouragement from the 14ers.com community, *TalusMonkey* suffered alone.

David may have spent the first hours after the accident watching Caroline descend until she was no more than a faraway dot in the valley below. Then he began to serve time in his wilderness prison. The mountains and valleys he cherished for their gifts of freedom had now incarcerated him.

Time ticked away on the cold snow high on Humboldt as he likely tried to manage his pain. The injuries David suffered would have been excruciatingly painful. He would have lived every slow minute with burning agony, perhaps feeling it was the longest day of his life. As the agonizing minutes ticked by, his characteristic optimism may have faltered when as he noticed storm clouds building. Soon, snowflakes would begin wafting down and as the daylight faded, he would have seen no sign of help coming his way.

An uninjured climber may become stranded overnight on a mountain, stuck in an unplanned trap somewhere on high, dangerous ground as darkness falls. They may have no other choice but to stop and wait for daylight. It could be in a small area, exposed to the mercy of the elements, without food or water. Confined to a ledge, it is impossible to move enough to keep warm. They don every shred of clothing they have and stick their legs in their pack shell. And still they are cold. They hope for dry weather because rain will drive them to the very edge of survival. They try to pass the time with mental games, thinking about their next trip to a warm beach. But cold, thirst, and hunger only remind them how slowly the night ticks away.

Like a medieval torture, David probably suffered all of this and more as he tried to tolerate the pain of broken bones, unable to move to keep warm. And perhaps even more painful than his physical wounds was his broken heart, knowing he could have avoided it all by changing one simple step. One single step. He could have been downing a shot of Captain Morgan chased with a Colt 45 beer, regaling his tale on 14ers.com of his conquest of Humboldt, escalating his public flirtations with Caroline as the irreverent but harmless swashbuckler he was.

It was an unplanned turn of events. Like most climbers of his experience level, David probably gave little to no thought of ending up alone and disabled on a relatively easy-to-climb route. Sure, falling off a cliff, being struck by lightning, or being swept away by an avalanche were possibilities under the right circumstances. Perhaps he thought he might twist an ankle while descending talus at his trademark speed.

But to crash into rocks during an *intentional* glissade without an ice axe? Based on his nonchalant attitude as described by Caroline, David apparently thought very little of his decision to slide down an unknown snow slope without an ice axe. Because he was tired from the previous sleepless night, malnourished, and dehydrated—and he had done the same thing recently—David may have lapsed into thinking this slope would be similar or benign. It wasn't and it caught him like a steel trap. Now David would suffer far worse than he likely ever imagined possible.

Eventually darkness came and still David would have seen no sign of help. Not one person, not even a distant headlamp, appeared in the valley as he endured his second night on the mountain, this time hurt and alone in shivering cold.

Second Morning

Josh and his contingent of five rescuers had driven as far as they could up South Colony Lakes Road by 1:00 a.m. New snow had prevented them from getting far. They quickly organized their gear, shouldered their large packs, and began the slow process of breaking trail through 18-inches of new snow. Each rescuer retreated into a world of tiring physical labor, hauling 50 pounds of rescue gear to add to the previously cached gear. They hiked uphill in the gloom of darkness, broken only by the circle of light from their headlamps on the snow in front of them, with the cold and wind penetrating the small openings in their clothing. "You're thinking there's a guy up there injured and laying in that storm. We were pretty cold hiking, so he must have been worse off. I thought there was a 90 percent probability we'd find him dead," Josh remembered.

They continued slowly trekking in the dark for three hours, arriving at the cached rescue equipment at 4:00 a.m. They took a break at the cache, waiting for dawn in the blowing snow. The team was in place, they only

View from the cockpit of a rescue helicopter just after takeoff.

needed daylight to evaluate the slope and snow conditions above them.

They sat for an hour continuously scanning the dark blue mountain above. They were soaked from the sweat of their labor and shivered in the pale beginnings of dawn, while the snowfall and wind abated. As the darkness slowly relented, they could see their next challenge—a steep, fully loaded avalanche chute.

"At dawn we studied the route up to stay out of avi danger as much as possible. We stayed on the edge of the avalanche chute all the way up. We could tell things were unstable. We heard a noise and looked across the valley to see an avalanche sliding. We knew we were taking on dangerous conditions," Josh said.

Josh is also a member of 14ers.com, going by the screen name *CO Native*. He knew their mission was to rescue *TalusMonkey*, the most famous member of the website. "I knew I was rescuing David and would not have gone out in those conditions for any other reason."

Meanwhile, back in Westcliffe, Caroline was waking up. She had listened to the rescue updates on the radio late into the previous night and was offered a place to stay in a local church. The snow had not yet started when she fell asleep exhausted early the night before. She was shocked when she looked outside the next morning. "There was a foot-and-a-half of new snow," she said. "The whole town was amazed at how much snow fell that night. No one expected that surprise storm."

Alive

Josh went out on point up the snow slope on Humboldt. "I went on ahead to find David and see if we had a live victim or not. If he wasn't alive, we could take our time and stay out of danger. The rest of the team carried a lot of gear. Six-hundred-foot-long ropes and all that stuff. Clouds were rolling in, visibility was poor. I lost radio communication at one point," Josh described.

"I saw his bag and yelled it down to the rest of the team. As soon as I yelled I saw a hand stick up out of the bag and wave. And seriously, man, my heart went through my chest. I yelled down three times HE'S ALIVE! Then I had to make myself take my time to get to him safe through the adrenaline rush."

SNOWFALL ON THE 14ERS

Late July in Colorado is usually the warmest time in the state, when the "flatlands" can experience triple digit temperatures. Snowfall anywhere in the state seems unthinkable in the middle of the summer. However, high on a 14er, it can and does snow any month of the year. Any accumulation is usually temporary and may not be noticed from way down below. You will certainly notice it, though, if you are caught unprepared for such a storm, which may be intense and can induce hypothermia.

It may seem crazy to pack a warm coat when it's 100° F at home, but you won't regret it if wind, rain, hail, and possibly snow pummels you far from the trailhead. The 14ers, and all Colorado mountains, experience intense weather of all kinds, from a hurricane force wind in winter or a blizzard in July.

Using his 14ers.com screen name, Josh introduced himself as *CO Native*. "He answered, '*TalusMonkey*.'" To someone unfamiliar with David, it would have sounded nonsensical, like the ramblings of someone with a head injury or hypothermia. But Josh knew exactly what it meant and who he was. He knew David was coherent. "I wonder what someone else would have thought hearing that response.

"I put chemical heat packs on him, gave him water. He was quite excited to get something to drink. He was lucid; I could ask questions and get responses." Other rescuers followed closely behind Josh and began treating David. Excitement ran high; he was alive and speaking. But the rescuers also recognized that David was in deep trouble and that his injuries and hypothermia were sapping away his life force. He had survived with severe injuries in a high-altitude blizzard for more than a day.

Time was critical if they were going to save him. They could probably get a medical helicopter into the valley, saving hours of evacuation time, but they needed to evacuate David to an LZ, or landing zone, first. The closest place was hundreds of feet down a dangerous avalanche slope. They prepared the evacuation.

It was 10:30 a.m. The race began.

The Age of the Internet

14ers.com was started by Bill Middlebrook as a clearinghouse of information about Colorado's 14ers. As it is a free website, it attracts thousands of users with a wide range of abilities including a high number of newer, less experienced mountaineers looking for route descriptions, trip reports, partners, and advice on climbing these famous mountains. They form a large community, know each other by screen names, and when not climbing together, have lively and sometimes heated discussions about various mountain topics. The energy is real and generally positive—but it is also potentially dangerous.

The website is no different from thousands of other open internet community forums. Anyone can join and read anything they like. And except for off-topic and poor decorum postings, anyone can post whatever information they like. An old, grizzled hiker can expound from decades of experience just as easily as the newbie who has hiked a single 14er. Most of the information posted is in good faith, but this does not make it correct. Intentionally misleading posts, though likely rare, are difficult to discern if written in an authoritative manner. The newer and less experienced climbers are attracted to the site both because they want the information and because it's free.

The community attempts to moderate this information by praising or denouncing certain posters or postings, but this is neither authoritative nor efficient, and a newbie would have difficulty knowing what is good or bad advice. Unfortunately, these forums also have the tendency to be cliquish and to foster groupthink. A single member can sway opinion, whether correct or not, based solely on their popularity or clever writing style. *TalusMonkey* was one of these charismatic characters, and Sarah Thompson recognized it.

Sarah, a Ph.D. researcher in physics and an extremely active mountaineer who has climbed all the 14ers plus the glaciated peaks of Mounts Rainier and Hood, met David on Longs Peak early in his 14er quest. She climbed many peaks with David over a two-year span and knew him well. "He had extremely low experience on snow," she said. "I don't think he had any formal training. He talked about formal training once or twice but never went through with it."

Sarah was also a member of 14ers.com, going by the name of *SarahT*. She read all the praise *TalusMonkey* was receiving after his accident and something disturbed her. Many of the postings expressed disbelief that David could have gotten hurt at all, as if his accident was like a lightning strike out of the blue. She thought this implied that he had far more experience than he actually had, and that struck her as wrong. She thought people should know that his accident was possibly related to his lack of experience on snow. In the midst of well-wishing, she wrote:

> TalusMonkey is one heck of a guy, passionate about the mountains, a great friend and hiking buddy, but he is not one of the most experienced people around here. That's just the plain truth. I am not trying to be

PART I: FLIRTING WITH DISASTER | 63

negative, but a lot of more inexperienced folks here need to realize that the most popular people on the forum aren't necessarily the most experienced. Hiking the 14ers in summer does not qualify someone as an expert, especially for hiking during the winter/spring seasons. This horrible accident could have been prevented with more experience leading to better judgment. It sucks having to learn the hard way.

I am no expert myself, but I've been noticing around here lately that younger, less experienced people have been taking big risks and getting lucky. That encourages more inexperienced folks to try similar things.

Sarah went on to describe her concerns for what she felt was David's reckless behavior on Lakawanna Peak, where only a week before he had lost control of his glissade in a similar manner:

Just last week I was mentioning this to a few 14ers. com members and I expressed my worries that it was going to take a bad accident for folks to realize the seriousness of their endeavors. It totally sucks that this happened to our beloved TalusMonkey and I was totally creeped out this morning when I heard the news and thought about what I'd said last week. I had no idea that in just a few days this would happen to a friend of mine.

I guess I just want to urge people to BE CAREFUL out there and realize the risks they are taking. Just because hero Mr. X did it (climbed Capitol in mid winter for example) doesn't mean you should try it until you fully understand what you're getting into and accept the risks involved. Sorry for the lecturing, but I have felt strongly about this lately and this latest

incident finally prompted me to speak up. If you
disagree, feel free to send me nasty emails. I only
have the best intentions.

I hope you recover quickly TM, talk to you soon.

Attempting to put a balance in the discussion, Sarah did not expect the negative response she got. "I really got attacked publicly for that," Sarah said.

Responses complained about her timing and being critical at a sensitive time when David was struggling to survive. Analysis and criticism should come later, they chastised. But should it come later? Now was the time people were paying greatest attention—the teachable moment. She was merely pointing out the truth and attempting to counteract the "popularity equals experience" factor very prevalent on such websites.

This unregulated information is not new to the internet. But despite its downside, the internet has opened up another fascinating door, and it did so quite unintentionally. It became the real-time news feed for a mountaineering accident. There were no editors, information officers, or censors to massage the story as it developed.

In 1996 the internet was the center of news about the now infamous disaster that unfolded on Mount Everest. Websites posted real-time updates of the climb and subsequent accident, something never done previously. The drama was heightened by the genuine surprise and candor of the stories, from the ecstatic summit news through a heart-wrenching U-turn to death and mayhem. The information was not always accurate, but was presented the way it happens in real life. However, during that tragedy the news was essentially related on websites run by commercial ventures interested in spinning the story as best they could to their advantage.

David's mountain disaster, with news centered on 14ers.com, took the internet a step further. The events were reported and commented on by a community of friends with almost no experience with death or accidents in the mountains. They had no vested commercial or publicity interest. It was revolutionary for Colorado, and perhaps the first time ever that something like this happened on this scale. It turned David's accident from a two-paragraph story buried in the newspapers to a multi-media event spanning multiple days.

Everyone got their chance to say anything and everything they wanted. They could express their shock and fright for David's experience, write their hope for his speedy rescue, exclaim joy when he was found, or criticize David's choices that day. And *everyone* could read it, anywhere in the world where internet access was available.

The reporting of events added to the drama. Consider the implications of the posting by *Jcwhite* at 10:23 a.m. on Monday, the morning of the rescue:

> Just talked to Custer County Sheriff. Quote: "He is
> alive, he is well, they are with him." Good news.

Jcwhite had called the sheriff's office to confirm the find that he probably heard locally over the mountain rescue group's radio frequency. He then relayed this message to the 14ers.com forum.

The time stamp of this posting is literally within minutes of when Josh actually found David. It confirmed the find and gave hints of his medical condition. A television station helicopter hovering directly over the scene would not likely be able to report these details. But there was something else remarkable about this information. It was not correct—David was *not* well.

That one sentence fragment, "he is well," is the kind of phrase that emergency agencies avoid like the plague unless they are absolutely sure it is true. If the Custer County sheriff's office literally said this, they had little understanding of the difficulties of mountain rescue, quite a frightening prospect. They also did not understand that one person could, and did, tell the world. Not a reporter, simply a member of a web community.

"He is well" dramatically shifted the mood of the 14ers.com postings:

> I never doubted it for a minute. If anybody can survive
> an overnight blizzard at 13,000 feet with serious
> injuries, it would be the Talus Monkey. Thank God
> you're OK David!

1:09 p.m. *Sdkeil* (Shawn Keil)

> I am careful as to how much I say, but I will confirm a
> couple broken bones. I also know SAR is still with him

on the mountain assessing his condition, my guess
is that he is/was suffering from hypothermia. He is
slowly becoming more and more coherent and the
plan is to have him airlifted once he is stabilized and
they can bring him down off of the mountain. Lets all
continue to hope for the best.

1:16 p.m. *Blue5oone*

I am glued to my screen, hitting refresh every few
minutes (like many people I am sure). I have never
met either but the information from both TM and USA
K has helped me on many trips. Positive thoughts
and prayers to both.

Shawn Keil expressed great wisdom in his posting. He stuck with the
facts, broken bones and possibly hypothermia. In no way could this be considered "well," as described by the Custer County sheriff's office, especially
given that David had suffered for more than 24 hours exposed in a storm.
But again, this news was being related as it happened, with no one re-pack-
aging it for public consumption. After a night of waiting and anticipating,
the rescue was in full force with events being relayed out as they happened.

As the day wore on, the news turned worse:

At 6:57 p.m. from *Freeze* (brother of Josh Friesema)

GUYS, PRAY NOW FOR TALUS MONKEY. HE WAS
STRUGGLING AT THE END OF THE RESCUE.

Sunshine1 responded:

Do you know something that we all don't know? Is he
alright? Last report was that he was down and doing ok?

9:12 p.m. *OBX Fisherman*

His condition is critical. Hypothermia. Lets hope for
the best.

The rescue team had struggled to evacuate David down the mountain for five hours. A medical helicopter was able to land in the valley near the base. Though he survived a terribly difficult night alone, his body did not have the strength to continue. As sometimes happens on mountain rescues, his condition deteriorated as the rescuers performed their time-consuming lowering toward the helicopter. By the time David arrived at the helicopter, which was loaded with advanced life support equipment, he was in cardiac arrest and CPR was being performed. He was flown as quickly as possible to a hospital in Pueblo, only minutes away by air.

Death

The type of death David experienced causes one to reflect on life itself. There are many ways that a life can end: old age, genetics, and disease are considered natural. Suicide, self-inflicted, and no-fault accidents are tragic. Of the three, self-inflicted accidents generate less sympathy, especially for the victims of dangerous sports. The level of perceived tragedy granted to a matador killed in a professional bullfighting match is less than that of an innocent woman crushed by a car motor in a highway accident.

Though it was not as if David was drag racing, his death has to be

THE EVOLUTION OF SOCIAL MEDIA

Social media was very young in 2007 when news of David's accident seemingly spread like wildfire, generating intense interest. Today, the expectation is that news is available immediately and continuously updated, a vast sea change from only a decade ago.

What has not changed is the lack of access to the internet on remote 14ers. A similar accident today would likely unfold in the same fashion at the same speed.

Another thing that hasn't changed is the time and effort it takes to understand what actually happened in a mountaineering accident. Speculative analysis on social media sites is usually incorrect in one aspect or another and unfortunately leads to incorrect conclusions that are not educational.

considered, without a shadow of doubt, self-inflicted and so may seem less tragic. Maybe this is true but David died while mountaineering. He was doing something he loved. This gives a sort of consolation to the survivors: his friends, relatives, and those who knew his online persona. They can rest assured that while all death is inevitable, they are given meaning to what otherwise seems senseless. David did not die from a mere accident, yet his ending was as final as any losing at high-risk games.

9:29 p.m. *OBX Fisherman*

> It's with a very heavy heart that I must tell you that David did not make it and died tonight. Please pray for his mother and his sister and his father. I've known David for 24 years and he was my best friend.
>
> I would talk with David weekly and he was always telling me about his adventures on the mountains of Colorado and with all his 14er friends. I am deeply touched that so many of you care so much for David. He was a good person and will be deeply missed by many people.

What followed were literally hundreds of postings of disbelief, sadness, and condolences, most by people who had never met David or Caroline. Outpourings of grief turned into memories and then memorials.

Caroline drove to the hospital to see David that night.

"I'd asked everyone to leave so I could say goodbye to David. I held his hand and talked with him. I could feel him telling me he was still there. He died in the Sangre de Cristos, it means Blood of Christ, and he was a firm believer in Christianity. I think that meant something." Caroline let go of his hand.

David's official cause of death: The cumulative effect of multiple traumatic injuries and hypothermia.

Breaking the Rules

Rule Number 1: Watch out for yourself.
Rule Number 2: Watch out for your teammates.
Rule Number 3: Watch out for the victim.

—First Rules of Mountain Rescue

These rules are not about self-preservation; they are about preventing a worse situation. The accident has already happened; the victim is already hurt. If a rescuer is injured during the course of a rescue, the situation becomes far more drastic. An injured rescuer requiring an evacuation eliminates a potentially high-value player from the team and also more than doubles the overall effort of the remaining team.

Of course, the reason the rescuers are there in the first place is to rescue the victim, so this balance often becomes blurred. In the aftermath of David's rescue, Josh illustrated this blurring to the world. He cracked open a fascinating door into the operations of an actual mountain rescue while at the same time revealing recklessness and what can be described as a botched operation.

One day after David's death, Josh posted a blow-by-blow account of his experiences on his personal website, including photos of the mountains, conditions, and the evacuation. It was a way to release, decompress, and manage the wrenching emotions burned into his psyche. Josh's website was, among other uses, a tool he used to communicate with his extended family. "My website is my hobby and a way to let my family know what's going on," he said. It was not unusual for him to write about the hikes he had taken, his rescue group trainings, or his children—all the happenings in his life. David's rescue was a life event for Josh, so, of course, he would write about it.

Like the 14ers.com site, Josh's website became a news portal, an unprecedented timely glimpse into David's rescue. "I had no idea it would get this reaction," he told me. "The website got linked to like crazy. I went from ten hits a day to six thousand." And also similar to the 14ers.com site, Josh described the rescue in an honest, unsanitized, and personal manner. The photos revealed graphic details of the high, remote, snowy peaks where David spent his last day of life. Now the world could see what it had only imagined, and it was an eye-opener. One member's posting said it all:

Tradgal on May 11:

> I also didn't have a full appreciation for SAR before
> the posting by CO Native, which left me speechless
> and shaken to the core. I like many people wondered
> throughout the day on Monday and Tuesday why
> it took so long to get him off the mountain and the
> answers to those questions were made crystal clear.

Josh's story was not available long. His rescue team pressured him and the post was gone in a matter of days.

"There's an unspoken rule in SAR to not talk about what we do, not make it glamorous. My site had a glamorous appeal, amazing conditions and all that," he said. Though it did not cross Josh's mind at the time, other rescuers who saw it were indignant. "All these SAR teams saw it and thought I was seeking glory. I happened to have pictures of the rescue on it. They thought I was playing it up."

On the contrary, it was unblinkingly honest. He repeatedly underscored the fact that the operation was extremely, and unnecessarily, dangerous. Josh's website posted proof of this:

> I now also had time to pause and realize the risks we
> were all taking. I had seen four avalanches actually
> occur during the day. As I looked around I noticed far
> more had occurred than what I had seen.

> I took this shot to show the slope actually was 40
> degrees [the prime avalanche risk slope angle] since
> most people overestimate a slope angle.

> This is a zoom of the upper portion of the photo
> above on a small avalanche that occurred above us
> while we were on this slope. Praise the Lord it didn't

go any farther than it did. It would have taken out a
lot of people.

This was the cause of major rumblings in the mountain rescue community, but *not* because it appears heroic. "Scene safety" is the first thing every first responder, from an emergency medical technician to a firefighter, is trained to think about when they arrive at the location of an accident. It means that the responder's first job is to make sure the scene is safe, to evaluate the scene for hazards to yourself and others before entering.

In defense of first responders, total scene safety is not always possible. Rescuers are there to rescue, not to stand around. Thus the first two rules of mountain rescue are forgotten more times than any rescuer wants to admit.

David was evacuated directly down an infamous avalanche chute. *Dawson's Guide to Colorado's Fourteeners* describes the couloir as "an active avalanche path. It should only be climbed or skied on firm spring snowpack." Borneman and Lampert's *A Climbing Guide to Colorado's Fourteeners* describes this chute as one of several that "frequently discharge their burden of white death in the early spring."

It is the responsibility of mountain rescuers to recognize this risk and mitigate it. David could have been moved to the side of the couloir, to less dangerous slopes, and then evacuated. The tradeoff would have been a delay in the evacuation when speed was essential, but that is what the rules are for, to help make those decisions for the rescuer.

Another highly experienced rescuer on the scene, one with more than 10 years of both mountain rescue and general mountaineering experience, agreed. But his criticism was directed not to the danger to the rescuers, but the fact that the rescue was too slow.

"We busted our ass's to get this guy and he basically died on us. That's never happened to me," he explained. The experience caused him to question that particular mission as well as his fundamental dedication to mountain rescue. He was certain: "We could have gotten David to the chopper two hours faster than we did and that may have saved his life. I think it very well may have. It bothers me to this day that we didn't get him down faster.

"Nobody was in charge. There was a lack of overall mission coordination. No one knew who was doing what, where, and when. We had to make stuff up as we went along, doing the best we could in a very uncertain environment." This lack of coordination caused delays to add up. A more coordinated team, one with better leadership, would have saved two hours that day. David had survived overnight in a storm. Any unnecessary delay inserted in his evacuation pushed him that much closer to death.

This rescuer acknowledged that field personnel were as professional and dedicated as possible. They knew what they were doing in general, but the overall operation was confused by lack of direction due to the conglomeration of different teams with different training and techniques. In this situation, it was leadership that was critical, and leadership was severely lacking. And unfortunately for David, or anyone getting into trouble on a remote 14er, whether in Custer County or any one of the sparsely populated counties in the state, this was the best response possible. It wasn't good enough.

David's death shocked this particular rescuer so much that, nearly a year later, he told me he was "still deeply emotionally affected. Before that mission I was proud of my accomplishments as a mountain rescuer. I speak about other missions all the time but do not talk about this one. I get choked up every time. It made me doubt myself as a rescuer."

This is the reality of becoming hurt on a Colorado 14er. Rescue may not come for a very long time. Cell phones have helped shave hours, even days, off rescues, but in remote areas there isn't necessarily a useable signal. And in this case, Caroline's phone did not work when the critical time came. Sometimes a helicopter is available, but it takes a specialized high power or lightweight chopper to rescue from high on a 14er. And a chopper cannot fly at night, in high wind, fog, or heavy precipitation. Because of this, these rescue options cannot be relied on.

Rescuers on foot are the best bet in the mountains, and they are not always perfect.

Epitaph

TalusMonkey's last posting on 14ers.com, an answer to a question:

Eye Doc Hiker asked:

> My husband and I are flatlanders from Kansas, but
> get out to CO to hike several times a year. He is
> convinced we should have ice axes for these hikes.
> Any thoughts on the benefit of this equipment for
> these hikes in late May?
>
> I think he just wants to look cool with an ice axe. He's
> trying to convince me it may save my life some day.
> He's probably right.

To which *TalusMonkey* made his last response ever, on Friday, May
4th, 2007:

> For basic mountaineering just get a straight shaft axe.
> I call mine a "summer" axe or "glissade" axe.

PART II: COURSE TO CATASTROPHE

"Climbing is not a battle with the elements, nor against the law of gravity. It's a battle against oneself."

—Walter Bonatti

Introduction: Dynamics of a Climbing Party

The minimum size for a mountaineering party is considered to be the number of people who can handle an accident situation adequately. Traditionally, a minimum party of three has been standard. Thus, if one climber is hurt, the second can stay with the victim and the third goes for help.
— Mountaineering: Freedom of the Hills

All 14er climbers find themselves in one of three situations on the mountain: as a solo climber, as one of two as partners, or as a member of a group (defined here as three or more) that may or may not have a definite leader. The decision dynamics vary with each of these situations. The solo climber makes his or her own decisions. In the partnership, each can provide input to decisions. The group, or the partnership for that matter, may have a strong leader making most of the critical decisions. An extreme example of this is a group led by a mountain guide. Or, the group may have a less dictatorial leader or may even be democratic, making all critical decisions by consensus.

As recommended by *Mountaineering: Freedom of the Hills*, the situation that is safest, that can handle an accident best, and has the potential for making the best decisions, is a climbing party of at least three. If the climbers have nearly the same ability, the party of three or more has an excellent potential to make the correct decisions in critical situations.

However, there is at least one group situation that can lead to major difficulties, and that is a group whose leader puts their own ambition ahead of the safety of the group, and followers who expect the opposite. This situation is more common than it would at first appear. A climbing leader can certainly possess more charisma than skill, or simply desire to be viewed as a great climber, and may easily recruit followers of lesser skill but who crave the 14er experience.

A climbing party of two partners is a close second in terms of safety and ability to handle an accident situation. A party of two who have extensive experience with each other's climbing style, ability, and psychology is even safer than a larger party in certain situations because two climbers can be much more efficient than a group. A partnership can make decisions, execute, and move quickly.

The downside of the partnership situation is that the potential for trouble increases significantly if the partners are unfamiliar with each other's abilities, ambitions, or decision-making ability. When these duos attempt a route at the edge of one or both of their abilities, they are entering a dangerous zone.

A situation with a very high potential for catastrophe is with the solo climber because there is no one available to help with an accident, and also because the solo climber must completely rely on his or her own strength, ability, and decision-making psychology to make correct decisions in critical situations. And the solo climber is far more likely to encounter a critical situation.

Consider something as simple as a short technical scramble on a 14er such as North Maroon Peak. If a group or partnership has a member who gets stuck, they can be helped up or down by the other members of the party, even if the other members do nothing more than talk their partner through the difficulties. Everyone may forget such a situation almost imme- diately after it is diffused. If a solo climber finds himself stuck, he will have no help or encouragement, putting him in more peril.

Perhaps the most dangerous situation is when parties split up. One climber in the group may get tired or feel the climb is above his or her ability and turns back. Or a party of two may split up for whatever reasons including ambition (one climber wants to push on and the other wants to turn back), or non-climbing related conflicts. This is the worst possible situation because the weaker climber is then in the situation of a solo climber, except that it is unplanned and the climber is likely not prepared for such a situation. The basic climbing rule of not splitting up is to prevent such a situation.

Solo

Dylan Hettinger wanted a taste of how bad things could get.

He woke up to cold whiteness on Saturday, December 1, 2007. He had been sleeping in his car, which was parked at the Quandary Peak Trailhead just off Highway 9, south of Breckenridge. Outside his frosted windshield he saw the trail, which starts out as a road, slice into the snow-covered pines to the south. Though early in winter, several feet of snow had already fallen here at an elevation of 10,800 feet, and would continue to accumulate through winter and spring.

Dylan wasted no time preparing and packing his gear and bundling up against the cold. In the cloudy grayness of early morning he was off, walking up the well-packed trail. He was alone.

Dylan, who was 24, had moved to Denver from North Carolina just three months before this climb. Although he had some mountaineering experience—climbing Mount Washington in New Hampshire as well as a winter ascent of Mount Elbert in Colorado—he had never been to or even seen 14,265-foot Quandary Peak.

The East Ridge route on Quandary is considered to be very easy for a 14er route. In summer, it's not much more than a moderate hike that most can complete in six to eight hours. Winter conditions are more difficult, but Quandary is a comparatively easy winter ascent. The approach is short, route finding is not difficult, and avalanche terrain is avoidable. It is considered a good mountain for someone's first winter ascent.

Dylan wanted a challenge, so he decided to do a solo winter climb of Quandary. When he learned that a severe winter storm was predicted for the mountains that weekend, he decided it would just add to the challenge. He intended to climb a mountain he had never seen, alone, in winter, and in a storm. "I wanted a difficult experience," he explained.

Dylan drove up to the trailhead the night before and slept in his car. He left a note for his roommate describing his planned expedition. He brought no compass or map. But he did carry a GPS receiver he intended to use for navigation if necessary.

He had little difficulty walking down the initial section of road. After approximately three quarters of a mile, the route left the snowpacked road and turned west into a forest. Soon thereafter, the hike became much more difficult. He took no snowshoes or skis. "I didn't think I needed them. I just postholed in the deep snow," Dylan told me.

After another energy-sapping mile, the snow relented somewhat. At 12,000 feet, the wind had either blown the snow to bare rock, or packed it densely enough to walk on without punching through. Visibility was deteriorating. The sky merged in gray-white with the snow on the ground, broken only by ghostly black patches of rock outcroppings. He could only see within a quarter-mile radius. But the terrain was not difficult and this was the challenge he sought. He later told me, "The weather was not a big deal, I expected it."

After what seemed like days of blind wandering, he finally stood on the highest point he could find. It was the summit. He had met half his challenge and turned to descend. He soon came to the realization that his challenge would be far greater than he imagined.

The wind had picked up and the snowfall was thickening. "I could only see 30 feet in front of me," he said. He was having trouble finding his footsteps in the snow, and having essentially no other reference points, he became disoriented. "I wasn't as prepared to navigate in it the storm as I thought I would be. I thought my sense of direction would be stronger." The wind and his exhaustion took their toll.

His GPS receiver, his only navigational aid, had earlier failed due to the extreme cold. He wandered until the fading light of day forced him to stop and take whatever shelter he could find. He thought he was "somewhere above 13,000 feet" when he found a ledge to sit on for the night. It afforded him some shelter from the wind and snow. "I never felt any fear but did have great concern. People die in these situations," he said to me later.

He also had the fortune of having a bivouac (bivy) bag, a lightweight, body-length waterproof and windproof survival bag. Though not insulated, it would ward off the bone-chilling wind and allow some body heat retention. It wasn't meant for comfort, only for survival and he was lucky to have it. It wasn't by forethought he was carrying the bivy bag. "I never carried it before and don't know why I decided to take it." It probably saved his life.

Dylan's roommate had become increasingly worried as the hours ticked away that evening without word from Dylan. Finally, at 9:00 p.m. he called Summit County emergency services to report Dylan missing on Quandary Peak. The note Dylan left his roommate had detailed information about his plans and Summit County Rescue Group (SCR) immediately found his car at the Quandary Peak Trailhead. They were not able to search that night due to terrible conditions—temperature of -15°F with 50 mph winds.

Meanwhile, as SCR was discovering the impossibility of the weather, Dylan was hunkering down against a wind chill of nearly -60°F. Though he lost a glove while clearing snow away from his bag that night, he was generally able to keep warm through the extreme conditions. At some point the weather cleared enough for him to see sporadic house lights far below him. "That's where I need to go tomorrow," he thought, "to civilization down that valley."

At first light the next day he arose from his miserable bivouac and began moving down the mountain again. "The visibility was actually worse than the day before," he said. He did not recognize the ridges around him, but he remembered the direction of the lights he had seen and decided to hike toward them. Though he survived the night unharmed, he was ready to get out of the cold wind and devour a hot meal.

He soon found himself walking along the top of a steep, thousand-foot face, which fell to a valley on his left. It was nothing like what he'd seen the day before, but he wanted to maintain his direction toward the lights. To do this he had to descend the high angle face at some point. Multiple snow-filled chutes cut the face, and he chose one to descend. "The more chutes I crossed, the worse my options looked. I picked one and dropped down into it. I should have known the terrain better," Dylan admitted. The weather was clearing to blue skies above, but it remained freezing with high wind. He soon found himself on the north face of Quandary slogging though waist-deep snow.

In very little time he found himself in a precarious position above extremely steep rock. That is about the time an orange-colored helicopter flew by. He knew it was looking for him.

A wave of relief swept over him. He then stopped his descent and waited to be rescued. He let his guard down—oblivious of the hours he would remain in this position. He had assumed the helicopter would "drop a rope," but instead it flew off and did not return. He waited motionless in the cold wind for two more hours. "That's when I got frostbite and hypothermia; I

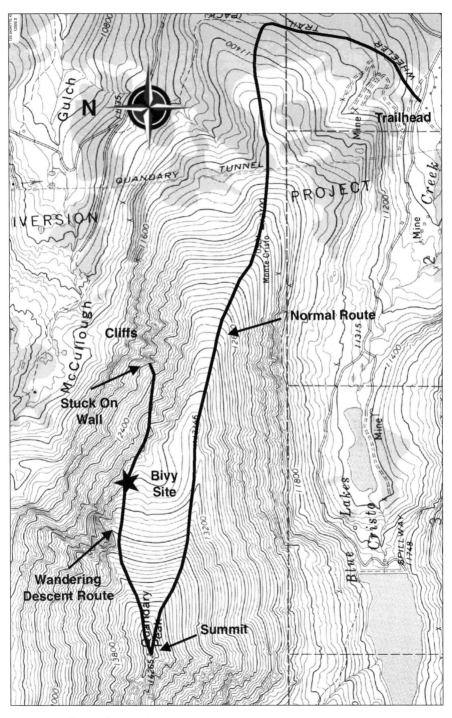

Topo map of Quandary Peak.

was okay up until then."

The helicopter that flew over Dylan was a Flight for Life air ambulance. Though not a resource generally available to rescue teams, air ambulances sometimes assist rescue operations if there is a possibility they will transport the victim as a patient. In this particular case, though, the chopper was unable to do anything more than search for Dylan by air.

If he had been on a level surface clear of obstacles such as large trees or boulders, the chopper may have been able to land and pick him up. The ship could not, however, pluck Dylan off the slope while hovering above. This medical chopper was not outfitted with equipment such as an external winch that could lift Dylan up. In Colorado, helicopters so equipped are not common and are generally unavailable for mountain rescue.

The helicopter crew did, however, alert SCR team members as to where Dylan was located. They were able to snowmobile to within several hundred feet of the face where Dylan remained motionless in the cold. Several team members approached the chute from below and shouted up to Dylan.

They told Dylan to climb down the steep rock face if he could. It would be the fastest way for him to get off the mountain. He was persuaded, and slowly began his descent. He was off the difficult section and down to the SCR rescuers within 20 minutes. The rescuers hurried Dylan away from the face and, while looking back, they witnessed an avalanche sweep the chute. Had the rescue been 10 minutes later, Dylan and his rescuers would have been buried.

The rescue team wrapped the hypothermic Dylan in big coats, put him on the back of a snowmobile and drove him to a waiting ambulance. At the hospital he was treated for his injuries including frostbite in all his fingers and toes. "All the frostbite and hypothermia happened while I waited to be rescued, not the night before," he said. "I just kind of gave up and waited for them to get me."

Dylan maintains, however, that he had never asked for a rescue and feels he would have hiked back to his car without incident if the rescue team had not shown up. "I had a plan and was following it. If I hadn't seen the helicopter I would not have stopped. I would have climbed back up that chute and gone a different way," he asserted. He would have gotten home a day later than planned and learned his lessons in navigation and survival on a winter 14er.

Despite his self-assurance in his determination, he was humbled by the experience. "The lesson I learned was don't push your skill and luck at the same time. You can't train for luck. I had bad luck Saturday but good luck on Sunday."

Back at home after his epic, Hettinger emptied his backpack. With his frostbitten fingers he pulled a 6x6-inch flat, plastic-wrapped package from the bottom of his pack. It was an unused 18-hour chemical warmer. He hadn't remembered placing it in his pack for just such an emergency. It might have prevented his hypothermia and frostbite.

But he took the experience in stride. "In the past I've come out worse, with broken bones," Dylan told me. I asked if he'd been involved in mountain accidents previously. "I was ice climbing and slipped off the top while walking down. I fell 30 feet to a road and shattered both of my heels. It happened five years ago." His doctor predicted he would never walk normally again, but the doctor was wrong and the bones mended nicely.

"Oh, and I had a cam pull," he added. A cam is a type of specialized technical rock-climbing equipment that is placed in a crack to protect a rock leader from a fall. Dylan had been rock climbing and fell, pulling out the cam that he placed to protect himself. He fell further and slammed into the rock below. "Got a compression fracture of a thoracic vertebrae and a broken wrist." I asked when that happened. "A year-and-a-half ago.

"It's not like I'm reckless, I pay attention. My cam pulled. And when I was on the ice, I just slipped; it wasn't like I was dancing up there. I don't know why it happened."

I asked if there were any other climbing accidents he had been in.

He responded, "No, not significant ones."

An article I wrote about Dylan Hettinger's experience on Quandary Peak elicited this anonymous on-line comment:

It's too bad that this unthinking neophyte endangered

not only himself but the dedicated volunteer mountain rescue team members that unselfishly responded and quite frankly saved his a**. Also it's too bad he probably won't be held financially responsible for the rescue costs incurred, and that there is no citation and fine that can be given him for being such an idiot. Reckless endangerment, perhaps?

Now that he will have some recovery time from his injuries I hope that he spends some of it reflecting on his great luck and his need for better mountaineering skills. ("Climbing skills or hospital bills.")

I also hope that he and his family pony up and make a sizable donation to Summit County Rescue Group and the state mountain rescue fund. Maybe the money they saved on funeral expenses could be given to SCR instead.

This chastisement represents a surprisingly common opinion among climbers and non-climbers alike. If you don't know what you're doing in the mountains, don't go there. If you do get caught in a tough or dangerous situation, then you deserve to suffer the consequences. Yet hikers of all ability levels solo climb 14ers often. Dylan happened to get caught but he is hardly alone in that unfortunate club.

There was the case in 2004 of a Longs Peak climber who had been turned back twice previously and was determined to get to the summit. He pressed onward after his partners turned back due to threatening weather at the Keyhole, a significant feature fairly near the summit. He was severely unprepared and displayed a disturbing lack of common sense as described in the following report from Rocky Mountain National Park:

On Saturday, September 4th, Sudheer Averineni, a 26-year-old Indian national, attempted a climb of the Keyhole route on Longs Peak, the park's popular "Fourteener." While attempting the summit, Averineni's two companions turned back near the Keyhole formation around

13,000 feet due to deteriorating conditions. Averineni continued on, though, and was last seen a short distance below the summit just after noon. When he failed to return that evening, a search was begun. Conditions on Longs Peak from Saturday afternoon through Sunday were severe—fresh snow, rime ice, recorded winds in excess of 60 mph, and temperatures well below freezing. Averineni's body was found on the summit around 1 p.m. on Sunday. He was dressed in sneakers, jeans, a cotton shirt, and a cotton sweatshirt. A cell phone was found in his pocket. The cause of death has been determined to have been exposure. This was reportedly Averineni's third attempt on Longs Peak this year.

Reports like these commonly elicit the "What the hell was he thinking?" reaction. But it may not be as simple as a black-and-white report implies. Surely, Averineni did not set out to kill himself, and it's reasonable to assume that he did not live his life on the risky edge of death either through carelessness or bravado. Most mountain climbers are quite the opposite, in fact. Hiking even the easiest 14ers requires more inspiration than walking along a park path. They demand more planning than a weekend car camping trip, more determination than playing a video game, more endurance than a 10 kilometer run.

Though it's easy to dismiss Averineni's disaster and shocking lack of preparation as the result of his novice abilities and knowledge, other soloist accidents are not so easy to explain.

Take the case of David Boyd, whose lifeless body was found September 4, 2008, on the rocky slopes of Little Bear Peak in the southern Sangre de Cristos.

Boyd began his climbing day on his mountain bike, pedaling up the four-wheel-drive road that leads to the Blanca Basin at 6:25 a.m. the previous day. The 47-year-old doctor from Houston, Texas, had planned to bike to Lake Como and climb the three 14ers accessible from the basin: Blanca Peak, Ellingwood Point, and Little Bear. This involved ascending 7,500 feet from the San Luis Valley floor to the summit of Blanca, then descending and re-ascending 2,000 feet to gain the summits of Ellingwood and Little Bear.

Boyd's ambitious plan was well within his athletic ability. He was a regular participant in hundred-mile biking and running endurance events. He had climbed 40 of the 14ers already, many of them as multiple peaks in a day. By all accounts he was a strong, thoughtful climber and had the background to safely climb the three peaks. He carried extra clothing, medical supplies, and a GPS. He wore a rock helmet and carried a SPOT beacon, a satellite phone/GPS device that, when a button is pressed, transmits your exact location to a predetermined email address so that loved ones or friends can track your progress, or, if the distress function is used, they can respond with help. Thus, the SPOT beacon is an excellent tool for the soloist as a sort of radio lifeline to civilization.

Boyd summited Blanca Peak, a relatively straightforward trail hike, signed the summit register, and progressed to Ellingwood Point, a relatively easy jaunt from Blanca. He then descended back to the basin below the ramparts of Little Bear Peak.

Little Bear is the high point along the ridge that forms the southern wall of the Lake Como Basin. Most of the southern wall is made of cliffs or steep ledges that require technical roped climbing to ascend safely. There is one couloir, however, that cuts up the wall from the basin floor to the ridge. It is the only easy route and thus begins the route up Little Bear. Boyd ascended this couloir, which tops out and cuts through Little Bear's west ridge just below the top, offering a gateway to the easy slopes beyond.

From the top of the west ridge, the standard route proceeds west about two-thirds of a mile to the base of a second couloir called the Hourglass. The trail is an easy, well-worn path paralleling the south side of the ridge, and Boyd likely covered this ground quickly.

The Hourglass is what gives Little Bear its reputation as one of the most difficult Colorado 14ers. It is a couloir that starts out as a shallow, wide rock pile at the bottom, narrows as it rises to a steep, solid rock wall a few feet wide in the center, and then opens up to a steep, wide bowl at the top. The narrow neck of this hourglass-shaped couloir cuts through a vertical cliff band on the west face of Little Bear and offers the easiest way up.

This neck consists of 150 feet of near vertical water-polished rock that must be ascended and later downclimbed. It is rare to find this section dry, as it usually contains a small flowing spring when not covered in ice or snow, thus rendering all the holds wet and slippery. The climbing is class 4, meaning that a rope is desired by most parties because a fall can be lethal. Many climbers of Little Bear bring a rope, if not to ascend then at least to rappel—a rope assisted descent—this route, avoiding a fearsome down-climb on the descent.

Above the neck, the Hourglass couloir is a very steep, crumbly concave-shaped bowl. Spontaneous rockfall is common, and because the route above the Hourglass neck spirals up through the loose bowl above, rocks dislodged by careless or clumsy hikers rain down like meteors on any unlucky soul clinging to the steep neck. The Hourglass has earned a nickname, the Bowling Alley, as several hapless climbers have been struck here like pins, being severely injured or killed. This concoction of hazards creates the most dangerous and difficult obstacle on the normal route of any Colorado 14er.

Boyd was wisely wearing his helmet during his time in the Bowling Alley and there is no indication he had any problem with the climbing or the rockfall here. From his SPOT beacon, it is known that he arrived on the 14,037-foot-high summit of Little Bear at 2:49 p.m. He had completed all three 14ers in just over eight hours from the trailhead, a feat that takes most climbers two or three days to achieve. It was a noteworthy accomplishment that gave testament to Boyd's high level of fitness. Boyd found the summit register, opened it up, and penned "3rd Peak Today! Nice & Dry."

Forty-two hours later, Alamosa Volunteer Search and Rescue personnel found Boyd's body. He was located at 12,400 feet in a steep, rugged couloir below the west ridge of Little Bear, far from the normal route. He had negotiated the most notorious pitches of Little Bear only to succumb on the relatively simple lower slopes, apparently trying to descend the west ridge too early, mistaking a steep, cliff-like couloir for the easy exit couloir further down the ridge that he had ascended only hours before.

No one witnessed Boyd's descent from the summit or the events leading up to his accident, but to those who knew David, as well as the SAR personnel who evacuated his body, it was a tragic and confounding ending to his life.

A friend of Boyd's wrote, "Word from one of the SAR respondents was that David was one of the most well-prepared hikers they had come across." He was also extremely fit and had plenty of climbing experience, all of which points to someone who would not make a simple yet fatal mistake.

After Boyd signed the summit register, he replaced it and likely began his descent almost immediately. He likely hiked down the steep, loose upper bowl and downclimbed the slippery rock in the neck of the Bowling Alley without incident, making his way on the much easier ground below to the west ridge, and then down to the access couloir.

It is easy for climbers to make the mistake of locating the incorrect access couloir on Little Bear's west ridge. There are six couloirs descending the ridge between the north face and the actual access couloir, and all are almost cliff-like in steepness. Several couloirs start out as a simple hike only to become exposed scrambles requiring a technical roped descent. However, the cliff sections are recognizably more difficult than the normal access couloir and a hiker can easily reverse his route and find the easy descent.

It appears that Boyd was downclimbing the difficult couloir where his body was found, raising the question as to why he did not reverse his route when he could.

But that mystery is compounded by the fact that he was in the wrong couloir in the first place. Boyd carried a GPS receiver that, if he was using it, would precisely locate the top of the correct access couloir. If he was not navigating with his GPS, the question becomes, why not? Little Bear's normal route is quite complex and use of a GPS receiver is a highly valuable tool, especially to the solo climber who is relying only on himself to navigate. Boyd must have understood this as evidenced by him carrying the receiver in his pack.

There are at least two possible explanations to Boyd's apparent lapses of judgment. The first was his physical state. He had ascended more than 7,500 feet, had expended an exorbitant amount of energy at altitudes above 13,000 feet, and had contended with the mental stress of negotiating the most dangerous 14er route before he was confronted by a confusing last set of couloirs. It is likely Boyd was not at 100 percent decision-making capacity.

Extreme athletes are very good at persistence. A 50-mile run or a

100-mile mountain bike course requires persistence but not much of the wide-range decision making that mountaineering requires. Also, altitude can affect cognition, especially when compounded by physical exertion, dehydration, and inadequate nutrition. These conditions are nearly impossible to avoid on the length of climbs that Boyd was attempting, regardless of physical conditioning.

The second possibility is that Boyd may have been caught in a storm. Witnesses noticed dark clouds in the vicinity of Little Bear during the afternoon at the time Boyd would have been descending. His summit register comment, "Nice & Dry" seems to contradict this theory, but he may have been referring to the condition of the Bottleneck rock, normally wet with runoff. Boyd may have made bad decisions while contending with freezing, wet, and wildly gusting weather.

It may seem surprising that Boyd would make a mistake as simple as falling down a retreatable rock section, but it was not a unique accident. Just five years before Boyd soloed into calamity on Little Bear, a father and son team descended into the same trap. Although they climbed as a team, similar circumstances and perhaps a similar decision process surrounded both tragedies.

Fifty-three-year-old John Boyles and his 20-year-old son, Aaron, had gotten a late start on the morning of August 2, 2003. They "had gotten in so late the night before" that they slept in until 8:00 a.m. The pair decided to climb the Northwest Face on Little Bear, a less traveled and much more difficult route than the Hourglass. They struggled to stay on route over hundreds of feet of fourth class scrambling. The pair had rock climbing skills but limited mountaineering skills, having summited only 20 14ers, and burned precious daylight attempting to find their way. The time-consuming ascent combined with their late start placed them on the summit at 2:00 p.m.

They found themselves enveloped by dark, menacing clouds that soon broke into a severe thunderstorm of drenching rain and wildly whipping wind. Static electricity buzzed and crackled in the air and the rocks around them as they descended the normal Hourglass route. The storm was so intense that it dislodged the rubble above them, forcing the pair to dodge random rockslides hurling down the slopes. They eluded lightning strikes as they watched the "hail pile up like snow" on the ridges below. Though dressed in waterproof shells, hypothermia threatened.

They managed to downclimb the dangerous Bowling Alley and reached the easier ground below as the rain began to let up. They could see tents and lakes in the valley below the ridge. It seemed they had dodged a bullet and only needed to descend an easy couloir to camp.

John picked a couloir on the ridge and began descending with Aaron following. The descent was tricky, but John persisted in looking for a way down. He yelled back to his son, "Aaron, I think I found a way over here." He then fell and landed in a sitting position on steep, wet slabs several feet below.

Aaron watched in shock as his father struggled to cling to the slippery surface, but he scraped down and went out of sight over a second cliff. He came into view again much further down, tumbling down the face of the rock. He disappeared over a third cliff, coming back into view as his lifeless body came to rest 500 feet below.

Aaron screamed for help, and a hiker emerged from one of the tiny tents below and was able to shout up to Aaron, directing him to the correct access couloir further down the ridge. Aaron was lucky. It is difficult to know what he would have done without help, in a state of shock after seeing his father fall, and not knowing about the easier descent route.

Though both men could have made the decision to return up the couloirs to the ridge as the climbing became difficult, neither did. The Boyles, who ascended a different route, may have felt the couloir was no more difficult than anything they had climbed that day. David Boyd's decision is somewhat more of a mystery given that he had ascended the correct couloir. Though the Boyles pair made many errors in their ascent—getting up late and burning time on a difficult route—we don't know what other mistakes Boyd made, if any. What they had in common was a storm and fatigue, something that may have caused both men to make one fatal decision.

Kevin Wright, director of Alamosa Volunteer Search and Rescue, has seen the results of many accidents on Little Bear over the years. "Little Bear is not like the Crestones [14ers bordering Alamosa County], it is loose and dangerous. The Bowling Alley is highly dangerous. The route is very difficult."

As for why climbers like the Boyles and Boyd choose the incorrect access couloir, Wright comments, "There are three lakes [Como, Blue Lakes, and Crater Lake] and five couloirs. People mistake one of the upper lakes for Como and descend the wrong couloir." In other words, many climbers intend to key off of Como Lake, the lowest of the three, as an indicator that the access couloir is near. By mistaking one of the upper lakes for Como, climbers descend the wrong couloir. "Each of those couloirs looks reasonable at the start but gets steeper as you descend." In difficult conditions, this simple mistake has proven to be fatal for more than one. There is a cairn at the top of the correct gully to indicate the proper descent route, but climbers must be paying attention on their ascent and look for it on the descent.

There was one final twist at the end of the soloist David Boyd's story. Concerned friends called the Alamosa County sheriff to report a strange event they were observing from David's SPOT beacon data. Though his data showed that he progressed continuously through his climbs of Blanca, Ellingwood Point, and Little Bear, he appeared to stop for 12 hours in a curious location below the west ridge of Little Bear. Several data points were sent from the same spot before stopping. The data points mysteriously resumed hours later, indicating the same location. For twelve hours they received sporadic stationary data points. They had not been able to contact David during this time. Alarmed by these strange and ominous events, they reported this information to the Alamosa County sheriff.

No one received an emergency 911 transmission from David's beacon, only the repeated location data. The sheriff provided the Alamosa Volunteer Search and Rescue team with the GPS data, and it led precisely to David's body. This raised two questions: Why did David fail to press the 911 emergency button on his beacon, and why was there a gap of several hours in the data that was transmitted?

Summit of Little Bear Peak after a summer hailstorm.

The first question was easy to answer. The rescuers noted that it was apparent that David was killed instantly. He would not have been able to press the emergency button on his beacon if his fall was a complete surprise to him.

The explanation to the second question is that David may not have ever pressed any button on his beacon. The SPOT beacon has an automatic mode that transmits location information on a periodic basis. The beacon continued transmitting data after David was killed. The reason for the sporadic transmissions could be explained by the fact that the beacon was receiving and transmitting from a couloir.

Portable devices that receive and transmit data to satellites, including satellite phones and GPS receivers, require a clear view of the sky to work. Because the satellites responsible for communication and GPS data orbit and move relative to fixed locations on the earth, locations with a limited view of the sky can lose visibility to these satellites at times.

The rock walls of the ridge and sides of the couloir surrounding the beacon severely limited its view of the sky, thus communication may have been lost as the satellites orbited, only to be regained hours later. Those mountaineers using technology that relies on satellites should be aware of this limitation.

Though David's beacon triggered the search for him, it did not help him to survive. It is likely nothing would have helped once he made the decision to descend the wrong couloir, but a solo climber who dies rarely leaves a record of the thought process leading to his last decision.

The Dangerous Leader Syndrome

A climbing team with a strong leader has a well-defined group dynamic. Essentially the leader makes all the important decisions on a climb. The team follows the leader, and depending on the strength of that leadership, decisions may never be questioned. This can be one of the best situations for a climbing team if the leader is careful, experienced, and puts the needs of the group ahead of personal ambition. It can be a disaster otherwise. A strong leader who has little experience or is only driven to get him- or herself to the summit can rapidly get a group into trouble. And sometimes a leader's comfort with risk places an entire group at risk.

I ran into such a person in Colorado in the 1990s. He had the unfortunate characteristics of appearing to be a strong and safe leader, but in reality was an extreme risk taker who led his followers into extraordinarily dangerous situations. He did this not because of a disregard for the welfare of his followers, but because he accepted a much higher level of risk and expected other mountaineers to do so as well.

On the last climb of his life, the leader took one step onto an overloaded snow chute and instantly sensed something wrong. He heard a deep, rumbling *whoomf* and saw the surface around him move. It was like the surface of a vast still lake beginning to flow after the dam breaks.

He turned to run out of the slope but felt the unstoppable weight of a thousand tons of snow pressing him downward. His mind probably screamed for escape, but like an insect caught in a spider's web, his flailing only drew him deeper into the trap. He would inevitably feel ice invading his clothing as the white tide contorted his form. His body was scraped around trees; his bones were shattered against boulders. He was flung over a cliff and crushed by the waterfall of snow. Surely seconds became hours as he was flung like a rag doll down the slope. When he finally came to rest he was encased in the frozen mass, unable to move even a finger. If he was still conscious at this point, he felt his lungs burning as his diaphragm pulled to no relief. He would have quickly lost consciousness and succumbed to death in minutes. It took rescuers three weeks to find his body.

And so was the death of 38-year-old Valerin Anton below the 14,018-foot-high Pyramid Peak on January 27, 1996. He was caught in a 300-foot wide avalanche that ran 1,400 vertical feet to the valley floor. Val, as his friends knew him, was the only victim. He was leading a climbing party of four up the peak despite an extreme avalanche warning in the Maroon Creek Valley outside of Aspen, Colorado.

An excerpt from the accident report in *Accidents in North American Mountaineering* 1997 described Val's apparent wanton disregard for safety:

> Due to the avalanche danger, snowmobilers were not using the road at the time; it is exposed to numerous avalanche runouts. The climbing party encountered an employee of the snowmobile operation who advised them of the avalanche hazard. On the group's approach to the 14,018-foot Pyramid Peak the climbers snowshoed over several large, fresh avalanche debris piles lying across the road. After snowshoeing approximately eight miles, the party began an ascent of the steep, northwest facing side of the glacial valley. This ascent was begun in darkness around 7:30 p.m.

Not only did Val ignore verbal warnings and the danger signs in his immediate environment, he and his party didn't even prepare for such

Rescue team on a probe line searching for a buried avalanche victim.

conditions. The surviving members were not carrying avalanche shovels to dig up a potential victim, were not wearing avalanche beacons, and had little to no training in either evaluation of avalanche risk or recovery of those caught in an avalanche. Val seemed to be asking for trouble, having deliberately climbed into such an extreme hazard.

The threat posed by avalanches in Colorado is insidious and remains one of the states most feared and mysterious mountain hazards. Coastal climates, such as Washington and Oregon, produce prodigious amounts of wet snowfall on the high mountains there. Avalanches in those climates are more predictable; when the snow falls, avalanches occur. The threat tapers off after two or three days. Though there are the occasional surprise slides, the vast majority of avalanches happen within a predictable timespan after a weather event such as a large storm or rapid warming. A climber can easily, though sometimes frustratingly, avoid these dangerous conditions and climb on a relatively avalanche safe day. These climate conditions exist on Denali and the high peaks in the Alaska Range, Mount Rainier in Washington, Mount Hood in Oregon, on many of the high peaks in California, and in the Himalayas where the tallest mountains in the world are located.

The climatic conditions in Colorado are vastly different from these areas. High-country winters produce a thin, dry snowpack, while air temperatures get extremely cold, commonly falling below -20°F. The combination of a thin snowpack and cold air temperatures generates *depth hoar*, a layer of snow below the surface that has very low bonding strength as compared to other forms of snow. This layer can release much more easily and allow the snow lying above it to slide down a slope.

Depth hoar forms in cold temperatures, usually generated at night under clear winter skies. The weak layer can lie at any depth below the surface of the snowpack and remain dormant for months while subsequent storms pile up more and more snow, producing extremely dangerous conditions. And this danger is invisible, waiting to spring unexpectedly on an unwary climber whose footsteps cause just enough disturbance to set it loose.

MOST DANGEROUS 14ER

I have often been asked, "What is the most dangerous 14er in Colorado?" My answer is, it depends on how you define danger. Technical difficulty such as Longs Peak may seem dangerous to some but not to others. Remoteness, like on Humboldt where a misstep can mean a rescue that takes days, may seem dangerous. High rockfall potential such as on the Maroon Bells may seem more dangerous to some. But really what most people mean is, "Where are the most accidents happening?" But even that question is deceiving. Some mountains have far more climbers and thus more accidents than others.

But if I had to select just one, I could make a good argument for Quandary as being the most dangerous. This may surprise some, but easy access during winter, nearness to the Front Range urban areas, and variety of routes make this a dangerous mountain. Of all the 14ers, Quandary has one of the highest accident rates.

Colorado is not the only climate that produces these snow conditions. This hazard is also endemic to the Canadian Rockies. But the Colorado mountains are notorious for consistently having the highest number of avalanche deaths per year in North America. And climbers suffer many of these deaths.

Understanding the hidden avalanche hazard produced by depth hoar requires education as well as diligence in looking for that hazard. The only way a weak layer can be found is by digging a snow pit from the surface of the snow all the way to the ground below. The pit must be dug on the slope the climber expects to be on because even the direction the slope faces can have a major effect on the conditions of the snow on the slope. Wind will deposit snow differently depending on how a slope is oriented to the prevailing direction of the blowing snow. North-facing slopes experience colder temperatures than south-facing slopes and may have weaker layers. Only a direct examination of the snowpack in question can answer the question of if and where the weak layers are located.

But the cold air and thin snowpack of deep winter are not the only conditions that can set up avalanche hazards in Colorado. The weather in the high mountains can produce them in any season. During warmer months the sun loosens snow accumulated over the winter to produce deadly wet slab avalanches. Only three and a half years prior to Val's accident, an avalanche of this nature killed two members of a climbing team just across the valley from where he met his demise.

On June 13, 1992, a group of seven Colorado Mountain Club climbers began their climb at 4:30 a.m. Their goal was to ascend the East Face Couloir of 14,156-foot Maroon Peak, a snow route that would allow them to bypass much of the steep, crumbly rock normally encountered on the slopes of the Elk Range peaks. Maroon Peak is known more popularly as the "Left Maroon Bell," forming the backdrop of one of the most photographed mountain scenes in the United States.

The group arrived at the base of the couloir after a three and a half hour hike along the valley floor. Once there, they noticed avalanche debris from a recent event in the couloir. The debris did not cover the entire width of the couloir, a warning sign of continued danger. It was enough of a threat to cause one of the team members to turn back. The other six decided to continue up.

Even though it was still early, only 8 a.m., the summer sun had been thawing the east face snow for almost two and a half hours. Their next 1,500 feet of climbing would require an additional two-plus hours on the snow, placing them in an escalating hazard. *Dawson's Guide to Colorado's Fourteeners* recommends that skiers attempting a descent of this couloir be off of east facing snow slopes by 9 a.m. in late spring and early summer to avoid these dangerous conditions.

By 10 a.m. the team was high in the couloir but still some 300 feet below the ridgeline. The snow was noticeably soft and wet, and with each step they sank a little deeper in the snow until they found themselves postholing up the slope. As the higher two climbers crossed the fracture line of the earlier avalanche, they triggered a slab beneath their feet approximately 40 feet by 20 feet in size. This slab quickly crumbled into a current and swept the two lead climbers downward. They collided with the next two climbers below them, hurling all four down the face. The last two saw what was happening above them and luckily were able to scramble to the side and avoid being hit.

The four climbers caught were dragged 1,500 feet down to the base of the couloir. Two of the climbers were killed, and the other two suffered broken bones and lacerations. Although the amount of snow was not great enough to bury and suffocate the climbers, it was sufficiently massive to trap them in a torrent down the face where they were killed or injured by the fall.

That type of avalanche hazard exists almost exclusively in late spring, usually peaking in May through late June, depending on the particular year's snow depth and spring temperatures. That is when the freeze/thaw cycle destroys the underlying structure of deep snow accumulated through the winter. After mid-July, snow conditions are generally well packed and highly stable until new snow flies in autumn, which produces yet another type of seasonal avalanche hazard.

When new snow accumulates on the frozen surface of ice that has survived the summer, "permanent" snow commonly found in high, generally north-facing couloirs in Colorado, the adhesion of this new snow is tenuous and creates a late summer season (or early snow season) hazard.

On October 16, 1994, two young mountain climbers aged 26 and 27, experienced the tragic side of this hazard on their descent of 14,197-foot Mount Belford, located 15 miles northwest of the town of Buena Vista in central Colorado.

The pair had ascended the northwest ridge route that day from their camp at treeline. Although the normal route is not much more difficult than a high altitude walk, they likely planned to glissade from somewhere high on Belford, as each was carrying an ice axe, a tool not required if the climber sticks to the normal route.

On their descent, they entered a north facing couloir that ran about 2,000 feet down from the northwest ridge to the basin below. They probably thought a fast glissade down this couloir would be an exhilarating way to wind up their climb, and so they started down with ice axes for self-arrest at the ready.

They unknowingly entered a death trap. A storm earlier that month had deposited new snow over the old ice layer in the couloir. As the pair zoomed down to the 13,600-foot level where the steepness increases, their added load triggered a slide. A layer two feet deep and 150 feet wide broke and swept them into the basin. One was buried and killed. The other survived, half buried, with a fractured pelvis and two broken femurs.

The survivor dug himself free using only his bare hands. Unable to walk or even stand, seeing no sign of his partner or any other climbers in the valley and with no way to call for help, he had but one choice to survive. He began what must have been an excruciating quest to crawl back toward his tent, located two miles away over rough, rock-strewn terrain.

Like Joe Simpson, who crawled for days with a broken leg in Peru as told in the book *Touching the Void*, he dragged himself for hours or perhaps days, toward his tent below. Unlike Simpson, however, he did not make it back to camp. Searchers, alerted to the fact he had not shown up for work the next week, found his frozen body only 100 yards from his tent. His partner was not found for 10 more months, when a hiker spotted his body melting out of the snowpack.

Nevertheless, avalanche risk encountered in deep winter is the most notoriously deceptive. The education, patience, and persistence it takes to find weak snow layers should be present in any team determined to climb Colorado mountains in that season. These were severely lacking with Val and his group, but even so, this does not explain why they ignored the explicit danger warnings all around them as they hiked in to Pyramid Peak. The commercial snowmobile operator was not an out-of-towner speculating about the conditions; he was a local who knew the area and had experienced the danger. And if that wasn't enough, snowshoeing across several massive piles of new avalanche debris should have set off deafening alarm bells even to the most novice climber. Yet it neither turned Val around nor caused his group to question his decision to continue.

Val probably had some understanding of avalanche hazards, but the speculation after the accident was that he did not understand the special conditions in Colorado. He was probably more used to the coastal climate that exists in the mountains of his homeland, and because no storms had passed through in the previous days, he possibly felt it was safe. However, he still had to ignore the slides they crossed that were plainly recent.

Even with all the warnings, it appears Val's group followed him indiscriminately, and that Val himself had some sort of blind ambition. But in reality the man himself was more complex. He was ambitious, but it wasn't likely that he wanted to die. Two more pieces should be added to the puzzle of his motivation. Val was a strong, experienced mountaineer with an obsession with his own version of *The List*, and he had personally beaten long odds on several epic adventures in his life that likely made him feel invincible no matter what he did.

Val, a climber from Romania, and I crossed paths four years before his death on the frozen slopes of the 14,110-foot-high Pikes Peak near Colorado Springs. He had been turned back on his solo attempt of the peak. He had not brought snowshoes, but that did not deter him from postholing for miles up Barr Trail before giving up. He was always focused on the summit. Lack of gear and difficult conditions merely slowed him. He was from the hard-core eastern European climbing tradition, having cut his teeth in the Carpathian Mountains bereft of even modest climbing gear.

I was on Pikes Peak training for a climb of the 22,850-foot-high Aconcagua, the highest peak in South America. He seemed impressed by my ambition, may have felt a kind of kinship, and prodded me to go on a climb with him sometime. The next year I agreed to a difficult winter attempt of Longs Peak with him, via Kiener's route.

Four of us hiked up to the base of the towering East Face cliffs of Longs Peak and set up camp at 12,000 feet. That night the wind built to hurricane speed, threatening to rip our tents from the ground and roll us all the way back to the parking lot. No one slept at all. The next day the winds had relented a bit but were still 40 miles-per-hour at camp and far worse higher up. The mountain rumbled in a wind that sounded like a hundred freight trains. Undeterred, Val still wanted to make the summit attempt. I was astonished—did he seriously think we could move up there? That we could survive such an environment, let alone climb in it? Was it his ambition or a kind of madness? "No thanks," I said, "we can come back when the weather improves; this peak is essentially in our backyard."

Val reluctantly descended with the rest of us, sullen and quiet except when he repeated, "we didn't even try." Later that night he phoned me to say he "felt bad. We didn't even try." I asked why it was so important to him. His response was that his goal was "to climb all the 14ers in winter by non-standard routes." This was his version of *The List*. I tried to explain that conditions would improve, that it didn't seem reasonable to attempt a difficult route in bad weather when it could be perfectly calm weather in a week. And still winter. There was no hurry.

I assume that Val had a different viewpoint. Maybe he felt that he did need to hurry. His past had taught him to take advantage of all opportunities no matter how small and risky.

In attempting to defect, Val had literally escaped from communist Romania in 1986. He was apprehended by authorities in Yugoslavia and sent back to a Romanian prison. He served several months and was released. A year later he saw another chance to escape from Romania and this time he was successful and made it to Holland where he was able to find work on a dairy farm. Eventually he was able to smuggle his fiancé out of Romania as well. They married and wound up in America. They settled in Colorado because of their love for the mountains, where Val worked as a welder during the week and climbed on the weekends. He quickly joined in the 14er mania, but not to merely summit all the 14ers by their easiest routes. He felt that was too easy, and he created the more challenging version for himself.

Val had been a member of a speed-climbing team in Romania. He learned techniques that would speed his ascent on roped technical climbs. Some of those techniques would compromise safety in the interest of speed. This is not necessarily a bad trade-off since many times speed equals safety on a climb. The less time you spend hanging out in the danger zone, the better chances you have of surviving it. He demonstrated his speed-climbing techniques one afternoon, to my horror, as I followed him up the Bastille Crack, a multi-pitch technical rock climb in Eldorado Canyon near Boulder.

I soon discovered a very uncomfortable secret to his speed: his gear placement was very poor and sparse, and pieces would fall out of the rock soon after he climbed past them. The wedges and camming devices he placed in cracks as he ascended were there to anchor the rope in case he fell. It is standard technical rock climbing practice to place protective devices in the rock periodically as the climber ascends. If the climber falls, the last device placed would "catch" him. Val had placed pieces of protection seated so haphazardly as to render them useless.

On the other hand, he was a consummate rock gymnast and would have had no problem soloing the route. Well, I thought, he was leading the climb and taking most of the risk, because the rock placements were there for his protection. I was just happy he took the time to belay me when it was my turn. I had no intention of increasing my personal risk on the climb. That was when I began calling him crazy. The label was part good-natured ribbing, part respect for his intensity, and part because he sometimes appeared not sane.

On one social visit to his home in Denver he showed me photos of the mountains of Romania, breaking out a map and tracing the route he took while training on backcountry skis. His ski routes were dozens of miles long. I was impressed. He had rock climbing skills and was an endurance athlete. He ran marathons regularly in the summer, skied long distances in the winter, and climbed mountains all year long.

He was an expert in every aspect of mountaineering, including equipment. The poverty of Romania drove him to learn whatever skills it took to make his own climbing gear. He tailored his own Gore-Tex shell wear. He constructed his backpacks and even made a pair of lightweight snowshoes. I knew of few people who did this; most spent money on expensive store-bought equipment. Val thought that was a waste and trusted his own equipment and clothing far more than something manufactured. He also trusted his own judgment more than others, a judgment tempered with a higher willingness to take risks, and a comfort level with higher risks than were acceptable to most climbers in Colorado.

It is tempting to assume Val's drive to climb blinded him to the risks involved. I don't think this was the case, however. I know other mountaineers who grew up behind the now-crumbled "iron curtain," and many of them display an attitude about risk that is rare in the west. There is a damn-the-torpedoes-and-go-for-it mentality expressed by these climbers. Mountain literature is replete with super-risk-taking mountaineers from Russia and Poland. They are not ignorant of risk, but accept a much higher level of risk. That acceptance frequently demands the highest price in the game of mountaineering.

It is important to note that the rest of Val's team could have, and should have, paid as much attention to their situation as if they were on their own. Would they have turned around, or would they not have been there in the first place? Val's group knew Val and his proclivity for risk, but why did they risk their own lives? My personal experience with Val was that he strongly resisted any attempt to turn back once he got going on a route, and it's extremely difficult for a climber to dissent if that climber has already relegated most of the decision making to the leader. In this situation, followers *must* trust that the leader has their best interests in mind, yet be prepared to question obvious digression from this philosophy.

Val, the super-athlete, the mountaineer from Romania who escaped his country twice and survived prison, had only one climbing mode in Colorado: go for it at almost any expense. He survived long odds all his life and probably felt it would go on forever. He ignored the fact that tomorrow or the next day or the next month, the conditions would be less deadly, and the mountains would still be there.

Winter Storm Warning

Longs Peak is the mythic challenge for mountaineers. Ranging from absolute beginners who have never set foot on a hillside, to world-class technical climbers seeking the most difficult routes, mountain climbers trek to Rocky Mountain National Park to undergo their trial by fire. Or more appropriately, trial by ice.

The 14,255-foot-high summit is protected like an ancient castle, completely encircled by steep walls and surrounded by a vast wilderness. It is the northernmost 14er in the state, rising so high above surrounding peaks that it catches the worst of the storms surrounding its summit. Summer thunderstorms form over and engulf the upper mountain, discharging lightning and dumping hail and rain on the surrounding cliffs.

The altitude and northern latitude of Longs Peak conspire to produce some of the most severe winter storms in the country. The jet stream regularly dips south and rakes the summit with winds in excess of 100 miles-per-hour for days at a time. Temperatures can fall below -40°F. More than 10 feet of snow may be produced by a single storm. Climbers training for Everest and Denali come to Longs Peak in the winter to experience the difficult climate conditions.

Longs attracts roughly 10,000 climbers per year, many who have never climbed a mountain before but wish to face its renowned challenge. The easiest climb, called the Keyhole Route, is seven-and-one-half miles from trailhead to summit, ascending nearly one mile. The route requires prolonged hiking above treeline as well as a great deal of scrambling over exposed terrain as the summit is approached. This is the "easy" way up Longs, but far more challenging than the easy routes on most other 14ers in the state. It is enormously difficult for those not experienced at hiking mountains and who live at lower altitudes.

The Keyhole Route is only a small part of the challenges offered by

Longs. The peak has more than 100 named routes, many of which are on the Diamond, a sheer, 1,500-foot vertical wall on the East Face of the mountain. Routes on the Diamond are extremely difficult and reserved for experts who can climb at high altitude under the threat of storms.

Lying between the extremes of the Keyhole and the Diamond are several routes that attract journeymen mountaineers—those climbers who yearn for greater challenges than a mere trail hike, but who are not looking for the technical challenges the Diamond. Several of these routes lie on the East Face, on the cliffs next to the Diamond. These routes are known as Kiener's, the Notch Couloir, and Alexander's Chimney. They make their siren call to the alpinists, most of whom overcome their climbing challenge, but some who infamously do not.

Take the example of 45-year-old Joe Massari, who attempted a springtime ascent of the East Face of Longs on April 20, 1991. Climbing alone into dangerous conditions, he vanished without a trace. Handwritten posters at the Longs Peak trailhead appealed for any sign or information about the man who was last seen at treeline, where he was warned of storms and high avalanche conditions, but continued on. He was an experienced mountaineer, but there were hints of trouble in his personal life. Perhaps he was attempting to temporarily escape to the mountains, to a place where he felt strong and more in control than he was in other aspects of his life. When he encountered the deadly conditions, he either ignored them, felt he could handle them, or perhaps even felt he had nothing to lose. Whatever he thought, he deliberately climbed into extreme hazard where he knew he would be on the razor's edge of survival.

At some point on the most difficult snow-covered rock scrambling of the route, the solo climber who took no rope or any safety gear, fell and plummeted more than 1,500 feet to the base of the East Face where his crushed body was buried under tons of avalanching snow. No one witnessed the fall and the storm soon erased any evidence he had been there at all. He was found months later as the summer melt-off exposed his body and other equipment he had been carrying, scattered and broken on Mills Glacier.

The position of his body confirmed that he had fallen from high on Kiener's Route, a passage seemingly cursed from the time of its discovery.

It is named after Walter Kiener, a Swiss guide who first climbed the route in the winter of 1925 while leading Agnes Vaille to the summit, and subsequently to her death on the descent. This route is also known as the Mountaineer's Route because of the wide range of skills necessary for anyone to successfully ascend it. It requires a long day of hiking, crampon work, technical rope work, and routefinding. This is the test piece route on which some mountaineers tragically fail, whether solo or not.

Why this particular climber continued on in terrible conditions is unknown, but he, like soloist Dylan Hettinger, may have wanted to see how bad it could get, and like David Boyd, got stuck in a difficult position that killed him. We don't know what these soloists thought in the end but it's clear that very poor decisions were made, and Kiener's is a harsh place to test your solo climbing thinking ability.

If the psychology of solo climbing raises the potential for practitioners to make dangerous decisions, this implies it is safer to climb with a group of like-minded partners. The more heads there are in the decision making the better. But, as discussed earlier, there is a situation where this benefit breaks down and a dangerous dynamic develops. It is between two partners who generally do not know each other's personalities or skill level very well, and who have little experience on the terrain they encounter. Throw in a desire to "go for it" and it becomes a recipe for disaster. Mix this dynamic with Kiener's Route and the outcome can be a frightening tale of suffering and disaster.

In the early morning darkness on October 11, 1997, Chris Sproul and Dave Sweedler began their climb of the East Face of Longs Peak. Their objective was to climb the Notch Couloir, a route just south of Kiener's and of similar difficulty, essentially a variant of the same East Face climb. Both routes share the same start on Lambs Slide (a wide moderate-angle snow gully) and Broadway (a ledge system half way up the wall). The Notch Couloir, however, continues above Broadway in a snow- and ice-filled gully steeper than Lambs Slide, and tops out several hundred feet below the summit. The route is completed with several pitches of moderately easy technical rock climbing similar to the Kiener's technical rock section. The descent is the same as Kiener's, usually down the easy North Face Route. The Notch Couloir, like Kiener's, is a route on which retreat is very difficult.

Sproul and Sweedler knew each other through their jobs at a Boulder biotech company. Sweedler had just completed the Colorado Mountain Club's basic mountaineering school course and felt the Notch Couloir was within his and his partner's climbing abilities, and "we just wanted to prove ourselves on the route," Sweedler said. The difficulty rating printed in the guidebook was well within their skill and ability, they assumed. However, difficulty ratings can be notoriously deceptive. The climb's rating is a simple descriptor that attempts to capture the complex mix of obstacles, maneuvers, environment, and the technical ability needed to overcome them, and distill these down to a single number. To fully comprehend the implications of that rating usually requires experience beyond what Sproul and Sweedler possessed.

Autumn of that year had been very mild and there had been little snowfall in the mountains. The Saturday on which they began their climb was tauntingly warm and windless, hiding the fact that a potential storm in October would have the likelihood of high winds, very cold temperatures, and deep snow. As a matter of fact, a major storm was predicted for later that weekend. "We knew there was a storm coming," Sweedler told me, but they chose to climb anyway, hoping to sneak up and down the mountain before bad weather started.

Sweedler and Sproul did not hike in and camp the night before as is the custom for many who climb the Notch Couloir, especially those who have never climbed it and may need more time route finding. They planned to make one long summit push, beginning at 2:30 a.m., hiking the easy trail to the base in early morning darkness, climbing the difficult sections during the light of day, and then descending on the easy trail again after dusk that night.

Dawn was finally breaking as the pair arrived at the bottom of the technical climbing portion of the route. They took a well-earned rest at the base of the wall. Sweedler recalled, "There were a surprising number of people on Lambs Slide, just climbing around up there. As we were watching them, one guy came sliding down the slope on his feet. I thought he had on a pair of short skis, but he didn't. He was sliding on his boots, he wasn't wearing crampons. He hit the rocks at the bottom of the slope and flew amazingly high in the air before landing in the rocks."

The man had fallen 200 feet down the couloir and suffered multiple serious injuries when he hit the rocks at the base of the snow. Sproul and Sweedler helped stabilize the man and spent an hour convincing the injured man's climbing party that he shouldn't walk down and he needed a rescue. And he did need a rescue as he was suffering a broken pelvis as well as a pneumothorax, air leading into the chest cavity, a critical injury that can lead to a collapsed lung. When they finally felt the climbing party "had it under control," Sproul and Sweedler continued up Lambs Slide. "We lost an hour and a half helping him," Sweedler explained.

"The accident somewhat freaked us out," Sweedler remembered. Their mental state had changed and they began to worry about the consequences of an accident. They twisted ice screws in and belayed the top of Lambs Slide, preferring caution over speed, and adding more delay to their race against the storm. "Maybe we should have just given up on the climb right then," Sweedler said.

As they ascended late into the day, the weather seemed to hold. Sweedler remembered, "There wasn't a sign of a storm until we got to the Notch, then it was a hurricane!" The Notch is a geological feature on Longs Peak, literally a narrow U-shaped notch cutting into the south ridge of Longs. The Notch Couloir runs from Broadway up to this cut in the ridge. The storm blindsided them from the west. They didn't feel the storm's wrath behind the bulk of the mountain, but when they topped out in the Notch, furious winds funneled through, threatening to blast them off the mountain.

"I think it was about 3:00 p.m. when we decided we couldn't top out on Longs," Sweedler remembered. They decided the best course of action was to traverse to Kiener's, dodging the fierce blast by staying well below the ridgeline, then swing below the summit and hike directly to the North Face descent. They felt they had no other choice; it was physically impossible for them to continue as planned as they were now experiencing one of the infamously intense Longs Peak storms.

It arrived on time, as predicted, and was as fierce as an angry dragon. The morning delay that Sproul and Sweedler experienced and performing their Good Samaritan deed for the injured climber brought them ever closer to facing the storm at a critical time in their climb. Had they not been delayed, they would likely have climbed the route without incident. Or, if they had abandoned their climb due to the late start, they could have merely congratulated themselves for being clever climbers as they looked back over their shoulders at the dark, storm-shrouded summit from the comfort of their car. But that was not their choice.

Sweedler and Sproul quickly discovered that traversing to Kiener's was not a simple matter. It required technical climbing as well as traversing rappels. "We kept climbing in the cold and the snow started accumulating." They were getting desperate. "A couple of times we had to cut the rope," Sweedler explained. As they rappelled across the face, their rope would get stuck when they tried to pull it. Instead of wasting time climbing back up to free the end out of the crack it was wedged in or the knob it wrapped around, they cut the end off instead. Again, they were desperate.

"We reached Kiener's at about 7:00 p.m., well after dark. Visibility was about zero," Sweedler remembered. They had to stop and bivy in whatever nooks they could find and suffered 10 hours of cold darkness. "We didn't sleep at all that night," Sweedler said.

Sweedler remembers the next day as being like a groggy nightmare from which he could not awake. "I guess my reptilian brain took over. My memory of that day is hazy, not because of the time that has passed since, but because of the state I was in. We kept talking about moving in the storm but it seemed to take us hours to get going. Time went by surprisingly fast. We had run out of water and food the day before and our hands were frozen. At one point Chris tried to climb a dihedral [a rock feature that looks like an open book with a crack running vertically in the corner]. He fell and hit me, knocking me off my stance and I went down 30 feet. All his protection ripped out, but one piece held. We both hit our heads and Chris's helmet broke." Many inches of snow had accumulated and the wind kept blowing, but they both had brought enough clothing to keep relatively warm. They just didn't know how to climb out.

"We tried to climb difficult cliff faces. I told Chris we couldn't be on Kiener's, nothing was that hard on that route. We couldn't retreat and couldn't go on," Sweedler lamented. They explored route options all day in the storm. "We even heard eerie, broken shouts coming out of the gloom of the storm. The rangers were yelling up from Chasm Lake 1,500 feet below, trying to contact us. "We shouted back but they heard nothing," he said.

They now faced a dreaded second night at 14,000 feet, but they finally caught a break. The storm was abating. The sky cleared a few hours after sunset. "It was strange, the freight-train sounding wind ended and it was silent. Chris spotted what he thought was an easy route and climbed it by starlight," Sweedler said.

Climbing out toward the top of the Diamond cliffs are several rock steps, each about four feet high, which lead to the top of the sheer 2,000-foot vertical drop of the Diamond. If one simply looks at the steps, it's easy to convince yourself that they couldn't possibly lead anywhere. But they do, they lead to a place where climbers can take one short, incredibly exposed step over the Diamond cliff and onto walkable ground above all the cliffs of the East Face. Walter Kiener discovered this escape while leading the first ascent of the route in winter, but he was a highly experienced alpinist. To those with more rock climbing than alpine experience, the dihedral, with a sling hanging three-quarters of the way up as bait, looks like the obvious way out.

Sweedler recalled, "Chris shouted back to me to follow him, but there was no way I was going to climb in the darkness. Our headlamps had failed long before." Sproul had found the easy route over the Diamond step and escaped. He left Sweedler behind and continued his desperate descent.

As Sweedler shivered in the darkness, he had time to contemplate their decision two days before to climb on, knowing there was a storm approaching. They now knew they made a bad choice. However, if Sweedler and Sproul had investigated recent history, they may have made a better decision and turned around after their delay. Their experience was becoming an eerie reflection of a highly publicized tragedy that happened only four years earlier on Kiener's.

On September 11, 1993, Bo Judd and Thomas Kelly hiked up the

Longs Peak trail to camp near Chasm Lake in preparation for their climb of Kiener's the next day. Judd, who worked in a mountain gear repair shop in Boulder, had immersed his life in climbing. He was a highly experienced rock climber but had only moderate experience in the alpine environment.

"What I knew of Longs Peak at that time I could fit in a thimble," Judd said recently. This lack of knowledge and experience did not deter their desire to prove themselves on the difficult route. "Kelly was enamored of Longs. He had read an old guidebook. Based on that and talking to friends, we thought we were comfortable. But we were unproven. We didn't have the depth of experience that we should have had."

They woke from their bivouac near the base of the shear East Face of Longs that morning, brewed up drinks and ate breakfast. The pair then donned their climbing gear and began their ascent.

Eventually, after hours of sometimes off-route climbing, Judd and Kelly had overcome nearly all the difficulties on Kiener's. They were standing below the last cliff blocking their access to the top of Longs as the sun set into the thickening clouds of an approaching storm. They discovered in their growing alarm, just as Sweedler and Sproul would four years later, that the top of Kiener's is notoriously deceptive.

Their concern spiked as it began to rain. Daylight faded and the wind caused the cold air to bite through their clothing. The wind increased dramatically as they huddled in whatever shallow nooks they could find in the rocks. Snowflakes began to fly, slowly increasing in number until the air was filled with white streaks.

They were now faced with the consequences of a second mistake—not heeding a winter storm warning. The storm that began blowing in had been predicted with a high certainty.

Judd remembered, "We knew weather was coming in but we had confidence we could climb the route. We knew the descent route and we thought we could do it in rain, snow, or dark."

Although weather in Colorado has a reputation of being generally unpredictable, especially in the mountains, some patterns are more certain than others. One of those patterns is the cold front that sweeps through in autumn, turning a mild, almost summer-like day into a raging blizzard.

The only thing more certain than the arrival of these storms is the severity of them. This one was no exception. Early on, Judd and Kelly could have abandoned their plans or at least brought emergency bivy gear in the face of this predicted storm, but did not.

Sproul and Sweedler made the same mistakes of not understanding the nuances of their planned route, as well as trying to outrun weather that was predictably severe. And like Sproul and Sweedler, Judd and Kelley had to deal with dangerously changing conditions. Initially the snow melted on the rock, making it wet and far more difficult to climb. This sent them into a near panic. Just as Sproul and Sweedler would do four years later, they had spent the last daylight hours frantically trying to climb a dihedral to the top of the cliff. It must have been the route, they thought, because there was a climbing sling embedded in the rock half way up.

They could not make the technical moves to overcome the dihedral, which is actually rated only moderately difficult, but requires unusual moves to surmount. By then all the rock was wet. They saw no other way up but also had not expected such a difficult pitch at the top. It was supposed to be easy at this point in the route.

Darkness descended on them, they were surrounded by slick rock, and they were immersed in a great tempest. They did not expect to bivouac at 14,000 feet in a storm but they had no choice. Like Sproul and Sweedler would later do in the same location, they would have to hunker down, survive the storm, and wait until dawn to figure things out. They were close to the top and almost out of the difficulties. But things got ungodly worse for Judd and Kelly.

They felt they had done everything right up to this point. Their only weakness seemed to be the inability to climb that dihedral. Why was that last obstacle so difficult? The answer was so terribly simple that neither considered it. They were off route, but only by a few feet. Exactly as Sweedler and Sproul failed to see, Judd and Kelly did not see the Diamond step. However, unlike Sproul, this psychological barrier was so powerful that it forced Judd and Kelly to make the decision to make a nightmarish retreat back down the way they came up, descending thousands of feet of steep snow-covered cliffs and ledges.

They could not descend that night and so they struggled to survive the cold on the same ledge that Sweedler was on four years later. Judd and Kelly witnessed an accumulation of 18 inches of snow while they shivered against the wind in an air temperature of zero degrees Fahrenheit that night. "We stuffed our feet in our rucksacks, used rope and gear rack as blankets. We were so drained and spent the night trying to convince ourselves we were in better shape than we were," Judd said.

Still alive the next morning but suffering from painfully cold temperatures and the debilitating effects of altitude, Judd and Kelly began retreating down Kiener's, not aware that this was extremely difficult even in the best of conditions. They were desperate and had entered a race for survival.

As they started their descent a voice called to them out of the storm. Both Judd and Kelly heard the voice and both, surprisingly, determined it was a hallucination. It was the very real voice of a Rocky Mountain National Park ranger who, alerted to the possibility of a climbing party in need on Kiener's, had climbed above the pair and was shouting down. He was trying to make voice contact since it was impossible to see any distance in the blizzard. He received no response.

Judd and Kelly continued down over the slippery rocks to the technical section where they set up the first of several rappels down the steep cliff faces they climbed the day before. They used their rock climbing gear to anchor their rope, which forced them to leave gear behind at each rappel. "We completely drained the rack on rappels and left the rope hanging above Broadway." Judd recalled.

On the last rappel above Broadway, they survived an anchor failure. With no rope or climbing gear, they would have no protection as they crossed the slippery ledge back to Lambs Slide. Hours later they were standing at the top of the Lambs Slide couloir, exhausted and hypothermic, but alive. At that point they felt they had won, having survived the most difficult descending in harrowing conditions. They both felt a resurgence of energy as their morale lifted for the first time since they became stranded.

Judd strapped his crampons on for the descent down the snowfield. Kelly decided to descend more quickly and began a glissade while Judd, who was older and slower than Kelly, walked down in a more controlled and careful manner.

Judd caught up with Kelly who was waiting for him at the bottom of the snow slope. Judd told Kelly to go ahead and not wait for him. "Among my climbing partners, I am always the slowest person," Judd explained. "They usually want me to go ahead of them so I'm not always playing catch-up. So even though Kelly was stronger and faster than I was, he told me to go find camp because he wanted hot chocolate and 'you're the only one who can work that damn stove.'"

Judd kept moving but later remembered that Kelly was acting somewhat out of character. "He had packed a lot of snow in his pants and parka, and I remember his lips being blue," Judd said. "He began jettisoning equipment from his pack, which was unusual for him. I assumed he just wanted to get to camp more quickly."

At this point they had spent the entire day descending. It was night again and they were utterly exhausted, hypothermic, and frostbitten. They continued to make a desperate run for their camp supplies, but now it was each man for himself. There was nothing either could do for the other except periodically yell back and forth in the gloom.

Judd's state of exhaustion left him with no choice but to focus on his own survival, and that depended on getting to the equipment cache where they had sleeping bags to warm and shelter them.

As Judd made his way across a boulder field to the cache, he slipped while making an awkward step. He crashed down on his ankle. "The pain was so great that I involuntarily evacuated my bowels. I put my head down and quite literally felt like I was giving up to die. But then I thought that I would be giving up on my friend and that got me going again."

Judd made it to the cache at midnight. At the very limit of his strength, he pulled out his sleeping bag and collapsed in it. "Over the night I kept waking up and taking a few steps out to look for Kelly but would start shivering and return to my bag. I knew there was something terribly wrong but was too scared to get far from my bag." He awoke the next morning alone. As soon as he could muster the energy, he emerged from his bag to search for Kelly. Judd found no sign of him.

Hours later, searchers found Kelly dead underneath a boulder on the

Kiener's Route
The Notch
Diamond Step
North Face - Cable Route
The Notch Couloir
The Diamond
Narrow Spot
Broadway
Lamb's Slide Couloir

The East Face of Longs Peak viewed from Mt. Lady Washington.

north side of Chasm Lake. They concluded he had collapsed before reaching camp and tried to shelter under a large rock. Exhausted, hypothermic, and without a sleeping bag, he died sometime during that night.

At the time, Sweedler did not know he and Sproul were reliving a cruel event in recent history. However, they fortunately caught a break when Sproul figured out the exit off Kiener's, thus saving their lives.

The same drive to climb Longs Peak was also driving them to survive. Two days without food or water in freezing conditions were not enough to kill Sweedler and Sproul, but they were getting dangerously close to the edge. Sproul eventually found the North Face descent and continued down the hiking trail and nearly walked past a group of rescuers staging, preparing to climb up to look for them. "Chris saw them but was so out of it he didn't think to talk with the rangers. The rangers yelled to Chris, asking if he had been on Longs. He said yes and my friend is still up there." Sproul described Sweedler's location. The rangers knew the position and prepared to launch a rescue.

The weather was excellent the next morning, October 14, so the rescuers were able to land a helicopter on the summit of Longs Peak. They descended to Sweedler and shouted down to him. "Even though I was mentally out of it, you can't imagine how happy I was." They talked Sweedler through the moves and he climbed himself off Kiener's with a belay from the rescuers. He was able to walk to the summit and take the 15-minute ride to Estes Park Medical Center where they began treating him.

Sweedler had survived two nights in a winter storm at 14,000 feet with no supplies or bivy gear. He suffered major frostbite, losing all his fingers to below the second knuckle, and both his big toes. "I didn't feel anything until I got to the hospital and started warming up. Then it was incredibly painful for a long time." But he was alive.

Bo Judd was also alive but lives with his tragedy to this day. "For the rest of my life I've thought there was one human being that could have done something and I didn't do it. The aftermath of this kind of thing is you can never forgive yourself, especially if you love the person. It's bad enough that you've deprived yourself of this person; you don't get to enjoy this person ever again, but add to that the torture of not being able to help him. I started out on this climb as an egomaniac and in the end didn't feel like I deserved to be alive. You may think the worst thing that can happen is that you die, but really the worst thing that can happen is that you live with something like this."

Though the partnership dynamics of Sweedler/Sproul and Judd/Kelly pushed them to make terrible decisions, they were all able to do one thing right. They dug deep and pulled out an unbelievable will to suffer the cold,

View looking down Kiener's Route from the Diamond Step.

Lamb's Slide

discomfort, lack of food and water, and to survive endless hours in an unmerciful storm.

Also, it should be noted that each party split up near the end of their ordeal. Splitting up, especially during times of severe distress, is considered a very bad decision. Everyone from highly experienced climbers to mountain rescuers would strongly advise parties finding themselves in such situations to stick together and take care of each other.

Two together have a much better chance of survival than two separated. However, these are cases of what happens at the edge of survival, when the rule of sticking together is actually counterproductive, and the chances of survival of one or both decrease rapidly if the parties do not split.

In the case of Sweedler/Sproul, the fact that Sproul was able to climb out and summon help may have saved Sweedler's life. For Judd/Kelly, split-ting up at the bottom of Lambs Slide was likely a factor in Kelly's death, but allowed Judd to live. Judd related that his rapidly fading energy was only enough to get himself to their equipment cache during that stormy night. There was essentially zero chance that Judd could have helped Kelly.

The rules of climbing may need to be reconsidered in extreme situations. It might be that the only rule that should always be followed is to think: Analyze the situation and determine the best course of action, even if it is a course that you would never take otherwise.

The surprising end to this story is that events leading up to both tragedies were shockingly similar to one that happened several decades before, during the greatest mountaineering tragedy to ever happen on the slopes of Longs Peak: The disaster of the Prince Willmon party—a group of climbers caught in an unforgiving storm.

Unforgiving

> The Colorado Mountain Club recommends a minimum climbing party of four. If one of the parties is injured or incapacitated then another can wait with the injured party and two can hike out together for help. This is especially true on multi-day expeditions or climbs involving difficult or technical terrain.

No mountaineering situation is guaranteed to be free from danger, and though a larger group can manage unforeseen difficulties better, even a strong party with a highly experienced leader can climb into disaster. A classic example of this unfolded in the spring of 1960 on Longs Peak to a team of four strong climbers. The epic of Prince Willmon and his climbing team was so unusual that the tragedy became a national news story.

Willmon, a 23-year-old University of Colorado graduate student, had spent the first days of spring break climbing on Ship Rock in New Mexico. He had returned to Boulder flush with success, having put up several first ascents on the difficult rock cliffs of the formation. With the few days of spring break remaining, he wanted to try to continue his successful streak by climbing a difficult route on Longs Peak.

He convinced three of his friends at the university to join him: David Jones and Jane Bendixen, both 18 years old, and 21-year-old James Greig. They would attempt Alexander's Chimney, a wide crack that ascends up the East Face cliffs. It is a moderately difficult route requiring ice axes, crampons, and roped climbing on both rock and ice.

The four drove to the Longs Peak trailhead and began their ascent in the dark of morning on April 19. They were a strong and motivated team, and moved quickly up the trail in mild conditions. It was cold, but not the bitter cold of winter. The air was relatively calm.

They intended to climb the peak in a single day. Probably in an attempt to speed their ascent and make the roped climbing easier, they went extremely lightweight. They did not carry the extra clothing and heavy coats that are standard fare for winter mountaineering. This was a similar philosophy to what was practiced by David Worthington before his uncontrolled glissade to his death on Humboldt Peak, though Willmon had much

AGNES VAILLE INCIDENT

On January 10, 1925, Agnes Vaille became the first woman to ascend the East Face of Longs Peak in winter. Her guide was Walter Kiener and their route was the now popular Kiener's route up the east face. The pair climbed through the night and summited at 4 a.m. when the temperature was minus 14° F. On the descent, the exhausted Vaille slipped and fell 150 feet. Her hands and feet were frozen and so Kiener went for help. The blizzard intensified and before rescuers could reach her she succumbed to hypothermia at 13,000 feet.

Herbert Sortland, one of her would-be rescuers, was alone at one point and broke his hip when he slipped in the Boulderfield during the rescue. He appeared to have frozen to death when they found his body a month later. The cone-shaped Agnes Vaille shelter near the Keyhole was built in 1927 and was named for this pioneering woman.

more mountaineering experience than Worthington. Willmon had a richer basis for his decisions as to what he would carry and what he would leave behind. However, their motivation was similar: speed.

They made great time during the five-mile hike in and arrived at the base of Alexander's Chimney at 10:00 a.m. Their fast pace produced one casualty, however. Greig had hit his limit. He was "sick and exhausted" at the base of the chimney, where the route changes from a hike to roped climbing, and decided to call it quits. He turned back while Willmon, Jones, and Bendixen continued on. Doubtlessly, Greig was bitterly disappointed that he could not continue on with Willmon and share his certain summit glory, but the twist of fate caused by his temporary weakness probably saved his life.

The remaining three continued up Alexander's Chimney and eventually to the upper portions of Kiener's Route, when the weather began to deteriorate. At about 3 p.m. a severe spring storm began to rake the mountain with high winds and heavy snows, reducing visibility and making the delicate scrambling in which they were immersed much more difficult.

Knowing that the upper portion of the route was dangerously exposed, Willmon decided it would be better not to go over the summit but to retreat to the Notch and traverse to the south side of the mountain. They would try to find the standard route, a route that was not much more than a walk down, where they would avoid the risk of being blown off a mountain ledge and falling a thousand feet down to Chasm Lake.

They struggled across slabs and reached the Notch at 4:30 p.m. in rapidly deteriorating weather. The terrain around the Notch is quite steep and difficult, but the Notch itself provides a relatively easy passage between the east and south faces of the mountain. The standard Keyhole Route summits from the south side, and Willmon knew he could get there from the Notch by traversing right and upward. But by the time they had moved to the South Face, the clouds and snow had obscured everything around them. They began to move west over broken slabs slightly less steep than what they had just traversed on the East Face.

They soon realized they were hopelessly lost. It's no real surprise they could not find the ledge called the Narrows on the vast West Face of Longs. The Narrows is a shelf only a few feet wide that gives the only easy, even if uncomfortably exposed, passage across the South Face. Large patches of snow on the giant face would double the difficulty of finding this small ledge even in perfect visibility.

Though moving in generally the correct direction, the Willmon party ended up below the Narrows and was forced to make rappels over steep cliff faces. At one point as light was fading, Jones rappelled to a ledge that was so small he yelled up to Willmon and Bendixen to make a shelter where they were, it was the best they could do. They were now split up, preparing to bivouac well above 13,000 feet in a winter storm on small ledges without warm clothing.

Willmon and Bendixen were able to dig a small snow hole on their ledge. Jones, having no other options, was forced to hunker down in a small rock cove. There, trapped as if on top of a frozen castle tower, they began their long, shivering night vigil.

While Willmon, Jones, and Bendixen squirmed against the storm, Greig was back at the trailhead. He had descended to the ranger station and began a long, uneventful wait. Greig noted the deteriorating weather that afternoon. Night approached, but as it was a long climb he expected his friends to arrive after sunset. After hours of waiting in the stormy night, Greig finally made the decision to call for help. It was just after midnight.

He may have delayed his call as long as possible because he was aware they were breaking park rules. The National Park Service rules at the time made Longs Peak off limits during the winter, imposing a fine on violators caught on its flanks before June.

That rule did not prevent climbers from ascending Longs but merely was a half-hearted deterrent. The park, as it does today, pared its personnel to a bare minimum during the winter months. It was highly unlikely any climber in the backcountry would ever encounter one of the few rangers on winter duty. But calling for help is a different matter because it was essentially an admission of guilt, which became trivial with the real prospect of his friends running into trouble on the mountain.

Greig phoned the Estes Park police department to get help. When informed that the missing persons were University of Colorado students and members of the mountain rescue team in Boulder, the Estes Park police contacted the university directly. They, in turn, notified Rocky Mountain Rescue Group (RMR), which immediately began preparations for a search and rescue operation.

Well aware that the park had no personnel available to conduct a search and rescue operation, and that they had no authority to operate in the park themselves, RMR leaders contacted park authorities to inform them of the situation and offer volunteer personnel to help with the rescue. Eventually, because of Willmon's connections in Boulder, a coordinated effort to save the climbers had begun.

During his five years at the university, Willmon immersed himself in the climbing culture. He was described as "extremely talented" and mentioned in the same sentence as other now-famous pioneering rock climbers of the day. He mentored and influenced younger climbers such as Gerry Roach. He was an active member of RMR, using his skills to save lives as much as for his personal enjoyment. He was charismatic and conscientious about climbing safety. He had witnessed firsthand the results of climbing disasters. Willmon had become ingrained in the small (at that time) Boulder rockclimbing and search-and-rescue fraternities. He and his stranded team could not have had better friends to get them out of their desperate situation.

At 4 a.m. on the morning of April 20, at the strong suggestion of RMR leaders, the park sent two rangers up the trail to check the shelters between the trailhead and the base of the peak. By 7 a.m., they had found no sign of the three missing climbers. By 9 a.m., RMR had a dozen climbers at the trailhead waiting for the park to give them authorization to enter the field, but the park authorities were reluctant. They held the large group of searchers in place.

Park officials were faced with a major problem that they had just begun to comprehend. They were completely unprepared for a large and potentially dangerous search and rescue operation. Perhaps park personnel assumed that a sign declaring Longs off limits would relieve them from ever having to deal with a rescue situation. However, it was widely known that many climbers were "breaking the rules" and ascending the mountain during that era.

Nevertheless, when faced with the reality of stranded climbers in need of a winter rescue, the park seemed more concerned with controlling their domain and did not trust the large group of climbers gathered at the trailhead. This group included Layton Kor, the legendary Colorado climber who had put up many first ascents around the state, as well as Harold Walton, a well-known mountaineer and technical rescue expert, was held back for hours as park officials decided what to do.

When finally released into the field, teams split up to scour the mountain. The storm had abated and visibility was excellent. A team was able to climb high enough to see tracks in the Notch and possibly Wild Basin, suggesting the missing team may have descended the south side of the mountain. Park authorities dismissed this idea, saying it was "unlikely because of the distance involved to get out," ignoring the obvious fact that no one had gotten out at the time. Kor's team searched for signs on another route but saw no sign of the missing climbers. They retreated just short of the summit due to dangerous avalanche conditions.

At the rescuers' suggestion, the park asked for aerial search help and got it from the military. Extreme turbulence around Longs prevented smaller aircraft from operating in the area, so the military sent a twin engine C-47 cargo plane to help. Making several passes around the summit, searchers in the C-47 could see ground teams clearly, but curiously saw no sign of the missing climbers.

The search teams returned to the Longs Peak ranger station as the day ended, the tracks seen in the Notch and Wild Basin being their only potential clues to the whereabouts of the Willmon party. Evening fell, and search managers began preparing for a larger assault on the mountain the following day. At 8 p.m., as planning intensified, word came that Jane Bendixen was found. She had wandered into a cabin in Allenspark, 10 miles south of Longs Peak. She was frostbitten and exhausted, rambling off an incoherent tale of desperate survival.

She was warmed and rehydrated before being transported to Boulder for medical attention. As she recovered, she was able to relate the details of her escape from the wilderness.

She and Willmon had survived the previous night in their small snow hole, but the night at high altitude and freezing cold had taken its toll. Willmon was alive but frostbitten and too weak to continue down the mountain despite the improved weather that morning. Bendixen was also frostbitten but had the strength to continue. Willmon told her and Jones to go for help.

She tied their two 120-foot ropes together, hammered a piton into a crack, and tied the end of the rope to it. She rappelled down past Jones, still on the ledge 100 feet below Willmon. Jones, too, was frostbitten and in bad shape but able to help Bendixen as she continued on a traversing rappel, attempting to reach hikeable ground to the side of the cliff band.

About 30 feet from the ground, Bendixen began to feel faint. She asked Jones to belay her as she downclimbed the final few feet and he agreed. She tied into the rope but passed out as she began her descent. Some time later she regained consciousness on the ground in a snow bank. She shouted for Jones but got no response. She untied from the rope and slid down the sloping snowfield to hikeable ground below. She began hiking into what appeared to be an endless forest below.

She spent the next 12 hours breaking trail through the deep snow in Wild Basin, following Hunters Creek out to civilization. She had no snowshoes or any means of floatation. She postholed or plowed her way through 10 miles of snow piled as deep as six feet. It's hard to overstate how arduous this must have been for her. Alternating with a partner to posthole even a few miles is exhausting and frustrating. Bendixen covered the entire distance solo after suffering an energy-sapping night in high altitude cold.

Bendixen's description of the location of the snow hole and her tracks up Wild Basin pinpointed the last known whereabouts of Willmon and Jones, both of whom, she assumed, were still alive and waiting for help.

RMR wanted to send in crews immediately, but the park authorities decided to wait until morning to avoid "possible night hazards." This condemned Willmon and Jones, already known to be debilitated, to suffer another night in the open.

At 5 a.m. on April 21, a team of RMR members hit the trail and ascended to the saddle between Meeker and Longs Peak in an astonishing time of four hours and forty-five minutes, a climb that usually requires six hours at a fast pace. Searching with binoculars, they spotted the rappel rope still in place. They were able to traverse to the bivouac spot and find the snow hole, but Willmon was not there. Another team approaching from below found the bodies of both Jones and Willmon. Both showed signs of major trauma caused by long falls.

Examination of the evidence suggested that Jones may have been pulled from his belay stance when Bendixen fell. His body was located very close to Bendixen's still visible tracks in the snow. He may have fallen and been killed at the time Bendixen passed out, which explains why she did not witness him falling. It is also possible that she repressed the memory due to the horror of watching him die.

The location of Willmon's body suggested that he fell while rappelling down the line. He was within 30 feet of safety at the bottom. He may have lost control due to severe frostbite in his hands, rendering them nonfunctional.

At some unknown time between the morning of April 20 when Bendixen left for help, and noon the following day when searchers found their bodies, Willmon must have felt desperate enough to attempt to climb out. Perhaps he saw Jones fall. Or perhaps, as the long day of waiting wore on, he decided he could not survive another night in the open and tried to follow Bendixen.

The bodies of Prince Willmon and David Jones were recovered by teams consisting largely of RMR personnel two days later. By that time, their harrowing epic had made headlines nationwide. The general slant of the stories was that the climbers were foolish or perhaps crazy to do something so dangerous. Park officials commented:

> Joseph Romberg, assistant chief ranger of Rocky Mountain National Park, said that the group was climbing in a closed area, clearly posted to that effect.
>
> —*Daily Camera*, Boulder Colorado, April 20, 1960

The death of Willmon and Jones and injuries to Bendixen were simply explained away as breaking rules. Never mind that the group was very strong and experienced. Never mind that dozens of people had died on the peak over the previous decades when the peak was "open." Never mind that the park was slow to react to the emergency and perhaps could have saved at least one of them.

Others simply chastised the climbers. An editorial in the University of Colorado newspaper parroted the view of the national park:

> The senseless tragedy on Longs Peak last week would not have happened had the students in the climbing party obeyed the rules designed to protect them from the fate they met.
>
> If everyone would use some good common sense and check with the authorities before climbing mountains, the men of the rescue teams will have their rewards.
>
> *Colorado Daily,* Boulder Colorado, April 26, 1960

These comments made over 50 years ago reverberate today when similar mountain accidents happen. Though they may be emotionally satisfying to those who know little about climbing, they are meaningless. If anything good comes from such tragedies, it is the lessons learned from climbing mistakes, to attempt to piece together their thinking process and understand why excellent mountaineers made disastrous decisions.

"They were inadequately prepared for Longs Peak at any time of year," one rescuer said in the aftermath. Harold Walton commented, "Willmon was not only a first-class rock climber but a good mountaineer who had winter experience. It is incredible that he should not have prepared to meet bad weather if it came."

Willmon's surprising lack of preparedness was rationalized as a lapse in judgment due to the lingering effects of having just returned from climbing in the warm desert. He simply forgot that in April, winter still has a tight grip at 14,000 feet in Colorado.

Unlike the teams of Sproul/Sweedler and Judd/Kelly in the 1990s, the Willmon party did not have the luxury of excellent weather forecasting or the readily available information on how extreme storms can get on Longs. That might explain how Willmon could have led his team into such danger, as he had no way of knowing a storm was bearing down on them. This isn't probable, though, because Willmon did have many years of winter mountaineering experience in Colorado and was well aware of the conditions they could encounter.

But there is another possibility. Willmon purposely went as light as possible. Even in moderately bad weather, a one-day ascent would not necessarily require heavy winter clothing if they did not stop. And on the upside, if their climb had gone off as planned, they would have successfully demonstrated "alpine-style" climbing. It is the fast, lightweight philosophy that would eventually come into popularity in the 1980s, more than a quarter century later. One acquaintance wrote that Willmon "often espoused the aesthetic need for unencumbered climbing," the basic tenet of alpine-style.

Alpine-style, like the ultra-light style preferred by David Worthington on Humboldt, requires much skill, experience, and strength, leaving little room for error, especially on a difficult peak such as Longs in winter, but they were characteristics Willmon possessed and were not beyond his abilities.

Ironically, the biggest mistake Willmon made was to be unaware of the history of Longs Peak. In the same way that Sweedler and Sproul could have easily made themselves aware of the traps on Kiener's, Willmon missed an easy opportunity for retreat when the weather broke as they neared the summit.

The first ascent of Longs did not start out on what is today known as the Keyhole Route, but on the south side in Wild Basin. L.W. Keplinger pioneered a route up a lengthy couloir on the South Face that now bears his name. Keplinger did not summit the mountain first but the first ascent party followed his couloir to what is now the Homestretch, the last 200 feet that access the summit just beyond the Narrows ledge.

Keplinger's Couloir descends without difficulty from the Notch to the relative flatness of Wild Basin. Had Willmon been aware of the first ascent route, he and his party would certainly have descended the easy slopes to Wild Basin and out, the way Bendixen did solo. But he was unaware of this simple escape—or of another alternative that easily connects to the Loft Route, which would bring them back to their car—and did not plan for weather contingencies.

The attitude toward climbing that existed a half-century ago in Rocky Mountain National Park has little resemblance to what exists today. Mountaineering is not restricted except for a few wildlife closures during certain months of the year. The park is far better prepared to effect a rescue when necessary. What has not changed is the eternal challenge of Longs Peak to mountaineers of all abilities—the remoteness, difficulty, and potential harsh conditions they face. A climber who gets stranded high on Longs is a long way from help.

PART III: WRONG WAY

"I had a bad feeling about that day from the start. I thought to myself, this was a recipe for disaster."

—Eric Sawyer's comment to investigators.

Over the Summit

The thumping of a helicopter rotor broke the quiet of a crystal blue autumn day above the high peaks in central Colorado. Inside the four-seat aircraft were a pilot, two trained wilderness searchers, and Ben Vanek. They scanned the terrain below them, a landscape of green valleys separated by rounded gray ridges. Within the valleys were splashes of yellow, like paint splattered on a green canvas. Dark blue and black lakes of varying shapes dotted the landscape to the horizon.

View from the summit of Mount of the Holy Cross. The Cross Couloir descends to the right from this view and is not visible.

They buzzed around the highest point on one of the rounded ridges. It was the 14,005-foot-high summit of Mount of the Holy Cross, known simply as Holy Cross. It appeared to be a grainy bump, like the top of a crumbling, crenellated tower of a sand castle, except made of tiny stones instead of sand. And there was something odd among those little rocks, something even smaller and almost invisible. They had to concentrate to see them. They were tiny specs of bright color: orange, yellow, blue, and white. What caught their attention was the way the colors did not fit in the gray landscape. The closer they looked the more colorful specs they noticed; they were all over the mountain, clustered into groups. These were the searchers, people wearing their orange or yellow shell jackets or blue pants or white shirts, hiking on the slopes of the mountain. Only then could they perceive the immense scale of the mountain rescue and surrounding wilderness.

They were flying over the wilderness where, while hiking with Eric Sawyer six days earlier, Ben's wife Michelle had vanished. Ben was being given a tour of the area that had been scoured by search and rescue volunteers for nearly a week. He was overwhelmed by the size of the mountain, the height of the cliff faces, the maze of ravines, and the endless pine and aspen forest.

The helicopter gently landed at the search base in the nearby town of Vail. One of the searchers turned a handle and opened the hatch. Ben unbuckled his shoulder harness and removed his flight helmet, opened the door, and stepped out beneath the still-rotating blades. His pent-up emotions burst forth. A friend of Ben's described what happened next.

> When Ben got off the helicopter he was hysterical, screaming that Michelle had no business being up there. It was then that they had to bring Eric down from Vail because we were worried what Ben may do to him in his state. Now let me say that Ben is the most kind and gentle man I know, so for him to respond this way made us all realize that neither Ben or Michelle had any idea what Michelle was doing.

The Decision to Climb

Two weeks before Ben Vanek's overflight of Holy Cross in September of 2005, he and his wife Michelle were having dinner with Eric Sawyer and his wife. Eric was 36 years old and had an athletic build on his shorter-than-average frame. He was obsessed with the 14ers and spoke of his hikes often. Over the years, Eric had ticked off 37 of the 14ers on his list. Eric's wife had hiked with him in the past but had lost interest.

Michelle was athletic like Eric, and a 35-year-old mother of four. She differed from Eric, however, in that she had never hiked a 14er in her life. However, Michelle exercised every day and was a marathon runner. Her husband Ben never had an interest in hiking 14ers, but the thought of it intrigued Michelle. Both families hung out together on occasion and "had dinner together once every six months or so," according to Eric.

During this particular dinner, Eric asked Michelle if she was interested in climbing a 14er with him. Michelle hesitated at first, but Eric persisted and she agreed to try an easy one, Holy Cross. It also happened to be a 14er Eric had never climbed.

Excited at the prospect, Michelle purchased new hiking clothing over the next two days and, under the advice of Eric, a pair of low-cost ski poles. Eric told her the poles would aid her balance over the uneven ground. She trusted Eric to make nearly every decision about the climb, from their climbing style (what equipment to bring, how fast they would travel), to which mountain and route they would hike. She placed a critical trust in him and he implicitly took the responsibility to make the best decisions he could for them.

Michelle probably assumed Eric was an expert, having talked of hiking 14ers over the years, and this was likely the basis of her trust. Eric knew Michelle was in excellent physical condition, a very desirable quality in a hiking partner. Even though the couples had known each other for "nine to 10 years," Eric curiously described their relationship as "casual friends," indicating that perhaps both were making many assumptions about each other's abilities.

Eric had never been to Holy Cross, but knew it was not considered a technically difficult peak. He had also considered an easy peak in the Blanca group, a cluster of four 14ers near Alamosa in south-central Colorado, the same group of mountains ascended by solo climber David Boyd before being killed on his descent. Eric had attempted to climb two of those summits on a recent trip but was only able to finish one. His other unclimbed summit, Blanca Peak, would have been within the scope of Michelle's novice ability, but he ultimately rejected the idea for a reason that had nothing to do with the difficulty of the climb.

The Blanca massif requires a four- to five-hour drive from Denver. Though technically easy, the peaks require a long day of hiking. The only practical plan to finish them is drive down the night before and camp, wake up early and refreshed for the long day of hiking before driving back.

Strangely enough, Eric was reluctant to suggest this very normal and frequently necessary part of mountain climbing. Even though they had known each other for a decade, he was still uncomfortable spending a night alone with Michelle. So he chose another peak closer to home.

Regardless of this almost childlike embarrassment, a dangerous social dynamic was forming. Michelle entrusted Eric with decisions affecting life and death. Eric may have understood this at some level, but he lacked experience leading novice climbers and probably didn't comprehend the serious problems they could encounter. And he created a potential conflict of interest as a leader because he was personally vested with an interest to check the peak off his *List*.

On the appointed day, Eric drove up to the Vanek house in the 3:45 a.m. darkness. He helped Michelle finish packing. They left at 4 a.m. in Michelle's white Toyota SUV and drove west on Interstate 70 for two-and-a-half hours. They zoomed by the town of Vail and finally to the Minturn exit where they left the highway and motored south. A few turns later the road transitioned to a rough gravel track leading deep into the White River National Forest, dead-ending at the Half Moon Pass parking lot.

By this time the sky had brightened enough that artificial light was unnecessary. There were a few cars parked in the lot as Eric stepped out of the car and looked around. The trailhead was not obvious due to several tall dirt piles from some sort of excavation, but he knew it was there; his guidebook said so. He circled the parking area and found a trailhead. It was the only one he saw.

Michelle is Missing

"He was kind of freaking out and shaken up," Jamie Nellis recalled when she and her hiking partner Tyr Johansen met Eric on their way up the North Ridge to the summit, "even more so two hours later."

Jamie and Tyr had come to hike Holy Cross as an overnight trip. "We hiked in that morning and left our heavier gear at East Cross Creek where we planned on camping that night. We then continued up to the summit. It was late in the day but it was September and the weather was good," she said, referring to the characteristic lack of thunderstorms in the fall.

They had hiked in via the normal route. The trailhead is at 10,400 feet and the route climbs up to Half Moon Pass at 11,650 before descending to a backcountry campground at East Cross Creek, located at nearly the same altitude as the trailhead. And this is the dirty little secret of what is otherwise an easy trail: A hiker must climb and descend 1,200 feet over two-and-a-half miles just to start climbing Holy Cross. There is no shortcut; this is the fastest and easiest way to the summit. And it must also be surmounted on the return, turning the end of the day into a mind-numbing slog back to the trailhead.

Jamie and Tyr took the option to split up the climb by backpacking camp equipment to East Cross Creek, where the valley flattens to gentle grassy meadows next to a gurgling stream. It is a designated campground for the wilderness area, the only legal place to camp, and they found several tents erected in the meadow when she arrived. They planned to set up their tent after going to the summit that afternoon, to camp there that night. The weather was good but it was getting late, and they wanted to return to their camp before dark. They stashed their camp gear and continued with much lighter loads toward the top.

A couple of hours later they approached an agitated man well above treeline on the North Ridge Trail. "We were about 600 feet from the summit when we first saw Eric. He was walking around like something was not right.

He had just gotten there and was surprised Michelle was nowhere in sight. It was about 2:30 p.m."

At the time there was no reason for Jamie to think this was a critical situation; it looked like just two people who had missed their connection. Eric asked them to keep an eye out for Michelle, describing her and her clothing. Jamie and Tyr then continued climbing up to the summit.

As they slowly ascended, Jamie recalled, "Another couple came up behind us. The female of that couple was blonde and had a blue jacket and we thought, 'Oh, awesome! Here she is, great!'" but it wasn't her.

"It took another half hour to get to the summit, we stayed there about 30 minutes and then we came down." They again encountered Eric in the same area as before, at about 13,400 feet on the North Ridge Trail. Eric was now frantic and recruited Jamie and Tyr to help him look for Michelle. They scanned the area with binoculars. Jamie had a whistle she blew repeatedly. They yelled for Michelle. "We didn't see anything that would make us think she was nearby," she said later.

At about 4 p.m. Jamie convinced Eric to call for help. "We said it was a good idea to get a search going even if she turned up later." Eric called his wife with his cell phone, who in turn contacted the Eagle County Sheriff at 4:13 p.m.

"We had to stop searching," Jamie said, "it was getting cold and the sun sets early in September. We needed to get down to our camp because we weren't prepared to search at night. We only had our daypacks and no headlamps." They gave Eric a shirt and some supplies in the fading daylight. Eric told them he would hike out to the trailhead and meet whoever was there for the search. And maybe Michelle somehow got ahead of them and was waiting for him in her car. Jamie and Tyr descended to their camp in the deepening darkness and plunging temperatures.

At some point during their descent, Jamie noticed a bright orange glow in the valley. "People camped near us had a huge campfire that night even though it's not allowed in the wilderness area. We could see it from far away coming down the trail. I think that if Michelle could have seen it from far off she would have wandered toward it."

The crisp autumn air of daytime chilled to freezing cold as the sun took away its heat. "It was cold, it got down to the twenties that night," Jamie recalled. They cooked dinner and crawled into their warm sleeping bags. "At that point we both felt and desperately hoped that Eric would return to the trailhead to find Michelle waiting for him."

In the meantime, the sheriff dispatch paged the Vail Mountain Rescue Group (VMR), who performed a "hasty search," covering high probability areas such as trailheads. The darkness limited their search effort that night but they began to plan for the following day, telling their members to prepare for a big search. It seemed to be a routine call-out and members prepared for an early start. They were used to looking for lost hikers on Holy Cross.

That night the moon rose just after 11 p.m., illuminating the barren summit rocks of Holy Cross with cold, pale light. The illicit camp bonfire that was visible for miles like a navigation beacon had died down to its embers. At 12:42 a.m. the moon entered the last quarter of its orbit, forming a perfect half moon as it hung like a direction signal over Half Moon Pass.

The next morning Jamie "awoke to the sound of people calling Michelle's name." They got up, fixed breakfast, packed their gear and leisurely hiked back over Half Moon Pass where they ran into more searchers. Jamie and Tyr told them what they knew and where they helped Eric search. They continued down with growing concern.

"When we got out to the parking lot the next day it was full of cars. They were parked all the way down the road; it was all the searchers. Eric told me they drove up in a white Toyota SUV. I remember seeing it when we arrived the day before and saw it still parked there. It hadn't moved."

It was day one of a search that neither Jamie, nor Tyr, nor Eric, nor any of the searchers could have predicted would balloon into a monster.

A Cascade of Errors

Everything seemed right when Eric and Michelle began their hike. Eric led out of the parking lot at first light, on the trail he selected among the jumbled piles of excavated dirt. Their pace warmed them quickly in the cold morning light. They weaved through the dense forest enjoying the air tinged with the smell of pine. It felt good to start working their legs, which had been immobilized during the long drive from Denver. Michelle anticipated summiting her first big peak, a 14er, and the first one on her *List*. Eric was excited to tick off another with a new partner, perhaps someone who would partner with him many times in the future. It was 7 a.m. and the blue-green light of a mountain dawn greeted them with the promise of good weather.

In such a benign environment, it is difficult for even the most experienced mountaineer to see the subtle beginnings of a dangerous cascade of errors, which grows like raindrops forming the beginning of a stream. The inexperienced usually don't recognize the coming flood until the errors coalesce into a river of unstoppable events, trapping a victim in the inescapable undertow of an accident.

It was shortly after they started hiking that morning when Eric and Michelle began experiencing a series of disturbing setbacks. Eric left his water filter in his car. This is a device that mechanically purifies water from a stream or lake by straining out microscopic giardia cysts, an intestinal protozoan parasite common in Colorado that produces a fever and diarrhea for many days. They would need this filter to replenish their water bottles as they drank them down. Though it would be reasonable for them to drink raw water when dehydration became serious, they would be reluctant to do so for fear of illness.

Eric also left his lunch in the car. Lack of food in itself isn't critical. Any hiker fit enough to climb Holy Cross can probably do it without food by using reserves stored in the body. As a matter of fact, it is difficult if not impossible to keep up with the caloric deficit produced on a long hike or climb without eating constantly. The body makes up for this temporary deficit by burning glycogen stored in the liver and muscles, as well as fat and muscle itself. Having available food, however, reduces the need for the body to dip into these reserves, thus reducing the stress of the climb, producing higher energy output and clarity of thinking. Eric did have some energy gel and bars, but this was far less food than he had planned.

These two mistakes might not have been noticed, but a third mistake was far more serious. Eric had led them down the wrong trail. They intended to hike the North Ridge Route, the "standard" route taken by 90 percent of

Holy Cross hikers. This route starts on the Half Moon Pass Trail, trending almost directly west from the parking lot.

Unknown to Eric, the Fall Creek Trail starts at the same point, but it trends south. The incorrect direction could have easily been noticed if they would have been aware of it. But perhaps because he was not aware of multiple trailheads starting at the same point, or because he was anxious to get going, he did not notice their incorrect hiking direction.

And his confusion may have been exacerbated by the jumble of high dirt piles and holes resulting from the heavy construction going on around the trailhead. The parking lot was being expanded and the normally well-marked trailhead was reported by other hikers at the time to be quite confusing. Eric said he walked around the lot but found only one trail, which happened to be the Fall Creek Trail.

Eric had not brought a compass or navigation map such as a USGS topo. He only had a photocopy of a small guidebook map intended for general route illustration. It showed route lines and large-scale terrain features but did not contain the detail needed to make good decisions about route finding or navigation. He apparently did not look at this map until they reached the Notch Mountain Trail intersection.

Eric finally recognized he was off route. And they were way off route, about two-and-a-half miles down the trail, one hour into their day. It would have been a super-long day even if they had followed the standard route to the summit perfectly, and now they were miles off course. It was frustrating, especially because the day was still young and the weather fantastic.

One thing Eric's map did show him was another route to the summit. He noticed a route that ascended Notch Mountain from where they were and traversed around to the summit on a high ridge. This is commonly known as the Halo Route on Holy Cross. It is considerably longer and more strenuous than the normal route, but there was a line on the map from where they were to the summit. This appeared to fix his navigation error; at least they could climb up Notch Mountain and look. And though the Halo Route was long, it was a far shorter distance to continue on it than to retrace their steps back to the parking lot and find the Half Moon Pass Trail. Maybe this would salvage their summit. It seemed like a good idea given their situation, except for one thing: they had been making one mistake after another. Their cascade of errors was growing.

At this point Eric had forgotten his lunch and water filter, and had hiked an hour down the wrong trail. He had insufficient navigation tools, had never been on Holy Cross, and was hiking with a complete novice who relied on him to make every decision. He was about to ascend a route he knew nothing about, and where he would see no other hikers en route to the summit that was many miles, and thousands of feet of climbing, away.

They could have called it a day, turned around, and hiked back to the car in time to have lunch in Vail before they drove back. They could have come back another day, having chalked up their mistakes to a learning experience, to probably never make them again. Michelle would have learned a good lesson on her first attempt.

With the summit very distant and mistakes mounting, this was probably the moment when a decision to abandon the climb would have been easiest. Each step up the mountain would make them more determined to finish, more reluctant to turn around and throw away their sweat equity. Eric decided they would continue.

Dawson's Guide to Colorado's Fourteeners rates the Halo Route at an advanced difficulty level, explaining:

A climber on an advanced route should be a seasoned mountaineer or an intermediate level climber accompanied by a guide or experienced friend.

Though Eric was arguably an experienced friend, Michelle was by no means an intermediate level climber. When asked later why he did not turn around when he knew he was off route, Sawyer rationalized that they would not have had time to reach the summit.

They turned west and began ascending the 2,000 feet to the summit of Notch Mountain. Eric said Michelle's pace slowed dramatically while ascending the steep slope and that he had to wait for her often. They marched on as the forest thinned and then abruptly ended. Above them the trail traversed upward, back and forth across an open, grass-and rock-covered face.

As they reached the top of the ridge at 11:30 a.m., they were rewarded with a breathtaking view to the west as the bulk of Notch Mountain fell behind them. The skyline was dominated by an undulating, gray rocky ridge, striated with lines of white snow of varying widths. The ridge rose out of a deep valley like the walls of an immense fortress.

Their eyes were immediately drawn to a symmetric pyramid rising high above the wall like a watchtower. At the base of the pyramid lay a blue mountain lake called the Bowl of Tears. An uncannily straight and deep gully cut the center of the 2,000-foot face of the pyramid between the Bowl of Tears and the pointed top. Another gully ran horizontally across, near the summit, the left side of which was more prominent than the right. Even late in September, there remained enough snow in the vertical and horizontal gullies to reveal the shape of a natural crucifix the size of the mountain. At their location they had the best view possible of this namesake feature.

This is where the world famous photographs of Holy Cross by William Henry Jackson were taken in 1873. Coincidentally, the last photo of Michelle was also taken near this point. It was one of the photos on a roll of film taken by Eric and developed by the Eagle County Sheriff's Department. It was the photo distributed in handouts to searchers and printed in newspapers around Colorado. It showed Michelle wearing her blue jacket, blue hat, and black pants and carrying her ski poles, hiking near the summit of Notch Mountain with the Holy Cross crucifix just out of sight in the background.

This is where the Notch Mountain shelter was built in 1924 to provide a location for religious services in view of the cross. Tens of thousands of devoted Christians have prayed here since the early 1900s. On that day there was only Eric and Michelle. A stiff, cold breeze nudged them to take refuge in the shelter. They rested for about 15 minutes before resuming their hike.

The Halo Route follows a U-shaped ridgeline connecting Notch Mountain to Holy Cross. The two main difficulties here are surmounting the intermediate summits rising along the route and the distance. However, from Notch Mountain, the distance doesn't appear to be too rugged or very long, and the then-visible summit was beckoning. They had invested hours in their climb, hiking five miles and ascending 3,000 feet. The sky was still clear, and even though they had made several mistakes, their goal seemed to be within reach.

However, this would have been another point where they could have called it a day. They summited Notch Mountain, got a rewarding view lost to most hikers of Holy Cross, and had put in an honest day's work hiking. It was already about the time prudent hikers would plan to be on a summit and Michelle was visibly tired. Yet they seemed to hardly have considered turning around, spending time only for a very short rest. Eric's motivations were clear—he wanted the summit.

But Michelle could also have suggested they turn around here, or insisted she herself turn around. She was an adult, and by Eric's account of their actions and discussions, had the mental capacity to make decisions. She had both the ability and responsibility to decide what was best for her. Perhaps she did discuss or even argue with Eric about turning back. Maybe she felt embarrassed about slowing Eric down, or thought this is what everyone felt like climbing a 14er. Whatever her thinking was, she ultimately followed him. Michelle relinquished all decision making to Eric.

They pushed on and soon found themselves struggling very slowly across the ridgeline. Eric was discovering that this route requires the hiker to remain on the traverse above 13,000 feet for more than three miles, climbing up and down a cumulative nearly 1,000 feet over three intermediary summits. Having never climbed a 14er in her life, neither Michelle nor Eric knew what the effects of altitude would be on her. She was dragging behind; Eric was constantly waiting.

Acute Mountain Sickness

Individual susceptibility to the effects of high altitude varies enormously, and a schedule of ascent that suits most members of a group may be far too rapid for others. These differences are inherent and have nothing to do with the individual's state of training.
The effects of altitude may mimic those produced by hypothermia, dehydration, carbon monoxide poisoning or hypoglycemia, all of which can befall climbers in the arctic environment of high elevations. Anyone ill at high

altitude should be assumed to have a disorder caused or
made worse by the altitude that can be cured or improved
by immediate descent.

—*Medicine for Mountaineering*

High altitude can cause several debilitating medical conditions. The most serious are High Altitude Pulmonary Edema (HAPE), which happens when fluid collects in the lungs, reducing their capacity to deliver oxygen to the body, and High Altitude Cerebral Edema (HACE), which occurs when fluid collects in the brain causing neurological symptoms such as severe loss of balance. These two serious conditions can rapidly kill or cause permanent damage, but are very rare at the altitudes encountered in Colorado.

The more common and generally less serious condition encountered in Colorado is Acute Mountain Sickness, or AMS. Though mild symptoms are little more than annoying, severe AMS can be debilitating. The symptoms vary, but can include nausea, headache, and a general flu-like feeling. All altitude illnesses are caused by less oxygen pressure at high altitude, making it more difficult for the body to deliver oxygen from the air to tissue. At 14,000 feet, the pressure of oxygen is only 60 percent that of sea level.

Michelle, who had a history of migraines, complained of a headache at the start of the climb. This headache may have been migraine related, or it may have been the beginning of AMS. Located at an elevation above 10,000 feet, it was well above the height where altitude sickness is possible (typically around 7,500 feet).

Michelle's slowness was an indication that she was probably experiencing AMS, perhaps to a high degree, something which she likely did not recognize. Though she ran marathons, her body apparently did not react well to the altitude of a 14er. Eric, who had climbed many 14ers, was far more used to high altitude but did not recognize the symptoms.

Eric described Michelle as constantly lagging "30 to 60 feet behind" him. Still, they pressed on. The ridge is not readily escapable. The easiest way off is to progress toward Holy Cross or back to Notch Mountain. Each subsidiary summit they climbed further stranded them. They climbed up and over Point 13,248 and back down to a low point. Then they scrambled

600 feet to Point 13,373 and descended, turning west across a boulder-strewn ridge.

It was there they that they were at their far point. Ahead they had to ascend yet another 600 feet to Point 13,831, which was still not the summit. Turning back would require climbing back over the two ridge points. Either way would require as much work, though reversing their course would allow them to return over now familiar ground. They pressed on. Eric helped Michelle up small steep sections that required easy scrambling.

ALTITUDE SICKNESS ON 14ERS

Elevations above 10,000 feet are the most common to get altitude sickness. You are likely to experience at least mild symptoms of acute mountain sickness while hiking high on a Colorado 14er, even if you live year-round in the "Mile High City" of Denver. Those travelling to Colorado from sea level are especially susceptible to the headaches, fatigue and flu-like malaise caused by reduced oxygen. Fortunately, there are ways to reduce and possibly prevent AMS from occurring. Drinking lots of water to prevent dehydration helps reduce most AMS symptoms.

If visiting from low altitudes, spending a few nights around 5000-6000 feet (which is the altitude of most of the urban Front Range) will normally reduce or eliminate severe AMS symptoms on your 14er hike. It takes about a week of exposure to altitude for your body to generate enough red blood cells to noticeably compensate and a full month to achieve complete acclimatization. Taking the prescription drug acetazolamide (Diamox) is the only proven method for preventing AMS after a large elevation gain, though there are many placebos sold for that purpose.

If you live on the Front Range, camping the night before your climb near the trailhead does wonders for your energy level the next day. Getting a good nights rest instead of waking at 3 a.m. to drive for a couple hours will help you feel better all day long. Hiking a 14er every weekend also has benefits both from increased red blood cells and enhanced fitness. Unfortunately, you lose most of those gains after a few weeks off.

144 | COLORADO 14ER DISASTERS

They finally topped the false summit and descended again. She continued to lag behind.

They finally arrived at the saddle between the unnamed Point 13,831 and the 14,005-foot summit. No doubt Eric felt the last hours excruciatingly slow. They approached a small snowfield lying across the top of the saddle and extending down the west slope of the ridge. Eric led across the snow, punching several inches in with each step, and Michelle followed in his tracks to the far side. The summit was now 550 feet above them. Eric saw his next 14er success finally within reach. Michelle saw the end of her climb.

Lost in the Wilderness

There is an ancient legend about Holy Cross from a time when it was a mythical mountain unseen by any Europeans. The story came from the northern frontier of Mexico in the 1700s, which at that time extended well into what is now Colorado. The story told of two Spanish priests who were hopelessly lost in the mountainous frontier. Close to death, the priests stopped to pray to God for direction. The clouds suddenly opened up to frame a magnificent view of the cross, which inspired the priests to choose the correct route south, back toward New Mexico.

Ironically, modern visitors to the mountain are more likely to suffer the opposite fate. Missing hikers on Holy Cross consistently trigger the greatest number of large search operations in Colorado. The mountain that pointed the way home for the lost Spanish priests has now become home to a sort of demon, enticing the unwary onto an "easy" 14er and leading them astray when their guard is down. It has changed from a beacon of hope to a labyrinth of lost souls.

During a typical summer season, lost hikers may generate more than a dozen organized searches on Holy Cross. Many make the common mistake of veering off route while descending the North Ridge, to stumble thousands of feet down to Cross Creek. They may spend a cold night, waking up the next morning hungry and tired but otherwise unharmed, able to walk out on their own or to be found by searchers. Others wander and spend many nights in the wilderness but eventually emerge alive. And some, like

Michelle, seem to have walked off the edge of the earth.

The disquieting fact is that this trend has been growing for decades. A sampling of lost hiker stories dating back 40 years shows ominous similarities to Michelle's case.

July 1968: A 16-year-old male from Philadelphia became separated from his companions during a driving hailstorm above treeline on the normal route. A rescue team of 150 people and six helicopters searched for him for 11 days. A couple days later, an Outward Bound group on the mountain found him alive, two weeks after he went missing. A searcher was quoted as saying, "Mount of the Holy Cross is that kind of country— remote, forbidding, and potentially dangerous."

August 1994: A 21-year-old male told roommates he was going to climb Holy Cross. He went alone to the mountain and likely saw no others on that Monday morning. He never returned. His roommates reported him missing on Thursday, and a search was launched. The search, which included as many as 150 people in the field at its peak, was called after ten days. The searchers "did not find a thing."

September 1996: A 32-year-old male became lost while descending in a storm. He was found the next day near Buffalo Lake, having descended into Cross Creek Valley and then back up 1,000 feet on the opposite side of the valley, to the lake.

July 1997: A 67-year-old female went missing when she separated from her partner on the ascent. She survived four days before searchers found her "taking shelter in a talus field."

August 1998: A 60-year-old female began to feel ill on her ascent, separated from her climbing partners to descend, and became lost. She was found two days later by searchers.

July 1999: A 68-year-old male spent four nights on Holy Cross before searchers found him. While descending, he became "lost in a ravine and was unable to climb out."

August 2004: A 47-year-old male became separated from his hiking group of 10 on the descent. He was found in Reed's Meadow the next day.

Michelle's disappearance in 2005 is next in the timeline. It is interesting to note how well it fits the historic pattern of missing hikers and, when described in this manner, does not stand out as a unique situation. It is also interesting to note that as time goes on, the missing person cases continue. Almost without skipping a beat, hikers continued to get lost on this mountain.

August 2006: A 54-year-old male became lost when he tried to descend alone after his three partners continued on to the summit. He was found the next day after wandering northwest of where he was last seen, at treeline on the Half Moon Trail.

August 2007: A 31-year-old female spent the night out after becoming lost on the descent. She had separated from her climbing partner, who had turned around on the ascent. She had a cell phone, called for her own rescue, and was found by searchers the next day.

October 2007: A 23-year-old male became lost on the descent when he "decided to go ahead because he was hiking faster" than his 24-year-old brother. When the slower brother reached their camp at East Cross Creek, no one was there. Searchers found the faster lost brother the next day after surviving a night of 18-degree temperatures and an accumulation of snow. He experienced hallucinations and heard voices "due to lack of food and sleep."

Note that the mountain does not discriminate its victims by age or gender. In addition, each person was either solo or had separated from their group when they became lost. Each lost person underestimated the mountain and the environment and was unable to navigate.

The First Five Days of the Search

After finding nothing the night Michelle went missing, a larger effort was mounted the next morning by Vail Mountain Rescue under the supervision of the Eagle County Sheriff's office. At first light, dozens of trained searchers entered the field in teams to cover areas mapped out for them. But that wasn't all; many "civilians" offered to help as well.

Michelle's father told the search leaders he wanted a helicopter in the air and would pay for it. Helicopters are expensive to operate and it was explained to him it might cost upwards of $600 an hour. He did not hesitate to offer payment, and helicopters can be valuable tools in a large area search.

One was soon chartered and flown over the area, carrying experienced search personnel. They saw no sign of Michelle as they scanned dozens of square miles of cliffs, forests, and mountainsides.

Many of Michelle's family and friends volunteered to help search. Though a noble gesture and certainly a way to vent frustration at waiting for information, untrained searchers can be a major headache to search managers. Experienced volunteers know what they are getting into and the managers can expect a certain performance level from them. Inexperienced searchers can be managed in small numbers, but crowds of them are a safety issue. An individual or two can be assigned to an experienced search team, but dozens of searchers are more difficult to assimilate. And volunteers who go searching independently can be even more of a problem. At best they cover undocumented areas or repeat sections that have already been searched; at worst they can themselves become victims and get lost or hurt and require a rescue operation that takes resources away from the main search.

Search managers in this instance did well to absorb these extras and make them useful. Eric himself was in the field with a team providing what help he could. But with the lack of clues about Michelle's location and growing concern that time was running out, it was soon apparent that a far greater number of trained personnel would be needed following the first search day. Search managers sent out the call that night via the CSRB for statewide response. Hundreds responded over the following days.

Daytime weather was mild and, though dipping into the twenties at night, the weather was survivable the first two nights Michelle was missing. The third night brought a severe storm to the area that included wind, heavy rain, and chilling temperatures. Michelle was wearing synthetic pants, neither windproof nor waterproof, and carried only a light jacket that would have provided little protection against the angry elements. It would have been very difficult, if not impossible, for her to survive this storm in the open. But it was also possible she could have found shelter. The area offered a myriad of opportunities, from shallow rock caves above treeline to dense trees or bushes below. With this in mind, the search continued undeterred following the storm. On search days three through five there were approximately 100 field searchers per day. On day six that number increased to 200.

And they did their job well. A trained searcher looks for the missing person as well as any signs she may have left behind. This includes footprints, messages, a dropped glove or candy wrapper, anything that could be connected to her and indicate where she may be or the direction she may have followed. Any place large, remote, and confusing enough for someone to truly get lost will present a myriad of clues to searchers, the vast majority of which will be unrelated to the lost person. Searchers found dozens of clues the first five days. The most intriguing among them raised questions, and even suspicions.

The Clues

On September 25, day one of the search, at 10:15 p.m., a searcher reported a strange encounter. Her team made contact with a six-foot-tall male on the Cross Creek Trail. Despite the darkness, he had no headlamp or flashlight and was wearing dark clothing. He initially tried to hide from the searchers in the trees adjacent to the trail. When the searchers inquired about Michelle, he acted strangely and avoided answering the questions. He avoided facial contact and eventually ran away from the search team.

Later that evening, searchers came upon what was described as a purple and orange tent two miles in from the Cross Creek Trailhead. Though a light was glowing within the tent, the party inside would not speak to searchers or unzip the tent.

The next morning, a man hiked out of the Cross Creek Trailhead and was approached by law enforcement officials. He roughly matched the description of the mystery man seen the previous night. He was uncooperative and gave evasive answers to the deputy's questions. He said he had been camping and reluctantly showed the deputies his tent—it was yellow.

On September 27 at 10:44 a.m., searchers found a watch hanging in a tree near the Notch Mountain Trail intersection. It was described as an "Indiglo Ironman Timer with a black band." Michelle was a marathon runner, so there was speculation she may have left this as a trail marker or

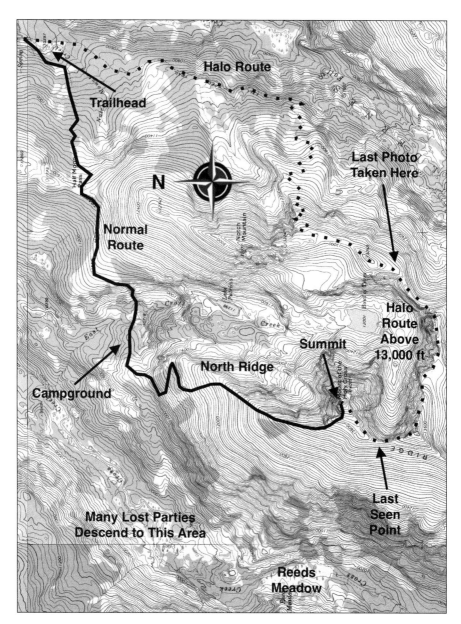

Topo map of Mount of the Holy Cross.

a signal to searchers.

On September 28, Team Seventeen finds a duffle bag 100 feet from the Cross Creek Trailhead in the forest between Cross Creek and the trail. The duffle contains, among other items, a shotgun.

On September 29, Team Five finds boot prints leading to and then ending at a cliff area on the western flank of Holy Cross. They request a helicopter search of the cliff. Nothing is found. The same day blood is found in the snow on the south side of the summit. It was later analyzed and found not to be human blood.

Many other clues were found by search teams but quickly discounted. The most interesting were also, in the final analysis, determined to be unrelated to Michelle's disappearance.

The Eagle County Sheriff investigated the "mystery man" encountered at the trailhead, who identified himself as Peter Martin and said he lived nearby. Despite what the investigators described as "suspicious" behavior, no evidence was ever found to link him to Michelle. The stealth man encountered on the night of the 25th and the person camped in the glowing orange tent were never identified and may have been one and the same, and may have been Martin despite varying descriptions of the men and the tents. These variations could be explained by darkness or by witness mistakes. Or they could have been two different men.

The Final Search Day

On Saturday, October 1, search managers took advantage of a weekend day when far more volunteers were available, and pushed for a final, all-out effort. Thirty-five ground teams comprising approximately 350 searchers and several dog teams swarmed over the mountain. Two helicopters flew, alternately inserting and extracting teams in remote locations, while scanning the landscape during their overflight.

Sadly, the day ended as it started and they were no closer to finding Michelle. They decided it was time to draw their monumentally frustrating effort to a close and accept the inevitable.

Final statistics on the search reveal the colossal effort put forth: Over a span of seven days, more than 800 searchers and dog teams worked well over 10,000 hours. Five helicopters were employed, including one with forward-looking infrared equipment used to spot heat sources. There were seven reported searcher injuries, some of which required medical evacuation.

Last Seen Point at Saddle

View from just below the summit looking toward the south saddle where Eric and Michelle separated.

Because a missing person incident is treated as a crime, everyone linked with Michelle's disappearance was investigated, including both Eric and Michelle's husband. Investigators did not find enough evidence to support a continued investigation of anyone in connection with the case.

The search revealed no clues as to what happened to Michelle.

Vanishing Point

Michelle sipped the remaining water in her Camelback water pouch at the saddle just below the summit of Holy Cross. Eric swallowed the water remaining in his bottle at about the same time.

What Eric thought at that moment only he knows, but he had worked hard for this summit and patiently waited for Michelle for nearly the entire hike. The summit seemed close enough to reach out and touch. According to Eric's account, this is when Michelle said, "I'm too tired to continue, you go on without me." And he did.

He told her to traverse to the North Ridge Trail.

Though it appears to be a freestanding mountain from certain angles, Mount of the Holy Cross is actually the highest point on a six-mile-long, north-south running ridge called Holy Cross Ridge. The summit is the northernmost bump on this ridge with the bulk of the ridge stretching south. The ridge to the north of the summit drops steeply down to Cross Creek. Along it runs the descriptively named North Ridge Route, the easiest

WHEN TO END A SEARCH OPERATION

A large-scale search operation such as what was mounted to find Michelle cannot continue indefinitely. At some point the managers must end the official search and the ultimate authority for this decision in the state of Colorado is the county sheriff. But when is that decision made if family, loved ones, friends, and even the general public want it to continue?

It turns out that most search operations have a natural ending point, which is determined by weather, the availability of volunteers, and the acceptance of the inevitable by family members. If a wet snowstorm moves in, it is unlikely a lost victim could survive after so many days. Large operations involving dozens if not hundreds of searchers demand many volunteers that are generally not available for more than a few days. And usually, when family members witness large operations and talk with experts, they ultimately accept that the search must end.

route on the mountain and the one most people hike to the summit. The summit block juts 1,000 feet east off the ridgeline. One could hike a line from the saddle where Michelle stopped across to the North Ridge, arriving at the trail and avoiding the last 500 feet of elevation gain.

Instead of sending Michelle across this expanse alone, Eric could have ascended and returned while Michelle waited at the saddle. Then both could have traversed below the summit and attained the North Ridge Trail. But as Eric reported, he thought he would save some time by having Michelle traverse while he summited, meeting up later on the North Ridge. This was the plan according to Eric.

Unfortunately, neither Michelle nor Eric considered the flaws in this plan. Again, Michelle was a complete novice; she was physically drained, and possibly even suffered from AMS. Given her lack of experience to draw on, compounded by the likelihood her mind was clouded by her physical state, this was an extremely dangerous situation for Michelle.

She would have no navigation aids on the traverse such as a trail or cairns (rock piles used to mark routes), and she would have to scramble over a field of boulders. "I pointed to where she should go, and that I would meet her on the way down," he told investigators. "I thought it was about 200 yards, an eighth of a mile."

He later admitted to investigators that he had vastly underestimated the distance. It was closer to a mile—a mile of confusing terrain without a guidepost.

Eric hiked on toward the summit while Michelle rested. He said he left her at 1:25 p.m. It was the last time anyone saw Michelle.

On the Summit

Though the Halo Route was barren of any other hikers that day, the North Ridge was not. Julia and Bill Taylor were about to complete their ascent of the North Ridge at about 1:30 p.m. Julia was slightly nervous about the late hour. She had trained herself over the years to be off the summit before afternoon thunderstorms built up and threatened with their lightning. But thunderstorms are not as common in autumn as they are in mid-summer, and the few clouds in the blue sky were smooth, white, and benign.

"I took a picture of Bill on the summit and you could see what time it was from his watch," Julia told me later. The couple donned warm hats and jackets to ward off a stiff, cold breeze that blew from the north, snapped a few photos, and sat down on a chair-sized boulder. They celebrated their summit with congratulations, food, water, and rest.

Their summit solitude was interrupted after only a few minutes when Eric walked up from the south. They exchanged greetings with him, and then Eric made two quick calls on his cell phone. During the first conversation he said, "We made it." On the second he said, "We will be late." When Eric was finished, the three exchanged pleasantries, as 14er climbers often do on summits, and he was off about five minutes later. "I don't think he even signed the summit register," Julia recalled. They descended shortly after Eric, worried about the late hour. "The weather wasn't threatening that day, but it was a long hike out," she remembered.

Starting gently over the summit stones, the trail soon steepened as it descended and began turning north. Perhaps 10 minutes down from the summit, Julia heard something very unusual.

It sounded to her like a muffled yell for help.

There are many thoughts that go through a climber's mind as he descends from a successful summit. One is surely the satisfaction of completing one more 14er, of persisting beyond the complaints of sore muscles and aching lungs, of ticking off one more from *The List*. Feelings of satisfaction are moderated by the dread of a long slog out during which the pain and fatigue are not masked by the anticipation of the summit and are only relieved by the finish at the trailhead.

Eric probably felt all of these feelings to one degree or another, but his immediate thought was to link up again with his partner Michelle. He surely must have thought he would come across her soon; she should be only minutes away down the North Ridge Trail. He said he was mildly surprised he could not see her already. He called out her name.

There was no answer.

A few minutes down from the summit, the Taylors came across Eric again. "He was shouting, 'Michelle!' His voice was garbled around the cur-

View from the North Ridge Trail toward the area from where Michelle was expected to traverse, coming toward the camera. Note the snowfield, which indicates a hidden gully that Michelle would have had to negotiate.

vature of the mountain and the second syllable in her name sounds like 'help,'" Julia said. They were only minutes behind Eric, perhaps a couple hundred feet, and yet his voice was distorted. One hundred feet further and Julia would likely have heard nothing.

This audio distortion is strangely inconsistent in the mountain environment. The clarity of voices over distance is dependent on weather conditions and the shape of the terrain. Whereas Aaron Boyles, whose father fell while descending the wrong couloir on Little Bear, could communicate with someone more than 1,000 feet below him, Julia, conversely, could not understand Eric's distorted shouts from one-fifth of that distance on the summit of Holy Cross that day.

Eric stated he arrived on the summit at exactly 1:42 p.m., only 17 minutes after separating from Michelle. He remained there for five minutes and descended the North Ridge Trail. Assuming it took him another 10 minutes to get to his intended rendezvous, it had then been more than a half hour from the time he left her. As evidenced by Julia's reported distortion of Eric's voice, Michelle could have easily hiked out of voice contact range over this time, but no one knows where. She might as well have been on the moon.

The Surprising Timeline

Rhythm is supremely important on a long hike. It is a natural pace comfortable to the mind and body, and different for each individual—some are faster, some slower. When a hiker settles into this pace, he wants to neither go faster nor stop, and the hours melt away into a pleasant memory. It is one of the secrets of enjoyable hiking or climbing.

Eric emphasized that Michelle was slow and lagging behind him for the majority of the climb. His pace was much faster and he repeatedly walked ahead and waited for her to catch up. This can be a supremely frustrating situation for both hikers—neither could get into their pace. Michelle was either forcing herself to go too fast or was too ill to achieve it, while Eric was going too slowly. Failure to achieve a rhythm makes the climb seem much longer and induces frustration. Eric certainly felt this based on his comments. Michelle was no doubt surprised and embarrassed at her relative slowness, but probably just felt exhausted.

But *was* Michelle's pace slow?

Here is a timeline for the climb based on Eric's account, witnesses, and a couple of good estimates:

3:45 a.m. .... Eric arrives at Vanek house in Denver.

4:00 a.m. .... Eric and Michelle depart Vanek house.

6:30 a.m. .... Arrival at trailhead.

7:00 a.m. .... Begin hike.

8:30 a.m. .... Arrive at Notch Mountain trail intersection.

11:30 a.m. .... Arrive at Notch Mountain Shelter.

11:45 a.m. .... Begin traverse to South Ridge of Holy Cross.

1:25 p.m. .... Separate at saddle south of Holy Cross summit.

1:42 p.m. .... Eric arrives on summit.

1:47 p.m. .... Eric leaves summit.

The Halo Route can be split up into sections with the distances and elevation gains measured on a USGS topographic map:

Trailhead to NM Trail intersection: .... 2.5 miles, 1,200 feet

NM Trail Intersection to NM Shelter: .... 2.6 miles, 2,100 feet

NM Shelter to Holy Cross South Saddle: ...... 2.6 miles, 1,600 feet

South Saddle to Summit: .... 0.5 miles, 550 feet

There are many qualitative factors that cause a pace to vary in the mountains, including terrain difficulties, steepness, altitude, and the state of the hikers such as how tired, hungry, and thirsty they are. For example, the first section above was hiked when Eric and Michelle were fresh, down at low altitude and on a developed trail. You would expect their pace to be faster on this section than in the third section, which is when they were tired, above 13,000 feet, and scrambling over a rocky ridge without a trail.

This data reveals some details about their pace:

From the trailhead to South Saddle took 6.5 hours.

Their pace on the first section of the hike, between the trailhead and Notch Mountain Shelter, was 1.1 miles per hour and 733 foot gain per hour.

Their pace on the last section of the hike, between the Notch Mountain Shelter and the South Saddle was 1.6 miles per hour and 958 foot gain per hour.

Eric's pace from the South Saddle to the summit was at 1.8 miles per hour and almost 1,950-foot gain per hour.

The first point reveals a very respectable pace. Though not fast, it was well within the norm for fit and experienced 14er hikers and very plausible for them.

The fourth item confirms how strong Eric was on that day and how different his pace was from Michelle's pace. His time on the last section to the summit was extremely fast, especially given that it was near 14,000 feet. He practically ran to the summit.

The second and third items are the most revealing to the psychology of the climb. At the time when Eric said Michelle slowed considerably, over the more difficult scrambling part of the ridge above 13,000 feet, she was actually climbing at a *faster* pace, and if the times are believed, a *much* faster pace.

Did she increase her pace to keep up with a newly energized Eric? Did Eric fail to realize he was pushing a much faster pace than before? Is the timetable incorrect?

The only unverified time the calculations depend on was the 7 a.m. trailhead departure. If they left earlier, it would result in a slower pace on the first section; leaving later would increase their pace. To match the fast pace on the ridge, they would have had to sit at the trailhead for nearly two hours after arriving, which is highly unlikely.

The times Eric reported may not have been exact, but he would have to be hours in error to describe a climb in which their pace slowed as they climbed. Simply matching their high-altitude to their low-altitude pace would have been an exhausting increase in climbing effort. This might explain why Michelle's motivation completely collapsed on the last few hundred feet of the climb. She burned her reserves trying to go faster, and yet Eric reported was that she was slower on this section.

Eric failed to recognize that she might have been in a highly vulnerable state on the saddle. When asked by investigators why he did not tell Michelle to wait for him at the saddle, Eric said, "It would have cost us 45 minutes on the descent."

The Last Question

Hundreds of Michelle's friends and family overflowed the church at her funeral. Having her life cut short so unexpectedly made her death unbelievably tragic for everyone who knew her. Her widower and four children struggle with the loss years later.

She is gone, but the burning question remains: where is Michelle?

Even if suffering from exhaustion, hunger, thirst, and the effects of acute mountain sickness, it seems unlikely she was so delirious she would stumble off the eastern cliffs of Holy Cross. It also seems unlikely she would reverse her course and hike back up over the 13,831-foot peak to the south.

If she had gone directly north as Eric directed, she would have eventually run into the North Ridge Trail and would have seen, or have been seen by, several people who were hiking at various points along the trail, but this did not happen.

What Michelle was attempting is known as "contouring," meaning she would follow an imaginary equal elevation line, neither ascending nor descending as she traversed. Hikers often use this technique to minimize the work of hiking up a hill or down a valley. And if they aren't careful, they find themselves losing elevation, arriving lower than they started. Contouring is deceptively tricky. Maintaining elevation on a traverse actually feels like climbing up, so there is a natural tendency to descend. And a sick, tired hiker tends to exaggerate the downward trend.

The eastward curve of Holy Cross's north ridge adds a double whammy to this contouring mistake. The slope contour would encourage her to hike more north-westerly, encouraging her to lose more elevation in a direction away from the North Ridge Trail, which trends northeast. If she had a reference point on the North Ridge, she would have lost it as the summit rapidly sunk behind ridgeline above and behind her, and then disappeared altogether below the curvature of the slope.

Soon she may have been descending directly downhill, more westerly and more quickly away from the North Ridge. This would take her toward the Cross Creek Valley, a place where she would be truly lost. She would have been hiking the wrong direction without a compass or map, looking for a trail she knew nothing about. On this course, she would have been out of shouting distance of the North Ridge within minutes and she would have never seen a hiker on the standard trail.

But simply being lost does not kill someone.

If Michelle had descended all the way to the valley floor without incident, she would have probably recovered a lot of her energy. The lower altitude and abundance of water could easily have boosted her mental and physical energy. The shelter and warmer temperatures of the lower, less exposed forest would have allowed her to live for days.

If she had descended to Reeds Meadow on the valley floor she would surely have recognized the Cross Creek Trail. The trail would have revealed an easy-to-follow route, much less difficult than the west flank of Holy Cross, a steep, rock-strewn slope that she would have descended to get to the valley floor.

She may not have recognized which way to go from there. South would take her to the head of the valley and eventually over Fancy Pass to the ghost town of Holy Cross City. But this would require hiking back uphill. Tired and lost people tend to travel in the easiest direction—downhill. Hiking downward from Reeds Meadow would have taken her to Tigiwon Road, the dirt road that leads to the Half Moon Trailhead parking lot, in only eight miles. It might have taken her until the next day to walk this trail, but she would have been found very soon afterward, having only suffered an open, overnight bivouac.

This scenario is so common that VMR routinely sends their first teams up the Cross Creek Trail to Reeds Meadow when called to search for hikers who have strayed from the North Ridge. And they did so on the first day of the search for Michelle, but she did not hike out and there was no sign she made it to Cross Creek valley.

If one assumes Michelle began hiking north, and then made the common error of descending toward Cross Creek where the terrain is fairly flat and benign, it is most likely she met her fate on the vast western flank of Holy Cross ridge. There are "terrain traps" on this face, cliffs and loose rock sections, but they are certainly avoidable if one is willing to backtrack and traverse around them. These cliffs are not the multi-thousand-foot monster walls that form the East Face of Holy Cross ridge. The largest "traps" are maybe 100 feet high and many are only 10 or 20 feet high and not vertical. It may not seem so intimidating to try a 20-foot downclimb of one of these cliffs if it saved you from re-ascending several hundred feet to avoid it.

Did Michelle, tired and wanting to get off the face as soon as possible, attempt to downclimb one of these cliffs and fall? Was she severely injured and unable to move, or even killed instantly? If so, this would explain why she left no clues as to her location. But then the question becomes, why couldn't the searchers find her remains after covering what appeared to be a tremendously large area?

The answer could be just that, it *is* a tremendously large area, and the truth is that searchers may not be very effective, especially as the days wear on. Ground searchers become tired and ineffective. Search managers may not be effective over time, losing information in the chaos of managing hundreds of people. Some areas are inevitably over-covered while others are severely under-covered. Search theory is a very inexact science, and there are many examples of searchers turning up zero clues, only to have the victim found long after the ground teams have left.

Consider an incident that happened exactly eight weeks before Michelle disappeared, just 80 miles north of Holy Cross. A ranger named Jeff Christensen mysteriously vanished while on backcountry patrol in Rocky Mountain National Park.

His case was similar to Michelle's in that it instigated a huge search effort that uncovered very few clues, but the circumstances were more disturbing than Michelle's. Christensen was an extremely experienced mountaineer, both playing and working in the mountains. He was a seasonal ranger who had worked for the park in the summer and a ski patroller for the Winter Park Ski Resort in the winter. He was on a backcountry patrol in the remote Mummy Range when he vanished. Though he was patrolling alone, he was carrying a radio and a pistol, both of which could be used to signal for help. He was also well equipped for backcountry travel and trained to survive life-threatening situations.

On July 29, 2005, a co-worker dropped off Christensen near Chapin Pass, the trailhead where he would begin his backcountry patrol, at 11:30 a.m. His intent was to hike the Mummy Range, which include a series of 12,000- to 13,000-foot peaks linked by popular, easy to hike trails.

He was seen in the saddle between Mount Chapin and Mount Chiquita at 12:30 p.m., where he spoke with two hikers. He was then seen at the summit of Mount Chiquita at 1 p.m., approximately three miles from the trailhead, where he spoke with several other hikers. He was not seen or heard from after this time. The weather that day was sunny, with a high temperature of 75° F at 12,000 feet, and no rain.

Headquarters tried to contact Christensen when he failed to check in at the end of the day. They received no response. He was not found at his residence in the park. A search was instigated and escalated in a similar way to the Holy Cross search, including the finding of intriguing clues that led nowhere.

A search area of 26 square miles was covered over the next eight days. More than 100 searchers participated each day, including several dog teams. Five helicopters were in operation at the height of the operation.

Several radio clicks were heard one day, and that led searchers to speculate that Christensen was trying to contact them but could not speak for some reason. Gunshots were also heard and again speculation was that Christensen was trying to signal for help. These clues ultimately led nowhere. Christensen seemed to have vanished without a trace, just as Michelle would two months later.

Then, just as the search was preparing to scale down, Christensen's body was found northwest of Chiquita Lake in a basin below Mount Chiquita. Despite their huge effort, the trained search teams did *not* find him. Instead, three hikers who happened to wander off trail found him in an area that had previously been covered by searchers.

Christensen died of a head injury that he probably suffered during a fall while descending the steep east slopes of Mount Chiquita. He was very much alive, conscious, and not disabled after his accident. He was found with his head bandaged using a t-shirt he had extracted from his pack. There was no evidence that he had fallen where his body was found, indicating that he hiked to where he eventually died, slowly losing judgment and consciousness as he bled into his skull.

His two-way radio was damaged but operational. Though there are radio dead zones in the park, he was not in one. He could have easily called for help, which may have saved his life. His sidearm was also undamaged and loaded with unused ammo.

Why Christensen did not call for help is forever a mystery, but why didn't searchers find him earlier? There are a couple of possible reasons. The area covered by each search team was huge and full of structure such as lichen-covered boulders, cliffs with cracks and holes, brush and trees, all of which can camouflage a body whose size, when compared, is insignificant. The standard ranger uniform worn by Christensen that day is dark tan and green, creating a perfect camouflage in the mountains.

If Michelle's remains are on Holy Cross, they too may be as hard to find as Christensen's were. The search for Christensen proved that hundreds of ground personnel and several helicopters searching for days might not find a thing.

But perhaps in time a hiker will stumble upon a clue.

Hikers Body Found 10 Years After He Vanished was the headline from an Associated Press story dated October 2, 2005; the day after Michelle's search was called off. The remains of Jim Mills of Fort Worth, Texas, were found near the base of Blanca Peak, a 14er located in remote south-central Colorado. He disappeared in August 1995, while solo climbing the mountain. Searchers combed the area for days finding nothing. Hikers stumbled upon his scattered remains on the east side of the peak. It was presumed he fell down the precipitous cliffs on that face.

The story described the relief Mills' relatives felt when he was finally found. But it was also a foreboding story for Michelle. As if to sate some horrific mountain demon that sadistically imprisons the bodies of hapless climbers for years, Michelle was taken just as Mills mysterious disappearance had been resolved. Her remains may be found years or perhaps decades from now, and that may bring final closure for her family and friends.

Meanwhile, the hazard remains, waiting to entrap the unwary or unlucky.

The lessons to learn from Michelle's disappearance seem clear, yet Mount of the Holy Cross will remain dangerous to climbers who underestimate it. Though its normal route is rated easy among 14ers, it has proven to be a difficult navigation problem for novices. This turns it into an insidious trap for these hikers, many of whom are attracted to Holy Cross because it is considered easy.

Holy Cross was once the most famous mountain in the country. It was steeped in religion and considered holy ground, itself a compass that gave direction in life and pointed to goodness. Its legacy has come full circle.

PART IV: THE CONTINUING SAGA

"My goal was to get to the top of Longs Peak so I continued climbing."

—Samuel Frappier's explanation as to why he continued climbing into unknown territory.

An Extraordinary Incident

Tuesday, May 27, 2014, began a series of events that over the following two days would add up to a truly unbelievable story. What happened to Sam Frappier was not miraculous, but to say he was lucky is a misleading understatement.

That day, at 7:30 a.m., Sam Frappier and Gabriel Fortin began hiking up the Longs Peak Trail intending to reach the summit via the standard Keyhole Route. The weather was excellent; there was little wind, no precipitation, and it was quite warm, as high as 65°F on the summit. Under these conditions on a weekend day during the high climbing season, which is typically from approximately July through Labor Day, you would find literally hundreds of others climbing the same route. But being early in the year, notably before the route is snow-free and relatively dry, and a weekday, there were few other hikers around.

Sam and Gabriel were young extreme athletes. Sam was 19 years old. Both had participated in long endurance races, including 50-kilometer runs and Ironman competitions. They were both, without question, at a much higher fitness level than most hikers who summit Longs Peak. You might expect, based on this information alone, that they would both summit and return in time for an early afternoon beer in Estes Park. Unfortunately, they were severely lacking in another area, namely mountaineering experience.

Both lived in French-speaking Quebec, Canada, where challenging peaks are few and far between. Sam's experience was limited to Mount Washington in New Hampshire. The Tuckerman Ravine route up Mt. Washington is 4.1 miles with a 4208-foot elevation gain. In comparison, the Keyhole Route on Longs Peak is more than twice as long, at 8.4 miles, with a 4875-foot gain. But the real difference in difficulty is the altitude during the climb. At an elevation of 6288 feet, the summit of Mt. Washington is 3100 feet lower than the starting point for Longs Peak, at 9400 feet.

Nevertheless, the difference in the difficulty of these mountains was not an issue for these two athletes; Longs Peak was well within their endurance abilities. Ironically, these abilities would actually be a negative contributing factor in the events that were to follow.

Sam and Gabriel ascended the Longs Peak Trail to just over 12,000 feet, where it forks, much more quickly than the average hiker who might take two to three hours. The Keyhole Route continues northwest along the lower slopes of Mt. Lady Washington. The other branch leads southwest toward Chasm Lake and the east face of Longs Peak and Mount Meeker. The trails are properly signed and this fork is not the first (it's the fourth fork from the trailhead). Sam and Gabriel incorrectly chose the Chasm Lake branch. If you are only looking at the peaks, the Chasm Lake branch appears correct, because it leads directly toward Longs. Sam and Gabriel were not the first to fall for this deception; many have made the same mistake.

This is a significant routefinding error for a novice to make as there is no easy route on that side of Longs. Had there been the usual throngs of hikers along the trail, it is unlikely they would have chosen this trail. But not having clues from seeing other hikers or being able to ask anyone, as well as ignoring or missing the direction signs and not confirming their location on a map, they continued to progress in this dangerous direction.

The Chasm Lake Trail ends at Chasm Meadows, located below Chasm Lake, in the giant cirque enclosed by the sheer east face of Longs and the south face of Mt. Lady Washington. There is no obvious trail into this cirque and there is no non-technical route out of this cirque (except to backtrack to Chasm Meadows), at least not in May when the snow is just beginning to melt at these high elevations.

Sam and Gabriel hiked past the Chasm Lake shelter and up to Chasm Lake, where they surveyed the cirque. There was no trail up the peak, only thousands of feet of sheer gray cliffs broken by a threadwork of white ledges and couloirs where the winter snow could cling. One of the couloirs appeared to ascend up to the ridgeline east of the summit. Though they didn't know at the time, this couloir is known as The Flying Dutchman.

The Flying Dutchman is normally climbed as a technical route up 13,911 Mt. Meeker. It ascends 1600 feet up from Chasm Lake, angling roughly south toward the saddle between Meeker and Longs. This saddle is quite large and forms a quarter mile long flat boulder field at the low point known as The Loft. From the top of the Flying Dutchman, a climber can descend a bit to the Loft and then hike to the summit of Meeker.

The Flying Dutchman is considered technical due to the gradual steepening of the snow as you ascend and the crux of the route, a 50-foot section where the slope angle approaches 60 degrees, where most climbers want a rope and belay protection. The condition of this section varies throughout the year. In mid to late summer, it has melted out to rock and becomes a 5.4 rock pitch. Prior to melting out it is covered in water ice (from melting/refreezing snow) and requires crampons and ice tools.

In spring, while the snow is still relatively thick and sticky, this section can actually be easier than other times of the year. These variable conditions are what make couloir climbing in Colorado an attractive challenge to mountaineers; you never know what the conditions will be like in late spring and early summer. Nevertheless, even when the climb is "easier," an ice axe and crampons are required for safety. A foothold could break off and send you screaming down the slope without warning.

Sam and Gabriel did not have ice axes, crampons, or ropes. As a matter of fact, Sam was wearing sneakers, not made for the wet snow conditions they encountered. He did not have gaiters, leggings worn to prevent snow from getting inside boots or shoes.

But the lack of proper equipment did not slow them down. They ascended 1200 vertical feet of the couloir up to the crux section. Gabriel was able to negotiate the steep face by climbing a 5.7 rock pitch around the water ice section. Sam decided not to attempt it and descended back down the couloir on his own. Being on difficult, unknown territory, Sam and Gabriel probably should not have split up during their ascent. They both could have descended when the climbing became too difficult for Sam, or Sam could have descended and waited at Chasm Lake for Gabriel to come down

But Sam was not satisfied with what he had climbed so far. On the descent down to Chasm Lake, Sam noticed a route that ascends up Mount Lady Washington, lying almost directly on the opposite side of the cirque from the Flying Dutchman. Sam decided it was a viable option out of the cirque and eventually up Longs Peak. He was correct about this; it is the easiest way out of the chasm, the only non-technical route up the peak from there. He chose to continue his adventure up Lady Washington.

From the summit of Lady Washington, it is a trivial hike over toward the Keyhole Route. Sam did not take this option, however, and chose to hike toward the North Face on Longs. The North Face is a much more direct route to the summit than the circuitous Keyhole Route, but it is considered a technical climb, with a couple of 5.4 rock pitches lying just above Chasm View, a thousand-foot-high sheer cliff descending to the Chasm Lake cirque.

Given Sam's route finding judgment, the North Face Route was probably a much better choice at this point than the Keyhole Route because the latter is difficult to follow unless you pay close attention and have some idea of where the route goes. During the high climbing season in the summer, most hikers follow the line of climbers in front of them and aren't required to do any real routefinding. Getting off route on the winding traverse between the Keyhole formation on the northwest ridge of Longs and the summit will put you in difficult fifth class rock climbing territory.

So given the likelihood of ending up in a worse situation, the North Face was probably a better choice. And in fact Sam claimed he had no trouble negotiating the technical rock pitches. He later wrote:

> My goal was to get to the top of Longs Peak so I continued climbing. I was getting very tired but I knew I was able to do it. My first mistake here is to continue getting up without being sure to have enough water to get down. I arrived at the top at maybe 5:30 pm, pretty tired but extremely satisfied.

At this point, Sam had ascended 6,000 feet. It had taken him 10 hours to complete his circuitous route, quite a bit more than he had anticipated, but he was on the summit. A hiker on the Keyhole Route, a much shorter route than what Sam had taken, might take seven hours to summit. Meanwhile, Gabriel had continued on his attempt toward the summit as well. He had arrived at the Loft and then turned directly west toward the summit. Gabriel did not realize this route would dead end at the formation known as the Notch.

The Notch is a deep cut in the ridge of Longs Peak that runs between the summit and the Loft saddle. When looking up from the Loft toward Longs' summit, it appears as a long scree slope. The Notch is deceptively hidden, frustrating unaware climbers. Just as they think they have the summit in the bag, the Notch blocks their approach, revealing itself as a sheer, impassible, 100-foot gouge in the ridge.

There is a non-technical route to the summit from the Loft called Clarks Arrow. This requires a traverse to the south slope of Longs from near the low point of the Loft and another traverse about equivalent in difficulty to the Keyhole Route. It traverses below the Notch over to the Homestretch to the top, the same finish as the Keyhole Route. It is not a commonly used route and it is not surprising that Gabriel was unaware of it. Gabriel's climb topped out on the downside of the Notch.

Sam spied his friend from the summit and was able to communicate with him. Sam wrote:

> I saw my friend who was on the peak just to the
> left of the summit: he couldn't make it to the top.
> We decided to get down at 6pm. As I was a bit
> exhausted, I decided to try going down by Kiener's
> Route. It was a very steep slope as you must know,
> but I managed to be careful and not take too many
> risks, though I sometimes feared a bit for my life.

What happened next is that Sam made the decision to descend the East Face of Longs in an attempt to save time. Gabriel had gotten to within a few hundred feet of the summit, and Sam could see their starting point at Chasm Lake 2000 feet directly below him. Surely the East Face was a faster descent, he thought. Instead of returning down the North Face, a route with which he was now familiar, he chose to negotiate the most difficult section of Longs Peak, which, unknown to him, has killed or injured many climbers with far more experience than he had.

Kiener's is a difficult technical route to ascend and it is exceedingly rare that anyone intentionally descends this way. Ascending Kiener's involves several pitches of low 5th class rock climbing with tremendous exposure over the Diamond. As described in the *Winter Storm Warning* chapter, it runs about 100 feet from the top of the Diamond to the Broadway ledge. Most of this distance is non-technical, and deep soft snow conditions encountered by Sam reduced some of the technical difficulties, though his shoes were now soaked.

It is likely that Sam Frappier's descent was roughly on Kiener's, as he himself does not know exactly. This is a good assumption as all other routes around this part of the East Face are highly technical and difficult. In any event, he ended up descending to Broadway, an amazing accomplishment for someone with no mountaineering experience or technical climbing gear. Compare this with Judd and Kelley's harrowing descent down Kiener's using multiple rappels and leaving the rope behind on the last rappel.

Broadway is a ledge that runs from the Lamb's Slide Couloir all the way across the east face complex of Longs. Between the Notch Couloir and Lamb's Slide it is not a single ledge but a system of parallel ledges. In winter and spring these ledge systems are piled with sloping snow. If the snow is hard, crampons are required. But if the snow is soft, conditions are much better, and you can plunge step through the snow, creating excellent footholds without the need for crampons. Sam was lucky that the snow was in this condition, making it far easier to not only descend Kiener's but also traverse across Broadway.

Sam was almost home free; there was only one last obstacle to overcome. There is a narrow section on Broadway that requires one to step around a protrusion in the ledge. This move is labeled "Narrow Spot" in the East Face photo on page 115. It's an easy step with good handholds, but it is fantastically intimidating because it requires you to make the move over 900 feet of cliff face. Many people belay this section, while others crawl underneath the protrusion. Sam arrived at this point and concluded he could go no farther.

It was approximately 7 p.m., the sun was still out, and the weather continued to be warm and dry with very little wind, which is about as perfect as it gets in late May at 13,000 feet. This was his second lucky break; the first was the excellent snow conditions. With darkness approaching, unable to progress down, and unwilling to retrace his steps back up and over the summit, Sam concluded he needed to be rescued. He had a cell phone, and being very high on Longs Peak, he was able to connect to a distant cell site.

This was his third lucky break.

He wrote:

> So I called 911. Here I'm gonna summarize: they
> told me I'd have to stay the night and that rescuers
> would come tomorrow. I stayed that night with all
> my clothes wet on a little rock (yeah, it was the most
> horrible experience in my life). Wednesday they sent
> people to look if they could help me, but they realized
> they couldn't climb straight up to get to me.

Sam wore a light windbreaker-like jacket. Otherwise, his clothing was all cotton, fabric that experienced mountaineers avoid. Once it gets wet from sweat or snowmelt, cotton is nearly impossible to dry and saps heat from the body faster than wearing nothing at all.

At this point it is interesting to note the differences between Sam's self-reporting of his experience and the official National Park Service (NPS) report issued a couple of weeks later. Longs Peak lies within NPS jurisdiction in Rocky Mountain National Park (RMNP), so the NPS was responsible for responding to Sam's call for help. The NPS report states that Sam contacted the RMNP rangers at approximately 6 p.m. and indicated that he was "stuck on the Keyhole Route." Because Sam's cell phone provided his GPS coordinates, the rangers concluded he was likely on the East Face, far from the Keyhole Route.

Surprisingly, Gabriel had by this time gotten back down to Chasm Lake, having down-climbed the difficult 5.7 rock pitch and the rest of the Flying Dutchman Couloir. The NPS report also states that Gabriel heard Sam's "shouts of distress" at Chasm Lake, and he subsequently headed down the trail to get help. Gabriel confirmed that Sam was probably on the East Face, so the NPS dispatched a "technical rescue team" that same night. They staged their rescue at the Chasm Lake shelter to begin a technical rescue the next morning.

Most rescue teams will not begin a rescue if the conditions are deemed too dangerous, and this was the conclusion the NPS team reached that night. Sam's exact location on the vast East Face cliff system was still unknown to rescuers, and attempting a search for him in darkness was considered to be risky and likely ineffective. Unfortunately, Sam did not have a headlamp or flashlight that could have indicated his position. He would need to remain in place overnight. The temperature would drop into the 40s, and Sam's sweat-soaked cotton clothing, light jacket, and sneakers were very ineffective at keeping him warm. He would need to suffer until morning.

Sam was about to have one of the most unpleasant experiences suffered by mountaineers: an unplanned bivouac. These usually happen when a climber gets stuck or delayed for some reason, darkness falls, and further progress is too dangerous. A planned bivouac, on the other hand, is a common practice on a long climb. Mountaineers, especially those who have suffered through an unplanned bivouac, usually carry some equipment to make themselves less uncomfortable, such as an insulated pad to sit on, or an extra lightweight down vest, gloves, and hat. Sam wrote:

> It was extremely horrible. My clothes were all wet, no exception. I was shivering uncontrollably all night. I was on a very small rock, trying to stay in a ball without risking a fall. Every 10 minutes I changed position. My legs were hurting and sometimes when I was getting into another position I realized that I couldn't feel or move my right foot. It was the worse and longest experience in my life, by far. I kept hallucinating about somebody coming near me, of my friend that was just below me. Just to open my eyes and realize that I was all alone in the dark, and change position.

This is a good description of the suffering that takes place. Having endured four of these myself, I have empathy for how terrible they seem. After spending a similar cold night above 13,000 feet on Maroon Peak, I was astonished at how I could be so cold for so long and not only survive but continue climbing for another 12 hours. One of the most beautiful and uplifting experiences in my life was to watch the frigid, black, star-filled sky turn blue and then see the sun rise, following an unplanned bivouac.

With a team in place on Wednesday morning, the rangers were able to see Sam's location on the Broadway ledge using spotting scopes. Another team approached the base of Lamb's Slide around 8 a.m., intending to climb up to Sam and get him down safely. That team was bombarded by snow and rock due to the unusually warm conditions and concluded it was too dangerous to climb while the sun was on the face.

The NPS also dispatched a short-haul capable helicopter from Jackson, Wyoming, where it is frequently used to extract stranded climbers in Grand Teton National Park. The helicopter was delayed due to the need to conclude the short-haul training already in progress at Teton. Given that Sam was relatively safe and uninjured, the rescuers chose to wait until this training was concluded and the helicopter could fly to Colorado to help them.

This is a special type of helicopter and rescue team. The helicopters must be able to perform at high altitudes, and the team must routinely train for what are called "short haul" operations. This requires a ranger to dangle on a cable winch below the hovering helicopter with the hope that the helicopter can insert the ranger at or near the victim in a precarious location, such as high on a technical mountain route. These are highly risky operations due to wind, altitude, and weather conditions and the fact that the helicopter flies so close to the terrain with a dangling rescuer. Teams must routinely train for this type of operation; it is not something that can be performed ad-hoc.

RMNP does not have an on-call short-haul helicopter and team because they are rarely needed. Short-hauls are routine in certain NPS jurisdictions, such as Teton or Denali National Park, due to the rugged and remote nature of those areas. The Teton team was the closest to Longs Peak, so it was dispatched.

In the meantime, a different helicopter was being used to shuttle rescuers and equipment up to the Chasm Lake area and was able to fly near enough to Sam to observe him and his condition. He watched while a helicopter flew near him and rescuers moved in vain 1000 feet below him. The Teton helicopter arrived that afternoon at 1:15 pm.

The NPS report states the short-haul helicopter attempted a fly-by but found downdrafts too unpredictable and dangerous to attempt a rescue.

The team decided to wait until "the intense sun" moved off the face and the falling rock and ice stabilized before ascending to Sam.

Sam had been contacting the rangers and family members intermittently using his cell phone and at some point that afternoon, his battery failed. After the short-haul attempted and then backed off his rescue, he began to panic. It was now late afternoon.

Believing that he would be spending a second night on the ledge, Sam suddenly became more innovative in attempting to descend on his own. He discovered that he could bypass the intimidating step-around to obtain a relatively easy route across the rest of Broadway and then down Lamb's Slide, though he had no clue what the rest of the descent would be like.

The rescue team had been keeping an eye on Sam this entire time through the spotting scopes. They watched him start to move after the short-haul attempt and were stunned. One rescuer told me, "Sam freaked, and ran/fell across snowy-filled Broadway (including navigating the upper step-around) and Lamb's Slide, around the lake, and then literally fell/slid down the slope from the lake to the flat clearing where the Chasm Lake shelter is, nearly sliding into the parked chopper. He did this all in what I think was just less than 30 minutes—we were all flabbergasted."

The official NPS report stated that he "started to move on his own at approximately 4 p.m. Frappier moved down toward rescuers staged at Chasm Meadows. Forty-six people and two helicopters were involved with this incident. The final cost is estimated to be $41,000. The National Park Service does not charge for search and rescue services."

Sam recalled:

> I wasn't and am not aware of what they did to help me except to send a first helicopter to see if they could send me supplies and a second helicopter from Wyoming that tried to get near me, without too much success (and I understand that it must be dangerous to get near me). The first time the Wyoming helicopter got away I got very desperate, even thinking about getting down on the way below me (which would have probably been fatal).

As I resigned to stay one more night in the cold, the helicopter came back to make another rescue attempt. I was desperate and looked for a better spot for them to take me off. I crawled through a dangerous path on my right to get to a spot I had seen before (but I had told myself that it was too dangerous to get there). Once I was there, the helicopter still couldn't get near me. But I am thankful because it is that way that I found the path that leaded me to the Chasm Lake (it was just behind the spot; I couldn't see that there was a trail behind it from where I was stuck). I was then extremely happy: I had finally found a way down, and it all ended well.

On the way back I saw the helicopter and I decided to go see them to say thanks for their help. That's when they brought me to a hospital, even if I would have been perfectly okay to get down the rest of the way by myself (and I would have preferred it this way, even if I liked the helicopter tour). I didn't have any injury except heavy sunburns on the face and eyes.

So you can understand there was NO help provided to me on the mountain, even if I am extremely grateful for them to have tried. I also understand why the media has changed the story to tell Colorado's population that I had been rescued by helicopter: it would be stupid to tell everyone 'Hey all, we spent a couple hundred thousands dollars to try to help someone but we couldn't help him and he got off the mountain all by himself.'

At this point I completely understand why Colorado's population is angry at me; I was stupid to get down this way. I should have had a better preparation

and knowledge of the mountain before going there.
I assure you that I won't do that again; I had way
enough time to think about that!

Thus Sam Frappier, who initiated a large SAR operation by asking for help, was able, in the end, to self-extract from the difficult and dangerous situation that he himself instigated, and was unbelievably fortunate to have survived.

A climber stuck on a cliff at 13,000 feet, shown with dramatic aerial photos, quickly became an international sensation. Many media outlets interviewed Sam, who admitted that he was "very stupid" and expressed profuse thanks to all who attempted to rescue him.

Mountaineering communities were understandably questioning the account. The media is notorious for both reporting incorrect facts and sensationalizing mountain rescue stories. It seemed beyond belief that a newbie climber could start out on the Keyhole Route and end up descending Kiener's and emerge unharmed. The media reported almost universally that Sam was rescued by helicopter when, in fact, he was not rescued at all. This was a believable but false story.

The incident was a perfect storm of strong athletes, mountaineering ignorance, and luck. It also illustrates the complicated decision-making process involved in a mountain rescue operation. It is a good example of how strength and determination can lead to a lot of trouble.

Sam's natural strength and ability allowed him to climb much further into trouble than most novices. These characteristics are highly desirable and necessary for mountaineering, but can actually be a liability when "summit fever" sets in. A climber should always be aware of the environment and consider its potential consequences. This awareness usually comes with experience and is a good reason to start a climbing career on less dangerous terrain and with someone who has experience.

A review of the rescue operation is also instructive. Sam wondered why there was no attempt to climb to him when the rescuers were well equipped and knew the area. Sitting on the ledge for the entire time the rescuers were there, he had ample time to observe conditions. Sam stated in his description of the rescue that he saw no rockfall and only minor ice and snow fall, nothing that he thought could have injured him.

Ground rescue is the most common approach for what is essentially a stuck climber. But from the rescuer standpoint, a large obstacle in climbing up to Sam was ascending 800 feet up the Lamb's Slide Couloir. It acts as a funnel and acceleration ramp for any debris falling from above. Rock and ice chunks can gain deadly speed tumbling down this couloir. Even a small rock can injure, and possibly kill, a rescuer.

Other rescue options included:

- Staging a team at the Broadway ledge early in the morning, before the sun rose. This is a standard climbing procedure for anyone wishing to climb the East Face. Broadway is the logical access point to anyone stuck on that section of the mountain.
- Climbing over the summit and rappelling or downclimbing to Sam.
- Rappelling from Chasm View, near the North Face Route that Sam ascended, down to Broadway. This is a common way that climbers approach the Diamond face routes, which all start on Broadway. The Broadway ledge is walkable all along the bottom of the Diamond to where Sam was stuck; it is not a technical climb. It is also not subject to much rockfall, as most of the Diamond overhangs Broadway and drops debris farther away from the face. It is fairly safe even if other parts of the face are dropping debris.
- Ascend to the Loft via a safe route (there are several) and descend a short distance down Lamb's Slide to Broadway, thus avoiding the bowling alley of lower Lamb's slide.

Rescuers considered these different approaches and each one was determined to have too much objective danger to get to Sam, who was essentially unhurt. Rescuers were also focused on a helicopter rescue. In addition, there was a language barrier, as Sam was a native French speaker. By the time he decided to down-climb on his own, his cell phone was no longer working and it may have been unclear to him that rescuers were in fact preparing to climb up to him when he showed up at Chasm Meadows.

In the end, Samuel Frappier descended by himself all the way to the staging area. He was not "rescued," although he did ask for a rescue, which requires the NPS to respond in some fashion. Given that Sam self-rescued, was the cost of the rescue operation justifiable?

The cost of this incident was certainly high because two helicopters were employed, one of which was flown in all the way from northern Wyoming. Helicopters are expensive to operate. In this case, one helicopter was used to shuttle personnel and equipment to and from the high altitude staging area. This takes many trips and is very useful for certain kinds of emergency operations. But Sam was neither injured nor in imminent danger, and he was in contact with the rangers at least part of the time by cell phone, so they had a lot of information regarding the nature of this incident. Was the use of a helicopter to stage people and equipment here a good idea, when the situation appears to not have been the type of high-level emergency where all stops are pulled?

It is worth emphasizing that helicopters are far from the rescue panacea they might at first appear to be. There are numerous examples in this book of the limited effectiveness of helicopters in SAR missions due to the difficult flying conditions in the high mountains. Another very important factor is the inherent danger of helicopter work in the mountain environment. This danger is, unfortunately, often not well understood even by the SAR managers who use them.

This fact is not surprising. Helicopter SAR operations are exceedingly rare in comparison to helicopter operation in general. Also, it is very difficult to define the risks of SAR operation helicopter accidents versus other alternatives. In other words, how much more risk is involved in using a helicopter rather than a ground operation? How is the benefit weighed compared to the risk?

One example of the risk of using helicopters happened on June 15, 2010. Kevin Hayne and Travis Windler were nearing the summit of 14,035-foot Little Bear Peak. They had hiked to the steep Hourglass Couloir and found the conditions icy and treacherous. They decided to stop and evaluate their options on a left trending ledge off the couloir when a hold that Kevin was clinging to broke. He fell several hundred feet down the steep slope below them. Travis quickly descended to his critically injured friend who had "two broken arms." Those were only his apparent injuries; he was in fact in much worse condition. Both Kevin and Travis were carrying SPOT beacons. But just like David Boyd's beacon on Little Bear as described in the *Solo* chapter, both failed. No help message was ever received. Travis suspected there was a problem and ran for help. It took him at least four hours after the accident to contact emergency services.

Because of the critical nature of the accident and the time it would require for a ground evacuation from such a remote location, a military helicopter was requested. A "Jolly Green Giant" two-rotor Chinook was dispatched from Buckley Air Force Base in Aurora, Colorado. Five volunteer Alamosa SAR team members were picked up. In their rescue attempt, as the Chinook was unloading the SAR team near Kevin, the rear rotor struck a rock and forced the helicopter to a "hard landing," in essence a controlled crash, on a high altitude basin 1,500 feet below where Kevin lay. The helicopter had broken its rear rotor, stripped off its landing gear, and buckled its fuselage, but miraculously no rescue member was injured. The SAR team found Kevin, who had passed away after suffering excruciating pain.

This mission turned out terribly. Kevin Hayne had died despite the heroic efforts of Travis and the rescuers, but it could have been far worse. Kevin Wright, a leader in Alamosa Volunteer Search and Rescue, resigned after witnessing this horrifically shocking chain of events. Wright had been a long time Alamosa SAR volunteer and is mentioned in the *Solo* chapter. He has since authored *Search and Rescue in Colorado's Sangre de Cristos*.

Even in the best conditions possible, helicopters can be treacherous.

On Friday, July 3, 2015, a helicopter crashed outside the hospital in Frisco, Colorado, killing the pilot and severely injuring a paramedic and flight nurse on board. The pilot was Patrick Mahany, a 28-year veteran of the air ambulance service Flight for Life. He was well known among the SAR community as he had assisted with SAR operations over those decades, not only flying patients out to hospitals, but also ferrying SAR personnel and equipment into remote high-altitude locations. I had flown with him on two high altitude missions. He was one of the best mountain pilots out there and knew well what his ship could and could not do.

The crash occurred shortly after take off. The crew was not responding to a medical call at the time. The chopper came down in a parking lot and was engulfed in flame. Flight conditions appeared to be excellent at the time and it's impossible to believe it was pilot error that caused the crash. But even if it was, this type of accident helps prove the point that with the best pilot, chopper, and conditions, these are dangerous operations, and accidents happen.

An academic paper, *Helicopter Accidents in Mountain Rescue Operations 1975-2013: A Review*, by Justin McLean, M.D. and Sean Slack (published in "Wilderness and Environmental Medicine Journal" (August 2014)), notes that the most common cause of helicopter accidents is high altitude. Colorado had the greatest percentage of the total number of SAR operation accidents of the total (22 percent) during the time period studied. The paper also notes that "death from helicopter accidents far outpaced all other causes of loss of life."

Any SAR manager in charge of a high altitude rescue in Colorado should weigh the facts from this study when helicopter operations are considered. As stated in the *Breaking the Rules* chapter of this book, the first rule of mountain rescue is to not create more victims.

For the Sam Frappier incident in Rocky Mountain National Park, the short-haul helicopter call was highly unusual. And despite the danger and cost, the NPS does this sort of rescue multiple times every year in Teton as well as Denali and Yosemite. The NPS does not routinely publish the cost of those rescues, many of which are far more expensive than the one involving Sam. On the other hand, the actual costs may not be as high as would be supposed at first glance. This is because NPS employees who do rescue work are paid regardless of whether they are rescuing someone or doing a trail interpretive program. In Sam's case, other rescuers were called from local volunteer SAR teams, such as Larimer County Search and Rescue and Rocky Mountain Rescue in Boulder. These members volunteer for their duty and pay for their own transportation, purchase their own equipment, and arrange for their own absence from home and paying jobs.

Because of the politics of federal agencies, and government agencies in general, it's difficult to ascertain the actual reasons for rescue decisions or whether the reasons given are exaggerated while other critical decisions are minimized or not explained. This is especially true when there is a national media spotlight on the agency. One solid takeaway from such incidents, though, is the fact that mountain rescue management in Colorado is highly inconsistent.

This rescue happened in a park under federal jurisdiction. If it had happened in on the Indian Peaks a few miles south of Longs Peak, then Boulder County would likely have managed the rescue, an agency with far fewer resources than the federal government. And if it happened on Mount Lindsey in Costilla County? There are essentially no local resources or rescue team. This is something to keep in mind.

Raining Fire

The summer of 2015 witnessed reports from all around Colorado of an unusual uptick of lightning activity. Lightning is common in the state every summer, produced especially in the afternoon and evening by towering thunderstorms that have been building throughout the day, but that year witnessed an unusual weather pattern that proved to be highly dangerous, especially for high altitude hikers. Even those who followed the rule of being off the summit before noon found themselves in peril.

The reports began in late June 2015 and grew more tragic over the following month. On June 24, a group of six people were struck by lightning on 14,115 foot Pikes Peak just before noon. They were not hikers but had been spectators watching training runs for a motorcycle race up the summit road. It was reported that only one was treated for an injury.

Four days later a more serious event took place. June 28 started out as a typical summer weekend day on Mount Bierstadt, a 14,065 foot mountain located in the Front Range just west of Denver. Bierstadt's nearest neighbor is the more well-known 14,271 foot Mount Evans, which receives far more visitors per year than any other 14er in Colorado, with the vast majority arriving at the summit of Evans by automobile. The highest paved road in North America runs from the town of Idaho Springs to the top of Evans, where sits a summit house and an astronomical observatory.

Bierstadt, located just a mile and a half to the west of Evans, is a different animal. Bierstadt's summit can only be reached by hiking to it. The most popular route starts at the crest of Guanella Pass, where a large

Mount Bierstadt on a clear June morning.

parking area enables access to the summit, starting at 11,669 feet. The normal route up Bierstadt makes it one of the easiest 14ers to climb. This easy access combined with its proximity to Denver (Bierstadt is very visible from the city) attracts hundreds of climbers every summer weekend.

That Sunday in June was no different. More than a hundred climbers were on the mountain that morning. The weather was calm and partly cloudy. The forecast called for afternoon thunderstorms, which are common this time of year. As is often the case, there was no indication that thunderstorms would be a problem on Bierstadt that morning.

Jonathan Hardman, along with his friends Mary Prescott, Will Chandler,

Matt Dayer and Hardman's German shepherd Rambo were among the many hikers on Bierstadt. They had arrived early and begun their hike from the parking area on Guanella Pass at 7:15 a.m. This would normally give them plenty of time to summit and be well into the descent by noon. This is a prudent plan on this type of route, which starts and remains entirely above timberline.

They found it to be unusually warm on their hike to the summit. Hardman reported that they had "been in t-shirts" all the way to the summit and the weather seemed perfect. Shortly after they arrived on the summit at around 10:30 a.m., they snapped their victory photos, posing with a handwritten paper sign that read "Mt. Bierstadt, 14,060 ft., June 28, 2015."

There are several photos showing the four of them and Rambo, smiling at their achievement on the highest point. But in the background something ominous is visible. The photo shows that the sky is crowded with dark-bottomed cumulus clouds and directly behind them, it is clearly beginning to rain and/or hail. Observed before noon, all mountaineers should take conditions like this as a red flag warning. Clouds that build to this point in the morning have a high probability of rapidly building to lightning-producing storms. It is prudent to turn back under these conditions.

The four had begun their descent when the weather "suddenly changed," according to Hardman. "It starting hailing like crazy," Prescott added. By 11:20 a.m. they were down nearly 500 feet when the bolt struck. Chandler later remembered it as, "just a light, just a bright light hitting the ground. Everybody was on the ground crying and screaming."

Hardman was coaxing his dog Rambo to "jump to where I was and the next thing I know, I just woke up, I couldn't move my hands, arms or legs," he recalled. When he was able to look around, he saw the lifeless body of his dog lying near him. Rambo had been killed instantly by the strike.

Prescott and Chandler were both knocked down on the rocks and sustained severe bruises and lacerations. Hardman was bleeding profusely. The lightning bolt directly contacted him near the rear of the top of his head, where it left a quarter-sized round hole in his skin. Currents through his body caused burns on his face, neck, shoulders, and chest that would later appear as thin, red, treelike fractal lines.

Nearby hikers felt the electric shock and some were knocked down as well, but none suffered injuries as serious as Hardman, Prescott, Chandler, and Rambo. Hardman felt that the proximity of his dog helped to disperse the energy from the lightning so that he himself wasn't killed, though it is more likely that Rambo's relatively small size simply prevented the dog's body from being able to disperse so much current and survive. Nevertheless, they were lucky to survive, especially Hardman, who took the direct strike.

Nearby hikers rushed to assist. At least one hiker activated a SPOT beacon emergency signal. Calls for help went out over cell phones. Bierstadt is located in Clear Creek County, so Alpine Rescue Team was called to respond. But the sheer number of potential victims was of high concern. Choppers could not fly into the ongoing storm and a massive response was requested from neighboring teams.

In Boulder County, a page went out to rescuers that read:

```
2015-6-28 11:51:06 ALPINE RESCUE IS REQUESTING
RESPONSE TO MOUNT BIERSTADT FOR 10 HIKERS STRUCK
BY LIGHTNING AT THE SUMMIT. POOR CELL SERVICE.
```

That number of potential victims in a difficult, remote location is a serious problem. Emergency responders refer to this as a "mass casualty incident" or MCI, and it requires a specialized response. Consider that an ambulance, a common sight in urban environments, can manage a total of one patient. An MCI requires a large fleet of ambulances.

Media outlets were reporting as many as 15 casualties from this incident. Fortunately there were only three serious injuries (plus the death of Rambo), and they were all able to self-evacuate to the trailhead. But one has to wonder, what would be the outcome if there were more, non-ambulatory victims? With the increasing number of inexperienced hikers on summits such as Bierstadt, perhaps the question is not if, but when will this happen.

Less than three weeks after the mass lightning strike on Bierstadt, a more tragic series of events began to unfold. During early afternoon on July 17, 2015, on 14,202 foot Mount Yale, newlyweds Katie Bartlett and Ryan Pocius were on their honeymoon and decided to hike this relatively easy

14er near Buena Vista. During their ascent, Katie remarked that "it was the most beautiful hike she had ever been on."

As they ascended, the weather did not appear threatening; small clouds hung in the sky, but no large storm cells were visible. Bartlett and Pocius summited a bit after noon and the weather still appeared to be fine. What was invisible to them was the potential for rapid storm development. They happily took their summit photos and began their descent.

Like Bierstadt, Yale attracts many hikers on summer weekends and this day was no exception. Among the other hikers that day were two brothers, Chip and Craig Lane. They had summited Yale just before 1 p.m. but were now descending fast, rapidly jogging down the trail to get below timberline in the relative shelter of the trees. They had seen a storm rolling in from Cottonwood Pass. Chip remarked that it looked "very far away." What they didn't take into account was that the storm was building fast, forming around and over them.

They had descended to 12,400 feet, nearly 2000 feet below the summit but still well above timberline, when they saw Bartlett and Pocius behind them, running down the trail. The Lane brothers decided to let them pass; they were running faster and trying to descend to the trees as well. Just then the lightning cracked, knocking all four to the ground, unconscious.

A nearby hiker descending in front of the four described the situation:

> All looked well until about 12:30-1 when a storm formed near Cottonwood Pass and expanded towards Yale. I was descending at about 13K with another guy when I decided it was time to boogie. We ran down and were just into the trees when a bolt and nearly simultaneous thunder hit just above me. There were many people still above me on the mountain and I hoped no one was hit. A bit later, a young man zipped past me and said a woman was hit just above treeline and was getting CPR.

Chip Lane was the first of the four to regain consciousness. He saw three bodies lying near him. Two of them came around soon after, but Katie appeared to be in bad shape. "Katie's clothes and shoes were pretty much off her, burnt and what not," Chip recalled. They all tried to revive her, trading off performing cardiopulmonary resuscitation. They continued for 45 minutes but it was a futile attempt. She had died instantly in the strike.

The SAR team got to the trailhead at 2:35 p.m. An air ambulance was called but was unable to evacuate the victims for hours due to the weather conditions. Ryan was hospitalized for two days.

The Chaffee County sheriff commented that it was, "really, really black over the area that afternoon." The storm that had produced the killer bolt was visibly ominous, but ironically produced very little lightning. Analysis from detectors would show that this particular storm produced a total of two lightning bolts.

Incidents were not restricted to the high peaks. There were other publicized lightning strike incidents that summer that affected several people in the cities of Aurora and Colorado Springs and resulted in injuries, but no deaths. These stories in the media illustrated what seemed to be an unusual season of very high lightning danger.

The climate conditions in early summer 2015 on the Front Range had been very conducive to the formation of thunderstorms with high humidity and heat, and that year saw a greater than average number of thunderstorms, beginning earlier that spring and running through mid-July.

Had hikers been observing the unusual weather pattern that year, they may have noticed this increased risk and taken extra precautions. The historical summer climbing season (about May through October) climate pattern in Colorado is generally an increase in thunderstorms from May through June with a dry spell starting about the third week of June. Then, sometime in July a monsoonal flow of moisture from the southwest drives a huge increase in thunderstorms, peaking in late July to early August, followed by a lessening trend through October, when the first snows fall on the high peaks.

The weather in 2015 did not follow this pattern in the Front Range. A large number of storms continued through about mid-July, when they tapered off to a very dry period from August through October. Experienced climbers pay attention to this pattern; some cancel any big plans in August when it is obvious the mountains are in the grip of the Colorado monsoon. But weather is weather, and predicting what will happen on a given day at a given location is nearly impossible even for the experts. So the best alternative for the climber is to pay attention to conditions in real-time and make good decisions, including decisions to alter summit plans.

Having made that statement, I have seen many hikers treat lightning differently than other objective threats in the mountains; they tend to under-react to the threat. The hiker's experience level doesn't seem to make much difference. I have been caught in thunderstorms while climbing, storms that I certainly could have avoided, and not because I was unaware or didn't take lightning seriously.

I lost a friend to a lightning strike. On September 10, 1995, 29-year-old Catherine Pugin was killed instantly on 14,204-foot Mount Princeton. This 14er rises dramatically above the Arkansas River valley, directly west of Buena Vista. It is also directly south of Mount Yale. Princeton, like many mountains in the Sawatch Range, is considered an easy hike on its most popular route.

On that Sunday, Catherine had hiked with a group of friends. By all accounts, the weather was excellent with few clouds. The group was a bit strung out along the route just below the summit as they began to descend. What was described as a minor cloud formed over them and produced a single lightning bolt, striking Catherine as she descended through 13,920 feet. She was killed instantly.

Her friends were unhurt and were stunned that the cloud had produced any lightning. Just after the strike, the cloud began to disperse and soon disappeared, like it never happened. But Catherine was dead.

When I heard the news, I found it inconceivable. Catherine was one of the more conservative and safe mountaineers I knew. She was a mountaineering instructor for the Colorado Mountain Club. She understood well the mountain environment and it was amazing to me that she underestimated her environment, but eventually I learned of the improbable storm that produced the strike. It had formed and dissipated very rapidly, and the only realistic way she could have avoided such a rare event was to not be there at all. Today there is a memorial plaque near the spot where she died on Mount Princeton.

Knowing full well the risks, I still found myself in the midst of lightning storms while high on mountains several times. In one incident, we were rock climbing on the Fifth Flatiron in Boulder when, near the top, we were caught in a storm that felt like it was literally raining fire, with thunder exploding rapidly around us. We rappelled off the ridge as soon as we could, but were exposed for at least a half hour.

On 14,279-foot Castle Peak in the Elk Range near Aspen, I had my closest call with lightning. My group did not ascend the standard Northeast Ridge Route where much of the climb provides good all-around visibility of approaching weather. Instead, we climbed directly up an easy snow route to the saddle between Castle Peak and its sub-summit, Conundrum Peak. Castle and Conundrum are connected by Castle Peak's Northwest Ridge.

On this route, the north face of Castle blocks the view to the south. The weather had been relatively clear that morning with few clouds. As we ascended the snow face, clouds began to fill the sky from the south, but they were not dark and didn't appear particularly threatening. We discussed the possibility that this could be an approaching thunderstorm, but if it did get worse, we could rapidly glissade the snow slope we were on to escape any lightning.

As we topped out on the ridge, only a few hundred feet below the summit, we saw that the clouds were indeed an approaching thunderstorm. We watched for a few minutes and it seemed to be moving slowly. The summit appeared to be very close and we noted that if we went over the summit, we could glissade the North Face Couloir that descended over a thousand feet down from near the summit. Our plan was to tag the summit, about 10 minutes away, and then rapidly glissade back to the basin.

But we underestimated the time to the summit and it took twice as long to get there. The storm moved toward us much faster than expected and by the time we got to the top, a large dark mass hung directly above. No lightning had been produced up to this point.

On the summit we met a limping, out-of-shape 60-year-old man who had soloed up the Northeast Ridge, the low difficulty normal route. There was no one else on the summit. The man was ecstatic that he had summited. He had climbed Castle Peak 30 years before and was very happy to repeat the climb that day so many decades later. I mentioned that we shouldn't remain there long; the storm was looking immanently threatening. He asked me to take a picture of him with his camera and I reluctantly agreed.

As he handed me the camera, I received a shock from the metal case that knocked me off my feet. I could hear the crackling of static discharge from the points of my ice axe. Realizing that we were in a charge field and lightning could strike any second, I told him to get off the summit as fast as possible and I began to run down the ridge. We left him there and got to the top of the couloir and jumped. Seconds later, we were about 500 feet down when we heard a BOOM!

We were unharmed and continued glissading down to the bottom of the couloir. I looked up and couldn't see the man we had left at the summit. Due to the danger, we kept descending as the storm slowly moved across the peak, dropping rain and hail along with more lightning bolts. I kept looking back trying to see any sign of life. About a half hour later, I saw the man coming down the ridge. He appeared to be moving well. He was limping, but it was the same limp we had noticed during his ascent and not a new injury.

He eventually made it down to the basin and was none the worse for the wear. This climber was highly inexperienced and didn't take the lightning danger seriously, but I assume he had a story to tell his grandchildren about how he survived the storm. Even if he was convinced that the lightning was a real danger, there is no way he could have descended very quickly given his slow, plodding pace. He could not have glissaded safely either, given that he had no ice axe.

Of course, given the dangerous situation we were in, it would have made no difference how fast we could descend if a bolt happened to strike us. We were all extremely lucky. We were also all in the same preventable situation despite the differences in our levels of our mountaineering experiences.

When I ask myself why we allowed ourselves to get into such a situation, I am reminded that many experienced mountaineers have also been caught out. Mountain weather is a temporary condition that is hard to predict. When it's sunny and warm in the morning, it's difficult to imagine that it could be cold, wet, and dark at mid-afternoon. As clouds slowly build over the day, the change from moment to moment is almost imperceptible and the weather can seem static, until the sound of thunder cannot be denied. In addition, the desire to summit must be managed; the drive that pushes through hunger, thirst, sore muscles, and fatigue can lead to more risky behavior. The only way to minimize the possibility of being struck by lightning is to ensure that you don't end up high and exposed on a mountain during a thunderstorm.

The best plan is to anticipate the possibility of being caught up high and prevent it long before it happens. The rule of "off the summit by noon" obviously does not apply to all situations, but it can be used in planning climbs. Make a reasonable estimation of the time it will take to climb a route and plan a start time accordingly. It is better to be conservative and add time to an estimate rather than planning to climb faster. Show up at the trailhead earlier rather than later.

Once on the mountain, however, the main rule to follow is: watch the weather and turn back before the storm. If clouds are building rapidly at mid-morning, that is not a good sign. If it's perfectly clear at noon, there may be no need to turn back. If you turn around and there was no storm, the mountain will be there another time. That is the safest way to manage lightning.

There are likely few accident victims who feel their risk-taking justifies the suffering they subsequently experience. In my many years of mountain climbing and rescue experience, I have never met a single one.

Lightning Myths

Lightning is a highly complex phenomenon that is not well understood, despite the fact that it is a very common occurrence. Lightning is actually the final stage of an energy dissipation event. The lightning strikes that cause concern travel cloud-to-ground rather than cloud-to-cloud or within clouds.

Thunderstorms act like a generator, building up an electrical charge separation like a battery. Stated simply, the bottom part of a thunderstorm is negative and the top is positive. The negative bottom side of a thunderstorm attracts positive charges from the earth. As a storm continues

Storm clouds threatening near the summit of Wilson Peak (14,017′).

to generate energy, a large voltage difference develops between the storm cloud and the earth.

Air normally acts as an insulator. This is why you don't get shocked as you walk past an outlet in your house or as you walk beneath a high voltage power cable suspended above you. All insulators have a dielectric break-down voltage. This happens when there is so much potential energy across material that the material can no longer "hold back" the voltage. Wood, rubber, air, and every other insulator will break down at a particular voltage.

When air breaks down in this manner, it forms a plasma channel that is extremely conductive. Current travels through this channel and equal-izes the voltage difference between the cloud and the ground to zero. The plasma channel exists for only microseconds but is extremely bright and hotter than the surface of the sun. This is what is observed as lightning. Thunder is caused by the sudden expansion of the superheated air surrounding the plasma channel.

There is an enormous amount of electrical energy carried by a lightning strike. It takes approximately 76,000 volts per inch of air to create a lightning bolt. Add up the number of inches in a thousand-foot-long lightning bolt and it approaches a billion volts. A negative lightning strike, which is the most common type of strike, occurs from the bottom of a cloud to the ground and can carry over 30,000 amps of current. It only takes a tiny fraction of an amp across your heart to kill you.

The positively charged top of the cloud can also produce a lightning bolt to the ground. This is called a positive strike, and though it is far less common than a negative strike. Positive strikes have been known to leap 20 miles from the top of a thunderstorm cloud to hit the ground nowhere near the storm. Such a lightening bolt would reach almost 100 billion volts. These strikes are notoriously deadly and can happen in the bright sunshine far from a storm.

Thus lightning is not as well behaved as the low voltage power that humans manipulate. Unfortunately, many assumptions about lightning are made based on observations of how low energy electricity works, which assumptions are not accurate.

Here are some common myths and facts:

MYTH: METAL ATTRACTS LIGHTNING.

Metal does not attract lightning, but sharp metal points and edges, such as the tip or spike of an ice axe, could be focal points of static discharge because of how they concentrate electric fields. This could be thought of as "attracting" lightning. The additional danger of carrying metal is probably miniscule, given the vast amount of potential energy that is already present.

Compare this to how lightning rods work. The theory behind lightning rods is to provide a highly conductive path from the ground to the bottom of the cloud, essentially bringing the ground closer to the cloud at a localized point that is more likely to be struck. Lightning rods must be higher than surrounding buildings and more conductive. Holding your ice axe in the air during a lightning storm is probably not a good idea. But keep in mind that lightning rods are not always the object struck first.

MYTH: CROUCHING ON AN INSULATOR.

This s often recommended in material about what to do in a lightning storm: If you're caught, crouch down and sit on your pack or minimize your contact with the ground. Crouching down might help, but insulating yourself from the ground is probably impossible. Crouching might reduce your path between the cloud and ground; it depends on the configuration of the charge fields, which you have no way of knowing. I'm not aware of any common material a person is likely to be carrying that can insulate from a billion volts of potential difference.

Also, there is no evidence that insulating yourself from the ground protects you from ground currents. Ground current behavior at that energy level s completely unpredictable.

MYTH: YOU ARE SAFE BELOW TIMBERLINE.

This is only partially a myth: You are safer, but not completely safe. This is due to the distance between you and the cloud, and the surrounding features. The greater the distance between you and the bottom of the cloud where the lightning originates makes a big difference in how much energy is required to cause a strike. The larger the distance, the higher the energy, and the less likely a strike will happen. The summit of a 14er is an exceedingly bad place to be in a thunderstorm, as is a high ridge.

The forest offers even more protection. Besides being thousands of feet lower than the summit, in a forest you are surrounded by objects much taller than you that can provide lower energy pathways for the lightning. This does not eliminate the risk entirely, but it certainly reduces it significantly. However, people have been killed standing next to a tree that was struck by lightning when the current jumped to them. And others have been injured following a strike when the tree exploded and sent out splinters like shrapnel.

MYTH: LIGHTNING KILLS MORE PEOPLE TODAY BECAUSE OF OUTDOOR RECREATION.

In fact, far fewer people are killed by lightning today. When humans were more of an agricultural society, the rate of lightning deaths was much higher.

Unintended Consequences of Experience

On June 23, 2013, a climber was killed while descending a peak near Aspen. Though these incidents are always tragic, this particular accident received a lot of attention from the Colorado mountaineering community because the victim was a highly experienced climber who was widely known and well loved by both his peers and protégés.

Steve Gladbach was a popular high school teacher from Pueblo. On that fateful day, he and two partners summited "Thunder Pyramid," a point on a ridge connected to the summit of Pyramid Peak, one of Colorado's 14ers. Thunder Pyramid is not an officially named peak but was originally christened "Thunder Peak" by a party that claimed the first ascent in 1970. It is not considered a separate peak but is often climbed by those attempting to summit all the 13ers in Colorado. If you think it takes a lot of determination to climb all of Colorado's 14ers, consider how much work and determina-

LIGHTNING DEATHS IN COLORADO

Data compiled by the National Lightning Detection Network show that between 2005 and 2014 there were a total of 17 lightning deaths in Colorado, which ranks the state third for fatalities, after Texas with 20 fatalities and Florida, which had 47 lightning deaths.

Colorado, however, ranks second for lightning deaths by population, just behind Wyoming at number one. On this scale, Florida is seventh and Texas is twenty-eighth. So though there are relatively few lightning fatalities, less than two per year, the chances of being hit are higher in Colorado than all but one state.

tion it takes to climb the more than 700 13,000 foot peaks in the state. Gladbach counted himself as one of these persistent climbers.

After summiting in the late morning, Gladbach intentionally separated from his climbing partners on the descent to check out a potential future route. They agreed to meet later at an appointed time and place below, and his partners continued descending. Gladbach never showed up and his partners called for help using a SPOT beacon at about 2 p.m. But because of the late hour when the call was received, and despite a quick helicopter search, Mountain Rescue Aspen was unable to locate Gladbach until the next morning, at which time they found him deceased.

No one witnessed the accident but it appeared he died after a fall of hundreds of feet. This was likely caused by loose rock, as the mountains in the Elk Range are very fractured, loose, and steep; they resemble a bunch of rocks stacked on top of each other like books for thousands of feet. Spontaneous rockfall in this area is common and makes the area extremely dangerous. A rock helmet is essential safety gear for climbing in this area but even that is no guarantee of safety. This is also true on the nearby14ers North and South Maroon Peak, Capitol, Snowmass, and Castle Peaks, where you might be hit by spontaneous rockslide or step on a car-sized boulder and cause it to roll down the face.

Gladbach was truly an experienced climber, having summited all the 14ers at least four times (including all of them in winter), as well as Denali, Elbrus, and Aconcagua. He loved the mountains and taught others the basics of climbing. He would even assist struggling strangers to reach summits by helping carry their packs the last few hundred feet, just so they could experience the unique magic of standing over 14,000 feet high.

Gladbach is a pointed example of someone who had a massive amount of experience—and was widely considered a very safe climber—yet succumbed to an accident that might have been preventable. If this accident happened to him, it could happen to anyone. But there is a caution here: experience can lead to over-confidence in one's abilities and create a false sense of "protection" against objective hazards.

No one knows what was going through Gladbach's mind at the time; his behavior was consistent with that of many experts. He was exploring new territory in an area with significant objective hazard. Pyramid Peak requires that climbers test every foothold, handhold, and boulder before weighting them. And the rocks here rain down from above without warning. The mountains have dangers that are not always preventable or avoidable. The best climbers can do is prepare by understanding this environment and how they interact with it.

Again On Holy Cross

On the crisp fall morning of October 3, 2010, James Nelson posed for a photo of himself at the Fall Creek Trailhead near the base of Mount of the Holy Cross. He was wearing a large backpack filled with necessities for his planned five day solo trek around the base of the mountain. Though somewhat overweight, the 31-year-old who lived in Chicago was an experienced hiker and loved the outdoors.

Nelson had never been to Holy Cross before, but had mapped out his route and discussed it with members of his hiking group in Chicago. His acquaintances agreed that the route didn't look difficult. He planned to trek along the Fall Creek Trail along the eastern flank of the mountain to the old ghost town of Holy Cross City. From there he would loop around the west side of the mountain and return to the trailhead via Half Moon Pass. He reportedly talked about climbing Holy Cross itself at some point.

After the photo, Nelson chatted with a couple of hikers and then headed down the trail. The autumn sun was warm and bright, but the aspen leaves were intense yellow or brown. Most had fallen from the trees by this time, foreshadowing what would soon be a long, frigid winter. It was Sunday, and it was the last time anyone saw James Nelson alive.

By the next Friday evening, Nelson still hadn't checked in with his fiancée in Chicago. Worried something had gone wrong, she called the Eagle County Sheriff's office and reported him overdue. Vail Mountain Rescue was summoned. They knew well the potential for a large, protracted late-season search in the Holy Cross wilderness, with the memory of Michelle Vanek's search only five years before. As was the case with Vanek, the first big mountain snowstorm would squelch any hope of finding their subject, and it could fall any day now.

Vail Mountain Rescue cranked up its search machine and worked for four days, putting in over a thousand searcher-hours trying to cover the vast wilderness that is Holy Cross. In a bitter parallel to the search for Vanek, they did not come up with a single clue as to Nelson's whereabouts or what could have happened to him.

The vanishing and the utter lack of clues after an intense search had people comparing the two disappearances and reinforcing their belief that Holy Cross was Colorado's "Bermuda Triangle." However, two years later, in May 2012, a local hiker came upon a cache of scattered equipment about 50 feet off the relatively popular four-wheel-drive road up to Holy Cross City. The equipment appeared to be the remains of an abandoned campsite not visible from the road. Investigators determined that the equipment matched the description of that belonging to Nelson. Further investigation also turned up human remains.

Then a partial human skull was found in August 2013. Initial headlines reported that a human skull was found on Holy Cross, and almost immediately there was speculation that it was Vanek. Only later did details emerge that it was found near Nelson's camp, and it turned out to be him.

It seems surprising that Nelson wasn't located during the search, especially because he wasn't deep in the wilderness; his camp was close to a well-used jeep road. It was reported that writing was found in his camp indicating that he had altitude sickness. It was also reported by the hikers who saw him on the first day of his trip that he was having problems with altitude.

Newspaper accounts reported officials as saying he was "a bit off his planned route." His camp was found below Holy Cross City. This helps to explain why searchers did not find him; a hundred searchers over four days will leave a vast area uncovered. Coordinators must guess the most likely places to search and cover those as best as possible. Nelson deviated from his planned route, thus decreasing the chances of being found by a search party in that area to almost nil.

A greater mystery is the circumstances of his death. On the surface, it appears that he may have been incapacitated by altitude illness. But there are a couple of inconsistencies with that theory.

Altitude illness progresses relatively slowly. It generally takes days to develop the truly incapacitating types of altitude illness, HAPE and HACE. The third, milder type of altitude illness is AMS, which while making you feel terrible will not kill you or prevent you from moving. According to *Medicine for Mountaineering*, HAPE is "very rare below 14,000 feet." Also, few individuals who have AMS develop full-blown HACE, and this almost always takes days to progress to a serious problem.

Nelson was probably not properly acclimated to avoid AMS. He was also overweight, though surprisingly, fitness level is not correlated to the ability to acclimate. It seems unlikely that Nelson could have developed one of the severe forms of altitude illness at the relatively low altitude where he was hiking or camped. And in the remote possibility that he did, why would he have not just gone to the road not 50 feet away and waited for help? Surely there were vehicles traversing this road while he was there.

There are of course other possibilities. Perhaps he got carbon monoxide poisoning by cooking in an unventilated tent. Maybe he had a serious medical condition that killed him quickly, though at age 31 this seems unlikely. There was no evidence of suicide.

Investigators reported that his camera, GPS receiver, and camp stove were not found. Also, though no details were reported in the press, his body was obviously not intact. Animals could have caused this over the two years following his death, but the camp equipment that was found was not scattered much and appeared to be in good condition. Foul play seems even less likely than altitude or medical problems, but the cause of his death will likely remain unknown.

James Nelson made some choices that may cost him his life, but are instructive:

- Hiking in an unknown area alone. This is not necessarily a bad choice, but one that has to be carefully evaluated given the individual's experience and capabilities. Many people routinely complete solo hikes with no problems.
- Lack of means of calling for help if he got into trouble. Even in 2010, SPOT beacons and Personal Locator Beacons (PLB) could be purchased and used to call for emergency help in the backcountry.

- Relying on a cell phone. To this day, a cell phone is of little use in the Holy Cross wilderness. There are no cell towers nearby and getting a signal requires being high on a peak. PLBs and SPOT beacons are far more reliable, though even these are not totally reliable.
- Deviating from his plan. While Nelson left a planned route description with his fiancée, unfortunately he deviated from it enough to prevent searchers from locating him in a timely manner. He may have changed his plan in an attempt to descend and walk out more quickly because he was feeling ill, but that decision may have been a fatal mistake.

Ten Years Later

As of this writing (2016), Michelle Vanek has still not been found and no clues have turned up around Mount of the Holy Cross in the more than a decade since her disappearance. Her case remains open for the Eagle County Sheriff.

I returned to climb Holy Cross in September 2015, just shy of the 10th anniversary of Michelle's disappearance. We hiked the normal route, packing over Half Moon Pass to camp at the Cross Creek campground and climbing to the summit the next day. The weather was perfect, with aspen leaves in full gold and red. The daytime temperatures were quite warm and comfortable at the summit, dropping to just above freezing at night.

The trail from Cross Creek up to about 13,000 feet was excellent and well marked. It has been vastly improved with giant cairns marking the route above timberline. This new trail should prevent at least some hikers from straying off route due to navigation difficulties.

What has not changed since Michelle's disappearance is the huge wilderness surrounding the mountain and the lack of cell phone service except when very high on the route. There were close to 50 other hikers on the mountain when I was there. Almost all of them were novices, and of the people we spoke with, none had heard of the propensity for people to get lost on this particular peak, or the disappearance of Michelle Vanek.

While hiking below timberline, I was reminded that the pine forest is amazingly dense. A disabled hiker could be less than 50 feet off the trail in many places and never be noticed by searchers. Above timberline are very large boulders and near the summit pyramid, the slope is steep enough to require scrambling over these boulders. But when we arrived at the summit, I noticed some aspects about the terrain that I had overlooked when I originally wrote of Michelle's disappearance.

The terrain between where Eric and Michelle separated and the planned meet-up point was not a line-of-site route. In the *Vanishing Point* chapter I describe the directions that Eric Sawyer said he gave to Michelle before separating at the south saddle. What I noticed in 2015 was that this route is far more difficult than the route going over the summit. Also, the meet-up point at the north ridge was not visible from their separation point.

There is a broad hump running up the west slope that blocks the view between the south saddle and the North Ridge of Holy Cross. It appears that Eric could have pointed only to an approximate meet-up point and, given Michelle's lack of experience and debilitated condition, it would have been easy for her to end up somewhere else.

The undulation in the slope and the unstable boulders that she would have had to bypass make this route more strenuous than climbing the trail over the summit, even given the additional several hundred feet of elevation gain. This is not apparent from a map and many hikers have mistakenly assumed that it's easy to shortcut a bump on a ridge by traversing. Not only was Michelle likely trending steeply downward, she was doing so in worse terrain than either of them imagined.

But assuming she started across initially aiming for a spot that Eric pointed out what was that spot? The point at which the North Ridge connects to the summit pyramid, the meet-up spot, appears completely nondescript from the south saddle. There is no obvious landmark to aim for, the slope appears to be continuous to the skyline, and the summit pyramid looks like a continuous slope. Given that Eric had never been to Holy Cross and the lack of navigation aids, it is hard to believe he could pick out the meeting place he thought was the north ridge.

Lastly, and perhaps most tragically, Michelle would have been highly visible from above to any hiker on any part of the summit pyramid, but only if someone was watching. She would have been visible to Eric for *the entire traverse*. If she were not visible, this should have been an instant alarm that she was off-route.

In the *Michelle is Missing* chapter, I describe how hikers Jamie Nellis and Tyr Johansen came across Eric Sawyer at the meet-up point at approximately 2:30 p.m. He had been watching for Michelle for a bit prior to that, and possibly from the point he started to descend.

The three facts that drive people crazy about this case are that (1) a huge search did not find anything, (2) there were no witnesses (other than Sawyer), and (3) there is still no new evidence 10 years later. These facts motivate people to make wild speculations about what "really happened." A web search of Michelle Vanek's name reveals the rumors and disbelief that the actual facts are true.

We still don't know exactly what happened to Michelle after she left home that morning. But there is actual evidence that must fit into whatever scenario you care to believe. My own investigation of the incident was quite extensive, from researching the sheriff's case file to examining the location and interviewing witnesses. When I applied my considerable mountaineering and mountain search and rescue experience to this situation, I arrived at a highly probable scenario about what happened, which is published in this book, and that discounts the rumors. My scenario presents evidence that the three "unusual" circumstances surrounding Michelle's disappearance are actually possible and have happened in the past: Other large searches have turned up nothing, other people have been missing for years, and people vanish without witnesses. These circumstances prove nothing about Michelle's disappearance but demonstrate that her case is not completely unique.

RUMORS CENTERED ON FOUL PLAY

Law enforcement investigators are trained to suspect foul play and they certainly did in this case. Two people went on a mountain climb and one returned. There were no witnesses. The Eagle County Sheriff investigated Sawyer for several weeks and did not find any solid evidence that a crime was committed, nor did they find any possible motivation. Other characters described as "suspicious" on the mountain were also found to have no involvement. This isn't to say there was no foul play; there just isn't any evidence of it.

RUMORS THAT MICHELLE WAS NEVER ON HOLY CROSS

These usually start with the incident being staged, claiming that she snuck away and is hiding somewhere like Mexico or, more bizarrely, was assisted in committing suicide for some reason, and she wanted it to look like an accident.

It is a fact that Eric Sawyer was on Holy Cross on the day Michelle disappeared; many witnesses placed him there. It's also a fact that Michelle was also on Holy Cross, and more specifically, well along the Halo Ridge. The proof is the last photo taken of her, the same one seen by all the searchers, splashed across TV news screens and on posters. She is wearing the clothing she bought the week before specifically to wear on the climb of Holy Cross with Sawyer.

During the search, rumors spread among the searchers themselves that the photo could have been taken "anywhere" and maybe it was staged somewhere else. It shows Michelle hiking with a rocky mountain in the background that was nondescript. But the actual evidence presents two problems with that conclusion.

The first is that the film became evidence and thus was in the hands of the sheriff prior to being developed (this was before the era of digital cameras). Eric had not even seen the photo he took before handing the film over to the sheriff, who then developed it. On that roll of film there were at least two photos of Michelle showing Holy Cross from a point on the Halo Ridge. What the searchers saw was a zoomed in photocopy of an original so that her face and clothing would be very recognizable; the distributed image had a cropped background. Also, the evidence file has more than one photo, and the photos clearly show Holy Cross in the background.

Perhaps more fascinating, the technology developed since Michelle's

This is the last photo of Michelle Vanek; a cropped version was used on the missing person flyer.

disappearance can show the position the distributed photo was taken from on any home computer. Google Earth allows you to place yourself on the Halo Ridge and zero in on the approximate location the photo was taken based on the angle of the features in the background. Simply place yourself in the approximate location and move along the ridge until the view matches the background photo. It is not exact because the Google Earth view is a morphed overhead satellite photo, but it's amazingly close. Michelle was definitely on Holy Cross and on the Halo Route.

RUMORS THAT MICHELLE'S DISAPPEARANCE WAS STAGED

The photographic evidence placing Michelle on the Halo Ridge eliminates all the speculative scenarios about this incident being staged, simply because those scenarios claim she was never there. That of course doesn't

Using Google Earth and its 3-D photo morphing, this image shows approximately the same point on the Halo Ridge. Though the summit of the mountain looks different, many features are present. [Generated from 39°, 28' 01.36" N, 106° 28' 37.10" W, eye elevation at 12,890 feet looking WNW.]

eliminate the possibility that it was staged, but requires a new theory to fit the evidence.

Whatever you want to believe, you have to start with Michelle on the Halo Ridge on the day she disappeared. Is it possible she started there and ended up living another life somewhere else? It's possible, but highly unlikely. This has been tried before. A recent example of how difficult it is to pull off this kind of stunt is the Lance Hering incident that happened in Boulder County several years ago.

At 5:15 a.m. on August 30, 2006, a man named Steve Powers called 911 to request help for his seriously injured friend Lance Hering. Powers reported that Hering was unconscious just off the Eldorado Canyon Trail a couple of miles from the trailhead. Powers claimed he had to hike down the trail to get cell phone reception and there was no one with Hering. Powers led rescuers to the accident site within an hour or so, a quick response given the remote location. Hering was not there, but there was a small pool of blood where Hering supposedly had been.

The rescue rapidly evolved into a search under the assumption that Hering was wandering in the wilderness in a deranged state caused by his head injury. Steve Powers had said that early that morning, he and Hering decided to hike up to an overlook to watch the sunrise, a final celebration before Hering, a United States Marine on leave, was to be sent back to combat in Iraq. On the way down the trail, Hering tripped on a root and tumbled down the ravine where there was now a pool of blood.

The search grew rapidly in size and personnel. The military sent personnel to help with the ground search. Over the next four days hundreds of people expended 7,000 searcher-hours looking for Hering. A helicopter equipped with forward-looking infrared sensors was employed to search an area much smaller but at least as complex as where Michelle disappeared. Nothing was found.

On day five, Powers admitted to making the whole thing up so that his high school buddy Hering could slip away and go AWOL from the Marines. Hering was on the run in the Pacific Northwest for two years before being found and arrested.

This staged disappearance was planned down to the detail of Hering actually extracting his own blood from his arm to be placed at the "accident" site. However, there were many flaws in their plan due to their ignorance of what does and does not actually happen during real incidents of this nature. For instance, neither Powers nor Hering had a clue about how much effort would be put into a search for a missing injured person in Boulder County. Powers, who picked an "accident site", did a poor job of selecting a believable place. While someone could trip on a root at the location he picked, it was nearly impossible to believe that a young Marine could then tumble down the shallow slope off the trail and hit his head hard enough to lose consciousness.

The blood pool did not appear to investigators to have been caused by a head striking a rock; it appeared more likely that blood was poured there. And there were numerous other "suspicious" behaviors by Powers and others during the search period. But the bottom line is that the admission of the hoax came very quickly, within days. Approximately a week later the sheriff confirmed that Lance Hering boarded a Greyhound bus in Denver on the day he was reported missing.

One could claim that this staged disappearance wasn't thought out well and that a better prepared plan with a bit more forethought would have been more believable. That may be true, but such a plan would have to be very complex. The likelihood of covering every possible detail is pretty low, and the greater the number of resources investigating an incident, the greater the likelihood of the hoax being uncovered. The chances that someone who knows nothing about SAR or law enforcement techniques could pull off such a hoax are almost zero.

This rationale can be applied to the Michelle Vanek case as well. Law enforcement officials investigated Eric Sawyer, going as far as placing him under surveillance for several weeks. Sawyer had no inside knowledge of how law enforcement and SAR organizations operated, and neither did Michelle. It is exceedingly unlikely that these two could pull off a successful staged disappearance, even with the help of others. Also, Michelle was the mother of four children, and the youngest was two at the time. What is the likelihood that she could remain in hiding for any length of time?

The Challenges of Mountain Rescue

Many of the stories in this book describe some of the great challenges of mountain rescue on a remote Colorado 14er, from the evacuation of David "TalusMonkey" Worthington to the large-scale search for Michelle Vanek. However, these tales only reveal part of the larger organization required to pull off these major undertakings, and raise several questions: Who are the people who make up these teams? What motivates them? How do they train and how much time do they invest? If you find yourself in the unfortunate situation of needing to be rescued, what can you expect? What events need to be set into motion to get you out of the backcountry and back into civilization and medical treatment? What is happening unseen in the background and who pays for all this?

Mountain rescue in Colorado, and in the United States in general, is an extraordinarily specialized and unique emergency service. There are very few practitioners, when compared to fire or ambulance services, for example, and almost all are volunteers. Every country in the world that has a mountain rescue service manages its organization in a different manner. Swiss mountain rescue operates differently from Russia, which is different from Peru, and so forth. The systems within the United States are not uniform even within states; operations may differ depending on local jurisdictions.

In Colorado, sheriffs are responsible for search and rescue in their counties. The situation is different in Rocky Mountain National Park (RMNP), which is under the jurisdiction of the federal government. But even RMNP requests help from neighboring counties during busy times or big rescue events. So the organization of county rescue services in Colorado, which is fairly consistent, provides a good general framework for a description of what happens across the state.

Fire, ambulance, and law enforcement are organized around municipalities or districts within a county and are funded by tax districts. Mountain rescue is almost exclusively organized as a single organization for an entire county. Only about half of the counties require the technical services of a mountain rescue team. County sheriffs are grateful for competent volunteer mountain rescue teams, which may be described as:

Competent: The team can perform actual SAR operations in the safest possible manner. It can find victims, treat their medical condition, and extract them while minimizing team injuries. It has the ability to solve unique and complex problems encountered during missions.

Volunteer: The team is unpaid, but willing to expend extensive amounts of time to train and is willing to perform rescues that last hours or even days on a moments notice. Members are required to buy all or nearly all specialized personal equipment.

Mountain rescue: The team can perform technical extraction on any type of terrain found in the mountains and provide first responder medical treatment that may continue for hours. It has the physical strength and stamina to carry large loads of gear into the field, and help carry patient and gear out of the field. Members have rope, anchor, and navigation skills exceeding what is necessary for normal mountaineering and rock climbing.

Team: No SAR operation can be accomplished by an individual. Teams require dozens if not hundreds of participants who are able to perform all the above. Some members have the ability to lead a field team or base operations.

Mountain SAR operations are highly complex. Some of the issues SAR confronts are:

- Time of Rescue: This could be any time on any day of the year, at mid-summer in the early afternoon or early January at two in the morning. All weather hazards are possible, from torrential rain, lightning, and hail to wind-driven sub-zero blizzards to stifling heat. Most or all of the rescue mission may take place in complete darkness.

- Location: The first task is locating the victim who may be found at the reported location, close to it, nowhere near it, or the victim's location may not be known at all. The victim may be in a forest, on a cliff face requiring technical gear, or on a snowfield or avalanche slope above timberline. All rescues start as a search.

- Medical Needs: The victim may be severely injured with multiple compound fractures and internal injuries, suffering a critical medical event like a heart attack or diabetic reaction, or having a severe psychological event such as a panic attack or schizophrenic episode.

- Number of people and incidents: There may be more than one person suffering the above problems in a party, or there may be many rescue calls at the same time.

Some examples of how SAR situations occur are:

Scenario 1: Respond to a missing person buried in an avalanche at 12,000 feet in a late December blizzard at 10 p.m. His partner showing you the location is nearly psychotic with grief and is threatening rescuers. He could potentially disappear himself into the blizzard to search for his friend.

Scenario 2: Two climbers are stranded, one with severe head and

Hauling gear out the easy way after a rescue.

shoulder injuries, at an altitude of 13,000 feet. They are located on a sheer rock face several hundred feet from any ledge under constant rockfall threat.

Scenario 3: A missing party separated near the summit of a 14er six hours ago and has not been seen since. Initial search of likely areas turns up nothing, and a snowstorm is imminent in four days. The missing party is relatively young, very fit, and likely to survive unless and until the storm moves in. Family and friends are on the way to help with the search. National TV and media are waiting for comment.

MOUNTAIN SAR: BIG PICTURE

Simultaneous rescues will stretch limited resources and likely slow things down as well. I witnessed an example of this in the fall of 1998.

We were nearing the top of the West Ridge of Quandary Peak, a more challenging alternative to the normal East Ridge Route. The climb involves minor scrambling on a rocky ridge that includes its share of loose rock, requiring that each hand and foothold be tested to ensure it is solid. Earlier in the climb we had noticed several people on the ridge ahead of us. Just below the summit is a scree-strewn couloir running down the south face.

One hundred feet down the couloir were three people kneeling over another person sprawled out on her back. Obviously there was something wrong, so I descended to help. When I arrived I saw that the woman lying on the ground had a bruised and swollen face, was bleeding, and unconscious. She had tumbled down the slope, head over heel, when one of her holds broke on the ridge.

One of the people attending her was Mary Walker, a nurse with backcountry medical training, who was monitoring the victim's condition continuously despite the danger of rocks falling from above. But there wasn't much she could do otherwise. To keep the victim's airway open for what she correctly anticipated would be hours, Mary had used a safety pin directly through her tongue and lower lip to hold the tongue in place, a surprising improvisation technique she had learned in her training. I did very little except give Mary whatever moral support I could.

Someone near the summit had a cell phone (not so common at the time), and was able to call for help. A few hours later an air ambulance helicopter showed up, but with no way to land anywhere near us, it proved useless.

In the meantime, the victim was visibly deteriorating, looking more and more gray, though she was still breathing. Soon one of the first rescue team members arrived carrying a large medical kit. He intubated the victim so that she could be manually respirated, but unfortunately her head injury was slowly getting worse.

Just then a Blackhawk helicopter arrived. The Blackhawk is a powerful military chopper with an external cable winch that can lower and raise people while hovering. It hovered about 30 feet over us, lowered a crewmember with a litter, and then flew off. It appeared the victim would be saved, but not before a dramatic and dangerous operation.

Crestone Needle (left) and Crestone Peak (double summit center) from Kit Carson. The Ellingwood Arête runs up the left skyline of Crestone Needle.

We strapped the victim in the litter, but had to hold it in place to keep it from sliding down the slope before it was attached to the winch cable. The Blackhawk was called back for loading. Again it hovered about 30 feet above while we struggled to attach the litter to the cable. It was extremely loud and chaotically windy, tossing dust and small rocks in the air from the ground effect of its massive rotor. We could not speak to each other and could barely keep our eyes open.

I happened to be the one by the cable hook and the crewman pointed to me to attach the litter to it. I did, but was having difficulty inserting the safety pin that holds the hook latch. Suddenly, the chopper lifted away, nearly ripping my thumb out and knocking all of us back two feet. It was an emergency dust-off; the pilot was feeling a wind gust that could push the chopper into the nearby cliffs. But the victim was on her way out.

It was an amazing operation and she made it to an emergency room alive. Unfortunately she died soon after; her injuries were just too severe and not treated in time.

A few days later a friend from my rescue team told me that this Blackhawk helicopter and crew were actually en route to a different accident on a different 14er. A man had been injured high on a difficult and precarious climbing route on 14,203 foot Crestone Needle in southern Colorado. The victim was climbing the Ellingwood Arête when he fell and severely injured his leg.

The easiest route up Crestone Needle is considered one of the more difficult of the 14ers normal routes. It is rated 4th class, meaning it is a moderate scramble but the consequences of a fall are severe. This route has extreme exposure and is highly intimidating to most 14er climbers. Many prefer to have a rope and belay, especially for the climb down. There have been many occasions when climbers have fallen on this section due to a hold breaking or slipping on a wet rock. Other climbers get a bit off route and into much more difficult climbing territory and subsequently fall.

The Ellingwood Arête is far more difficult than the normal route and is considered a mountaineering classic route by expert climbers. It is rated 5.7, a technical rock climbing route that requires a rope for all but an expert few. Though there are only two or three pitches of fifth class climbing IF you stay on route, there are many hundreds if not a thousand feet of 4th class scrambling required.

An accident happens on this mountain approximately once or twice each year that requires a difficult evacuation. The Ellingwood Arête sees its share of these accidents and because the route is so steep, they are usually fatal if not very severe. On this particular occasion, it was a solo climber (no rope or partner) wearing hiking boots, rather than the preferred climbing shoes that help feet stick to footholds much better. He fell and a rescue was summoned.

Crestone Needle is located in Custer County, across the valley from where David "TalusMonkey" Worthington had his accident on Humboldt Peak. As is usual for accidents in this area, help must be summoned from far away. Because of the steepness and remoteness of Crestone Needle, a technical evacuation from the ground is dangerous, time consuming, and arduous. A specialized helicopter that can maneuver at high altitude and has a rescue winch is invaluable and is used frequently on such occasions.

As mentioned previously, helicopters cannot be used in many of the weather conditions encountered in the mountains. High or turbulent winds, storms, and fog prevent their use. On this occasion, though, it was something else.

Custer County requested helicopter assistance from the military and a Blackhawk responded. En route, it was diverted to the accident on Quandary. Unfortunately for the victim on Crestone Needle, his accident was not as life threatening as the one on Quandary. Because both accidents had been reported late on the same day, only one could be helped. The victim on Crestone Needle was forced to spend a cold, painful night before being evacuated the next day.

The bottom line is that a helicopter rescue from a 14er is not possible in many if not most situations. Rescue must rely on ground teams and the slow, difficult work of a ground evacuation.

I hope I have led you to an appreciation of two characteristics of mountain rescue. First, it requires a tremendous amount of preparation to perform an SAR operation safely and efficiently; and second, any given operation may take days to complete. SAR personnel who perform rescues are continuously training, usually for years if not decades, and are ready, for any accident that may happen, to perform quickly and safely. And they are volunteers.

MOUNTAIN SAR: WHAT IS THE REAL COST AND HOW IS IT PAID FOR?

The cost of mountain rescue is poorly understood by the media or general public. The process of extracting a victim from the mountains and delivering him to an emergency room usually involves more than just the mountain rescue team. The rescue team gets the victim to the road or to a helicopter-landing zone. After that, a for-profit ambulance service is likely

Rescuers evacuating a victim down treacherous terrrain.

to take over. The costs for these for-profit services are not discussed here because they are the same whether the accident happens in the mountains or on a road or in a home.

As discussed before, the vast majority of SAR team members are volunteers. Of the very few who are paid professionals, they perform SAR work as a part of a larger public service job function. In other words, a deputy sheriff may take over as incident commander for an operation, but is paid to be a deputy regardless of the specific duty the deputy performs. Similarly, a National Park Service ranger may participate in a rescue but is paid to be an NPS ranger, and participates in the rescue as part of his or her duty. The same is true of all public service agencies. There are no personnel paid solely to perform SAR work in Colorado. Thus, no additional money is paid for agency personnel for any operation at any time.

As to the specialized equipment necessary for SAR operations: There are two categories of this equipment, team and personal. The volunteer, not the team budget, pays for personal equipment. There may be a few exceptions, like helmets, but the majority of this cost is borne by the volunteer team member.

The team equipment includes items such as ropes, litters, anchor and belay material, vacuum splints, oxygen, and radios. It also includes rescue vehicles such as four-wheel-drive emergency vehicles, snowmobiles, and ATVs. This equipment, some of which is relatively high cost like an emergency vehicle, is usually paid for with money provided to the team as described below. But much of the expensive equipment can be reused often.

Many teams have a headquarters building that must be maintained. A new building may be potentially funded in a capital campaign, but these are rare. Also, a dedicated SAR building is almost never a requirement; many teams have survived decades by sharing space with another service such as a fire department or ambulance, or have not had a building at all. It is reasonable to argue that capital-building costs should not be counted toward SAR operations cost, though maintenance of the building should be.

Other annual costs such as insurance, vehicle maintenance, and miscellaneous services add up. Insurance is the main cost in this category because workers' compensation is usually required to participate in official county business.

These are the major costs to most mountain SAR teams. Today, these costs can range from, approximately, a low of $10,000 to $100,000 per year. The high end appears to be quite high, but in comparison many fire departments have budgets of over $1,000,000 per year. For example, the Rocky Mountain Fire Department has a budget of over $6 million per year and covers just a portion of Boulder County. There are numerous fire departments in the state whereas there are only a relatively few SAR teams. If the overall budgets for fire protection districts versus SAR teams in the state is compared, it is likely well over $100 million for fire protection districts but less than $1,000,000 for SAR.

When needed, helicopter operations are by far the majority of the cost of SAR operations. They can cost hundreds to thousands of dollars per hour to operate. On operations that require many days of constant helicopter support, such as the Michelle Vanek search, these costs can add up to significant amounts. However, these price tags can be deceptive. If military helicopters are used, the costs are high but would likely be spent on a training mission anyway and are never charged back to a county or individual. Sometimes a county will pay for a helicopter during a search, and sometimes a victim's family, for example, will pay. Air ambulances are ambulance services that are charged back to the patient they transport and not paid for by a county and thus not part of the cost of a SAR operation.

To summarize, the main costs of an SAR operation are amortized equipment and maintenance, and team operational costs, including training, medical supplies, and the use of a helicopter in special cases.

The actual cost of a rescue is paid for by a combination of money provided by local governments, donations, and grants. A county or city budget may have a line item for SAR teams, for which the county taxpayer pays a minuscule amount. These amounts are usually not enough to cover actual costs, so donations and fundraisers are employed. Grants usually

14ER ACCIDENT STATISTICS

Despite being one of the most popular mountain activities in Colorado, and a treasure promoted by both the outdoor industry and state, there is a severe lack of reliable statistics on accidents on 14ers. There is no official statewide archive, most rescue teams and sheriff departments have no statistics of this sort, and historical data is notoriously inaccurate or missing.

Surprisingly, there are also no accurate statistics on the number of visitors to the state's 14,000-foot summits. The best statistics are estimates and this makes the determination of accident rates difficult. Longs Peak may see many accidents, but it also receives far more visitors and inexperienced visitors than probably any other peak in the state. And what is the accident rate on Mt. Eolus, a very remote 14er in La Plata County? With the population of Colorado growing rapidly and information availability spreading via the internet, I hope that these statistics will eventually be compiled. This information would be invaluable for preventing disasters on the Colorado 14ers.

help with specific equipment, such as to pay for radios or to buy a vehicle, or for specific training.

Many teams spend a lot of time on fundraising events and sometimes large donations are made by those rescued, but unfortunately this type of funding is highly variable year-to-year. Grants from various sources must be applied for.

Another source of funding is often misunderstood: the Colorado SAR, or COSAR, card. COSAR card marketing is somewhat misleading and many people understand it to be a kind of rescue insurance. It is not rescue insurance and will not pay for a rescue, but no SAR team in the state will charge for its rescue services.

The misleading marketing of COSAR cards is unfortunate. When a COSAR card is purchased, the seller, which may be a rescue team, gets a small cut of the price. The rest goes into a Colorado state fund that also draws money from Colorado off-road-vehicle and watercraft permits. One of the uses of this fund is to reimburse county governments (not rescue teams) for some of the costs of a rescue. This money must be applied for and approved; it is not automatically distributed. Another use of this fund is for equipment grants to teams. Thus the COSAR card can be broadly viewed as insurance for a rescue team (but not necessarily the one that rescues you) but the SAR team won't charge you.

LESSONS LEARNED

Mountain climbing, and finishing *The List*, is essentially an intense game played far from any amusement park. It is a game that grants rich, if somewhat ethereal, rewards to the "winners" and, like a Roman gladiator event, severely punishes the "losers." From ancient Native Americans on vision quests at the summit of Blanca Peak to present-day list baggers, people have challenged themselves and played the game on the Colorado 14ers. And the challenge will continue far into the future.

The game will not end as long as humans desire to compete with themselves and nature. To pay the respect earned by these reverential summits, each mountain climber should understand the environment they are entering and face it as best they can.

Whether or not any of the 14er disasters in this book could have been prevented, they are lessons and can help us to understand how human psychology can work against us as we play the game. Even the most seemingly simple but deadly mistakes, such as the one David Worthington made by intentionally sliding down Humboldt Peak to his eventual demise, are not straightforward when all his actions and thinking are taken into account. However, there are ways to mute certain negative psychological patterns by understanding a few fundamental tenets that climbers of every experience level should follow to have the best chance of a long and successful career.

- Climbers should take responsibility for themselves no matter what their experience level. The novice climber must trust a more experienced leader, and that trust should not be given lightly. The novice relies on that person or persons to make potentially life and death decisions. On the other hand, the experienced mountaineer must continuously assess their skills and strengths, and avoid letting their guard down when on familiar ground or seemingly benign situations.
- A climber should fully understand and embrace his or her personal motivation to climb. This is not as simple as it sounds.

Is the motivation simply to participate in an activity with friends, or is it to escape from civilization on a beautiful summer day? Is it the physical challenge or is it to get to the summit? Are you only slightly motivated to summit or do you want to summit at all costs? Motivation will color your climbing decisions.

- Climbers should constantly evaluate their situation. This includes both the external environment and internal thoughts and feelings. Have you unintentionally climbed into dangerous terrain and could you reverse your course and retreat? Has the weather deteriorated enough to turn back? Will you lose daylight and do you have flashlight? Are you making a series of mistakes that may lead to an accident? If so, why are you making these mistakes and is it time to call it quits for the day?

- Climbers should understand their personal decision-making processes. What would you do if your partner decides to give up and turn around? What are the consequences of splitting up? Climbers should understand, or at least think about, how they would make decisions under extreme stress. What would you do if your partner broke his ankle on the summit of Crestone Needle with an impending thunderstorm moving in?

- Climbers should attempt to understand the psychology of their partners and others around them. Knowing how your group thinks gives you more of a chance of seeing when both good and bad decisions are being made. You will be more assured when good decisions are made and possibly be able to recognize and avert bad decisions.

- Climbers should understand that they are human and can make the same mistakes as everyone else. There are no exceptions; we all make mistakes. The mistakes made on Kiener's Route on Longs Peak are repeated surprisingly often. If you've never encountered the Diamond Step on Kiener's, your chances of attempting to climb the wrong way increase. Understanding these mistake patterns helps you avoid them. Study accident reports and put yourself in the same situation. How would you handle it?

When climbers are aware of their personal responsibility, motivations, current situation, and how they makes decisions, and have a general understanding how others around them will react, they will then have what it takes to make the best decisions possible.

Finally, climbers should understand that in some circumstances, the best decisions possible are not good enough, and someone may end up getting hurt, lost, or even killed, becoming the latest victim of the game.

Appendix A:
PREVENTING DISASTER

By Cindy Gagnon
Safety Committee Chair
Colorado Mountain Club, Boulder Group

There are many things that can cause an accident while climbing 14ers, leading to an unexpected wilderness survival situation. Planning and skills are what give you the best chance for survival.

Those wishing to ascend any Colorado mountain, including the 14ers, in a safe and efficient manner should do the following prior to the climb:

- Understand and acquire the abilities needed to do the climb (conditioning and skills).
- Understand the nature of the climb (nuances and difficulties of the entire route, how long will it take you, what are the technical skills needed, what are the risks and how do you assess them).
- Understand what gear you need.
- Understand the objective hazards: weather, location, seasonal issues, etc., and manage risk.
- Plan for the unexpected.

UNDERSTANDING AND ACQUIRING THE NECESSARY CONDITIONING, SKILLS, AND ABILITIES

The foundation of a mountaineer's skills and abilities is physical fitness. Aerobic and endurance fitness are required to safely and efficiently ascend any 14er. Keep in mind that the physical response to altitude varies among individuals and is not related to aerobic fitness.

Acquiring the necessary skills cannot be done solely by reading books. There are a multitude of "how to" books to cover just about everything one needs to know. However book knowledge, while useful, does not enable practical skills. Nothing replaces one-on-one hands-on instruction from a teacher skilled in mountaineering. Skills such as navigating with a map and compass, mountain survival, and how to plan a trip should be routinely practiced.

Some Colorado 14ers require only basic hiking skills, however many include terrain such as technical 5th class rock, or snow slopes requiring the use of ropes. The technical 14er routes demand basic rock-climbing skills as well as other alpine-climbing skills. Routes that consist of steep snow require basic snow-climbing skills and the use of ice axes and crampons.

UNDERSTANDING THE NATURE OF THE CLIMB

Planning your climb is perhaps the easiest part, due to the availability of Colorado 14er guidebooks such as *The Colorado Fourteeners: The Standard Routes* by the CMC, *Colorado's Fourteeners, from Hikes to Climbs* by Gerry Roach, and websites such as *14ers.com.*

One should not venture into the backcountry without navigation skills that include map reading and compass use. These skills are essential for staying on course and for determining location information if you find yourself off course. A GPS receiver is a navigation device that should be used in conjunction with a map and compass to help determine your location and how to travel to reach your destination. Keep in mind that GPS receivers do not always work, for instance when batteries run out or satellite visibility is minimal, and should not be relied on as a sole navigation tool.

Hikers should also understand terrain and weather hazards unique to Colorado 14ers. Severe weather tends to be more intense at higher elevations, especially above treeline where there are no sheltering trees. Summits and ridges are colder and more exposed to lightning, wind, and precipitation. In the summer months, it is strongly recommended to summit and begin your descent before noon to avoid lightning and other thunderstorm hazards. In winter, lightning is rare but days are shorter, the terrain is more hazardous due to snowcover, and storms are far more severe.

UNDERSTANDING THE GEAR REQUIREMENTS

Experience gained by mountain climbers over many years has shown that one of the most important ways to be prepared for emergencies, unexpected weather, or unplanned bivouacs is to always carry certain items. The Colorado Mountain Club (CMC), for instance, requires that each participant carry the following ten essential items on every trip.

1. Navigation: Map of the area, route information, and compass. A GPS receiver is an additional navigational device and should only be used in addition to the map and compass.
2. Sun protection: Sunglasses and an effective sunscreen or sunburn preventative.
3. Insulation: Extra clothing for both warmth and protection from the weather (wind, rain, snow, sun). Cotton should be avoided.
4. Illumination: Headlamp with extra batteries.
5. Body emergency/first-aid kit: First-aid kit and individual medical needs (for example asthma inhaler, insulin kit, EpiPen). First aid can be as simple as duct tape, an analgesic, and a pair of latex gloves. The CMC recommends you take a first-aid class geared toward the outdoors (minimally Wilderness First Aid).
6. Fire: Lighter or waterproof matches and two types of fire starter. Practice with your fire starter to make sure you know how it works.
7. Emergency tool kit: Knife and other tools or supplies you might need (specific to the gear you are bringing). Minimal recommended contents include multi-tool or small knife, a small pair of pliers, small scissors, whistle, signal mirror, and water purification tablets. Attach knife and whistle to outside of pack or around neck.
8. Nutrition: Extra food beyond what you expect to need for the trip.
9. Hydration: Wide-mouth water bottle and/or hydration bladder (full). Depending on length of trip, water purification tablets and/or water filter.
10. Emergency shelter: Bivouac gear (something waterproof in which you could survive the night). Examples include specially made space blankets, bivy bags, or trash bags.

Note that this list is considered the minimal amount of gear that one should carry on every hike, including a simple two-hour jaunt in the foothills. Keep in mind that carrying the gear is just the first step. Understanding how to use the gear is just as critical.

Every 14er ascent will require additional gear and clothing beyond the minimum list mentioned above. Factors such as weather, route condition and difficulty, length of route, and other personal needs will determine a mountaineers complete gear list.

UNDERSTANDING THE OBJECTIVE HAZARDS AND MANAGING RISK

Risk is inherent in mountain activities and the only way to be completely safe is not to go into the mountains at all. Risk management has three parts: hazard recognition, hazard analysis, and minimization of risk.

The traditional description of hazards categorizes them as either:

- *Objective hazards*—those that can't be controlled.
- *Subjective hazards*—those that are controllable.

Most hazards encompass both uncontrollable (objective) and controllable (subjective) aspects. A more useful categorization of hazards is:

- *External hazards*—presented by the mountain environment, such as weather, difficult terrain, darkness, falling objects, etc.
- *Internal hazards*—created by members of the party, and can be either physical (inadequate physical condition or technical skills,) or psychological (such as miscommunication, bad decision making, or group behavior)

Some hazards have both external and internal aspects, such as equipment failure, which can be due to external and cause internal hazards.

In most cases, hazards do not affect climbers in the mountains without warning. Mishaps or accidents are often not the consequence of a single event but result from a chain of seemingly unrelated incidents whose warning signs were not heeded. The warning signs can be "outer" or "inner" signs. Examples of "outer" signs are evidence of recent avalanche activity or a verbal disagreement among members of your climbing group. Examples of "inner" signs are your unease about conditions on the climbing route or about the dynamics of the climbing party, neither of which you can precisely put in words.

PLANNING FOR THE UNEXPECTED

Planning for the unexpected is difficult. But thinking about the unexpected, especially while in the comfort of your home, will enable you to handle an actual emergency more easily. Your survival attitude is the number one skill you have to rely on. Your will to survive is your greatest tool so try to stay calm—panic is the enemy. If you did your pre-planning, you're more likely to remain calm and able to create a survival plan.

So how does one plan for the unexpected? The first step is to understand your basic needs to manage an accident or an unplanned overnight stay:

- First Aid: Your number one priority would be to address any medical emergencies. The best way to prepare for this is to take some formal training. The CMC recommends certified courses such as Wilderness First Aid (basic) or Wilderness First Responder (advanced).
- Build a Shelter: You can survive the elements for FAR LESS time than thirst or hunger. Learning how to build emergency shelters from your surroundings (trees, branches, snow) or what you carried in your pack is essential to survival.
- Water: Prevent dehydration. Remember you can only live a few days without water, and much less at high altitude. Plan ahead and identify possible water sources from studying the maps.
- Fire: This is essential to provide warmth and can be used to signal help.
- Signaling: This skill increases your chances of being found if you are lost or stranded. You should understand how to use signals (audible, visual, and SOS distress) appropriately.
- Rest and sleep: It is critical to make yourself rest and sleep at least for short periods of time during emergencies to enable making rational decisions.
- Food: Believe it or not, this is the easiest need to survive without. You can live longer without food than any other requirement. Most people can survive for several weeks without food, although your strength, mental clarity, and temperature regulation improve if you have food.

Appendix B:
MANAGING DISASTER

By Alpine Rescue Team
Evergreen, Colorado

No matter how experienced you are, and how well you have prepared yourself and your party, mountain emergencies still occur. When it does happen, there are several steps you can take that will help your companions—and the search and rescue (SAR) team—immensely.

If an accident has injured someone, the first step is to immediately assist them, and ultimately assist the search and rescue team that will arrive to help.

ASSIST THE PATIENT AND RESCUERS

Carefully move the patient to stable ground if you can, without aggravating their injuries or endangering yourself and your companions. Be careful of neck or spinal injuries.

1. Using the first-aid kit always carried by your party, bandage all injuries.
2. Attract rescuers by blowing a whistle, hanging colorful cloth from a tree limb or outcrop.
3. Gather firewood before darkness.
4. Start a warming fire.
5. Rig shelter from impending.

If one of your party has gone missing, how you report that and what you report is critical. Most of this information is also needed for the rescue of an injured person.

You must eventually talk to the emergency authorities in the county in which the person went missing (or the accident occurred). Wired (land line) telephones will ring into the correct 911 center when called. However, 911 calls by a cell phone might reach a dispatch center in another county or distant city, depending on which cell tower the call goes through. In this case it is critical to first advise the 911 operator what county you are in and your location; they will transfer you to the correct 911 center for that area, and if the call is lost they can still notify the correct 911 center. Then be as specific as possible; e.g. the name of the trail or peak you are on, and specific location (e.g., 1,000 feet below the summit on the northwest ridge).

For a missing party, important information includes:

1. Name of the missing party
2. Clothing description (especially colors)
3. The intended destination
4. Your route plans
5. The missing person's medical history (if known)
6. Description of your group's vehicle(s), and where it's parked
7. How long the missing person is now overdue
8. Your call-back telephone number
9. The experience level of the missing person

CALLING FOR A RESCUE

The following information should be given to the 911 emergency operator when calling for a rescue for yourself or someone you have come across:

1. Your name and call-back number, whether a cell phone or a land line (do not hang up until told to do so by 911). Stay by that phone until instructed otherwise. Remember to conserve your cell phone batteries and keep them warm.
2. Your location and/or the location and elevation of the emergency. Be precise in reading every digit and character of your GPS receiver since it is capable of displaying the same position in several formats. For example, each of the following coordinates are different formats for the same location:
   A. 105° – 31' – 29" (ddd-mm-ss) (This is the historic map reader/navigator's format)
   B. 105° – 31.4833' (ddd-mm.mmmm)
   C. 105.5166° (ddd.dddd) This is the default setting on many GPS receivers
3. The nature of the emergency (e.g., fallen hiker, stranded climber, injured from rockfall, etc.)
4. How many are in your group, and how many need aid. This is

important information for the SAR team as an evacuation of two injured parties may require more than double the equipment necessary to evacuate a single injured party.

5. Any injuries
6. The current weather
7. The route in that you followed
8. Equipment that is available at the scene, such as a stove, sleeping bag, or tent
9. The experience level of those at the scene, especially in first aid or medical care.

Now that you have given as much information as possible to 911, it's important to remain calm and focused. Be ready to handle changing situations, such as deteriorating weather. It may take hours for a SAR team to reach you. Look for ground teams or a helicopter, which could be a bright-colored medical helicopter or a dark green military one. A helicopter may not be able to land anywhere near you but may spot you and radio your location to ground teams. Signal them immediately with a mirror, by waving a bright-colored jacket or large object, or even by waving your arms. When you see a ground team, blow a whistle (carries much farther) or shout to get their attention.

SAR teams may approach from an unexpected direction. They have to consider speed of access, inherent danger of a route, and a perhaps-not-obvious evacuation route that is different than a "standard" route.

Contact Information: Alpine Rescue Team, P.O. Box 934, Evergreen, CO 80437; 303.526-2417 (Alpine Rescue Team Headquarters); www.alpinerescueteam.org

Appendix C:
BACKCOUNTRY COMMUNICATION AND NAVIGATION EQUIPMENT

Recent years have seen a huge advance in the ability to call for help from the wilderness, and the ability to provide the pinpoint position of where help is needed. These advances are nothing less than revolutionary and give the hiker or climber an excellent chance of reducing emergency response time in the mountains by hours or, in some cases, days.

Note that all of these technology options have one common limitation—they are battery operated. Carrying spare batteries is always a good idea even if the unit is rechargeable. Expect heavy use of these devices in an emergency, enough to drain batteries at less than full capacity. There are various battery technologies, including rechargeable (nickel metal hydride and nickel cadmium), and single use (alkaline and lithium).

Low temperatures common in the mountains reduce the chemical action that batteries require to produce power. Though some batteries perform better than others (lithium and NiMH are best), *all* battery types perform worse at lower temperatures. Many times a battery that is "dead" can be revived by warming it to body temperature.

GPS RECEIVER

These are available as stand-alone units and are also built into a growing number of communication devices. A stand-alone GPS receiver is not a communication device but can be used to get extremely accurate information about your position that is invaluable in reducing response time.

Cost: variable depending on options

Weight: variable but as low as several ounces

Operational Complexity: High

Advantages

Position accuracy to within a few meters

Limitations

The unit must have a view to open sky for GPS satellite reception.

Reception can be blocked by canyon walls, rocks, trees, and interior spaces.

Battery operated.

SMARTPHONES AND CELL PHONES

This is one of the most common and useful backcountry communication devices. A myriad of models and services available, and smartphones can provide apps that function as a "stand-alone" GPS, including topo maps. Cell phone GPS receivers automatically transmit GPS coordinates to service providers, which can subsequently be provided to rescuers in emergency situations. A special precaution for smartphone users is to be aware of operational time limitations, especially when using GPS and other apps that tend to be power hungry. Operational time can be as short as a few hours even when starting with a full charge.

Be aware that cell phones will not have service in many of the wilderness areas of Colorado.

Cost: variable depending on model and service

Weight: variable, can be as low as a few ounces

Operational Complexity: moderate

Advantages

Potential to contact 911 service directly.

Potential to communicate situation directly with rescue personnel.

Most climbers have one.

Booster battery packs available.

Limitations

Cell phones must have a line-of-site visibility to a cell site.

Cell sites are limited to populated areas and are rare in the backcountry; therefore cell phones do not generally find service except on high ridges or the summit. When service is found in the backcountry, it is often weak or intermittent.

GPS receiver is less sensitive than stand-alone units, which have larger antennae, so trees or poor satellite locations more easily block readings.

Battery operated.

GPS-ENABLED SATELLITE PHONE BEACONS

These beacons combine the advantages of satellite phone, GPS, and web technology. They have become popular in recent years and have been successfully used in emergency situations where cell phone service is absent. The location acquired by GPS is transmitted via satellite phone service to email or text message accounts or directly to a 911 response center. The system uses web-mapping technology to display an exact location. These allow you to call for help or send an OK signal showing an exact location. A paid subscription service is required.

> *Cost:* $150 MSRP for SPOT Satellite Messenger beacon (sometimes free if signing up for subscription), $100–$150 per year subscription service.
>
> *Weight:* As little as a few ounces
>
> *Operational Complexity:* moderate

Advantages

> Combines communication and location information in one easy-to-use device. Uses satellite phone service, which is generally more available than cell phone service in the wilderness.
>
> Allows non-emergency messages to be sent.
>
> Useful worldwide.

Limitations

> The unit must have a view to open sky for GPS and communication satellite reception. Reception can be blocked by canyon walls, rocks, trees, and interior spaces.
>
> Unit cannot be used to communicate situation directly to rescue personnel.
>
> Battery operated.

DISTRESS RADIO BEACONS

This includes the Personal Locator Beacon (PLB), Emergency Locator Transmitter (ELT), and Emergency Position Indicating Radio Beacon (EPIRB). These devices are essentially radio beacons that transmit signals that can be received by both a satellite and air- or ground-based direction-finding equipment. Though any of these beacons can be carried and used by hikers in distress, the PLB is the beacon designed for such use. The EPIRB is usually used for emergencies at sea, and ELT's are intended to be used to find downed aircraft.

PLB's are relatively expensive. When a PLB signal is detected, the government contacts the local emergency services directly. PLB's must be registered by the user.

Cost: Mid-$200

Weight: 10 to 12 ounces

Operational Complexity: low

Advantages

Uses proven government managed emergency response system.

Useful worldwide.

Limitations

Unit does not require view to the open sky but trees, canyon walls, rocks, or interior space can weaken the signal.

Unit cannot be used to communicate situation directly to rescue personnel.

Emergency use only, heavy fines imposed for non-emergency use.

Battery operated.

FRS RADIOS

The Family Radio Service radios are relatively low cost and used by many recreationalists. Their range is limited and there is no standard distress channel, but the popularity of the service increases the chances that others are listening. Some models are equipped with GPS receivers that automatically transmit location information.

Cost: as low as $20

Weight: 6 ounces, varies between models

Operational Complexity: moderate

Advantages

Moderate cost for unit, no service fee.

No license requirement.

Useful as a general communication device within group.

Potential to communicate situation directly to rescue personnel.

Limitations

No standard way to call for help, must rely on others monitoring the
channel.

Range is very limited and line-of-sight, the radio waves cannot
travel around obstacles.

Antenna cannot be upgraded.

Battery operated.

AMATEUR RADIO AND OTHER RADIO SERVICES

Handheld VHF/UHF amateur radios operating are extremely useful in the
Colorado mountains. These radios operate line-of-sight; that is, they cannot
reliably transmit over the horizon. However, because amateur radio clubs
and organizations install and maintain repeaters statewide, the coverage
of these radios is much higher than other services, including cell phones.
A license is required for general operation, but no license is required for
emergency communication.

Other radio services such as citizen band (CB) and general mobile radio
service (GMRS) are less useful since few people monitor them.

Cost: variable, with costs starting less than $100

Weight: variable, as low as 6 ounces

Operational Complexity: high

Advantages

Moderate unit cost, no service fee.

VHF/UHF coverage is excellent in Colorado.

Much more powerful transmitter than FRS radios (5 watt vs. 0.5
watt).

Range can be boosted with a telescoping antenna.

With a license, can be used for general communication.

Can receive National Weather Service broadcasts.

Some radios can be modified (MARS/CAP mod) to broadcast on
sheriff, park service, and rescue bands (legal in an emergency).
This also opens them up to broadcast on FRS frequencies for
group communication.

Potential to communicate situation directly with rescue personnel.

Limitations

Operation can be complex depending on radio and intended use
area.

Requires a license for general communication use.

Battery operated.

HANDHELD SATELLITE PHONES

Hand-held mobile satellite phones are available and generally work anywhere in the world as long as the satellite is visible. Canyon walls and trees can block the signal. The service is relatively expensive as compared to cell phones.

Cost: unit as low as $500, service subscription required.

Weight: As low as a few ounces

Operational Complexity: moderate

Advantages

Backcountry coverage is excellent compared to cell phones.

Ability to contact 911 service directly.

Ability to communicate situation directly with rescue personnel.

Limitations

The unit must have a view to open sky for communication satellite
reception.

Service can be intermittent.

Battery operated.

GLOSSARY

Acute Mountain Sickness (AMS): Illness induced by altitude that expresses itself as flu-like symptoms of headache, nausea, dizziness, fatigue, and malaise. AMS disappears upon return to lower altitude.

Anchor: A point to safely secure a rope, person, or any other object. Examples are large trees, big boulders, or climbing equipment secured in cracks in solid rock.

Avalanche beacon: A hand-sized device that is strapped to the body when one enters a snowslope that has some danger of avalanching. The device is a transceiver, i.e., it will transmit or receive depending on which mode it is set to. While in an avalanche zone, the beacon is set to transmit mode. If the person wearing the beacon is buried in an avalanche, others can set their beacons to receive and use them to zero in on the buried victim.

Belay: The act of holding a rope for safety, which is tied to a person climbing or a litter being lowered. The rope is held using an anchored friction device to increase holding power. This allows easy control of a descent and will easily stop a falling climber.

Bivouac (Bivy): An overnight camp involving minimal or no extra camping gear. It may be unplanned such as when stranded overnight on dangerous, unknown terrain.

Bushwhack: Off-trail cross-country travel where one will whack or be whacked by bushes.

Cache: A stash of equipment.

Couloir: A gulley that runs down the face of a mountain. When filled with snow, couloirs make excellent climbing and descent routes.

Crampon: Metal spikes attached to the bottom of a boot to assist in climbing steep snow or ice.

Crux: The most difficult spot on a climb. Most climbs or hikes have one most-difficult spot that determines the difficulty of the overall route.

Depth Hoar: Ice crystals that form beneath the surface of snow. These crystals form invisibly within thin snowpack when the air temperature is well below freezing, a common occurrence in Colorado. They do not bond well and cause weak layers, increasing avalanche possibility.

Dihedral: A rock formation that forms a roughly 90-degree corner like the shape of an open book.

Exposure: A qualitative description of a climber's potential for a disastrous fall. Flat ground would have minimal exposure; a cliff face would have maximum exposure.

Glissade: A method to rapidly descend a snowfield. It is a slide down the snow, usually controlled with an ice axe. This is usually accomplished in a sitting position but can also be performed while standing using boots like skis.

Handwarmer: Small chemical packs that can fit in a glove and emit heat for a limited time period to assist in keeping hands or other body parts warm.

Heel-plunge: A technique used to walk down a snow slope. Rather than walking flat-footed, the heel is plunged into the snow to form a stable step.

High Altitude Cerebral Edema (HACE): A dangerously advanced form of altitude illness characterized by lack of muscle control and other severe neurological symptoms, caused by fluid build-up within the skull. Very rare in Colorado.

High Altitude Pulmonary Edema (HAPE): A dangerously advanced form of altitude illness characterized by breathing difficulties, noisy breathing, and coughing up blood, caused by fluid build-up in the lungs. Very rare in Colorado.

Hypothermia: Lowered core body temperature that can be caused by warmth depleting exposure to wind, rain, snow, or even laying on cold ground. Hypothermia progresses from mild to severe, with corresponding loss of mental capacity.

Ice axe: A tool to assist with climbing steep snow or ice. It consists of a long shaft with a specially designed head to grip snow or ice.

Kernmantle: The common structure of a climbing rope made of a protective but thin sheath (kern) and a high strength core (mantle).

Litter: A body-length basket made of a high strength material (usually metal) used for evacuating disabled victims of mountaineering accidents.

Piton: An early form of rock anchor still used today in certain situations. It is a wedge of metal a few inches long with a ring on the end. It is hammered into a crack as a rope attachment point.

Postholing: The act of walking through deep snow without the aid of floatation such as snowshoes or skis, forming "postholes" with each step. It is a very tiring, inefficient method of travel and usually results in exhaustion after a relatively short distance.

Rappel: A method of using a rope to descend vertical or nearly vertical cliffs.

SAR: Search and Rescue.

Scree: Small fragments of rock commonly covering large expanses of mountain slopes above treeline.

Self-arrest: A technique to stop a slide on snow with an ice axe. The basic procedure is to put one's body in a stable sliding position and then dig the pick of the ice axe into the snow to create enough friction to stop the slide.

Self-belay: A technique used to anchor oneself to a steep snow slope with an ice axe.

Snow shelter: A structure built into snow, usually as an emergency shelter. A snow shelter can range from a hole or trench dug into a snowdrift, to a full-fledged igloo.

Step chopping: A method of ascending very hard snow by "chopping" steps with an ice axe typically used when the climber lacks crampons.

Step-kicking: A method of climbing up a steep snowslope by kicking stable step platforms.

Talus: Same as scree.

Treeline: A well-defined elevation above which trees and large plants do not grow. The elevation varies with latitude and exposure to the sun (higher on south facing slopes, lower on north facing). On average, treeline is approximately 11,500 feet above sea level in Colorado.

USGS Topo: United States Geological Service topographic map. Produced by the government agency, it shows details that include contour lines indicating the altitude and shape of the terrain.

Wind chill: The effect of wind on the temperature of the body. The stronger the wind is, the lower the temperature of exposed body surface and clothing, thus turning cold weather into dangerously frigid weather.

ABOUT THE AUTHOR

Mark Scott-Nash was born and raised in Colorado, where he fell in love with the mountain wilderness at a very young age. He has extensive experience in all aspects of mountaineering and technical climbing, ranging from the local Colorado mountains to the great ranges of the world. He has taught and guided climbs from the basic level through advanced mountaineering, worked intermittently as a climbing guide and was a founding member of the Colorado Mountain Club's Advanced Mountaineering School in Boulder.

Mark has written extensively about issues relating to the mountain environment, adventure stories, politics and events. He is the author of two other books, *Forty Demons* (2012, Snowdragon Publishing) and *Playing for Real: Stories from Rocky Mountain Rescue* (2007, Colorado Mountain Club Press).

Mark has lead or participated in fourteen international expeditions to the Himalayas, Andes, and Alaskan mountains. He has been a volunteer mountain rescuer since 1999 and has been certified as an emergency medical technician. Mark has participated in more than one hundred search and rescue missions.

Blog at www.scott-nash.com

Get Outside.

COLORADO
MOUNTAIN CLUB

Become a CMC Member, today!

Explore the mountains and meet new people with the Colorado Mountain Club. Join us for trips, hikes, and activities throughout the state! Join today and save with special membership promotions for our readers: **www.cmc.org/readerspecials**

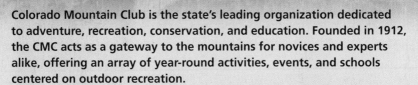

Colorado Mountain Club is the state's leading organization dedicated to adventure, recreation, conservation, and education. Founded in 1912, the CMC acts as a gateway to the mountains for novices and experts alike, offering an array of year-round activities, events, and schools centered on outdoor recreation.

When you join the Colorado Mountain Club, you receive a variety of member benefits including:

- 20% discount on CMC Press books
- Up to 70% discount off top outdoor gear brands on Promotive.com
- Discounts at select outdoor retailers and Colorado gear shops
- Subscription to Trail & Timberline magazine
- Lodging discounts at CMC backcountry huts—Brainard Cabin and Arestua Cabin
- Member pricing on mountain skills schools and courses around the state
- Access to 3,000 mountain adventure trips annually ranging from easy hikes and snowshoe trips to peak climbs and cross-country ski trips.
- Exclusive member pricing on events and tickets for Banff Mountain Film Festival, Radical Reels, Backcountry Filmfest, Backcountry Bash, American Mountaineering Museum and more.